The Unexpected Professor

by the same author

THE VIOLENT EFFIGY: A STUDY OF DICKENS' IMAGINATION
THACKERAY: PRODIGAL GENIUS
JOHN DONNE: LIFE, MIND AND ART
ORIGINAL COPY: SELECTED REVIEWS AND JOURNALISM 1969–1986
PURE PLEASURE: A GUIDE TO THE TWENTIETH CENTURY'S MOST
ENJOYABLE BOOKS
THE INTELLECTUALS AND THE MASSES
WHAT GOOD ARE THE ARTS?
WILLIAM GOLDING: A LIFE

as editor

WILLIAM GOLDING, THE MAN AND HIS BOOKS
THE FABER BOOK OF REPORTAGE
THE FABER BOOK OF SCIENCE
THE FABER BOOK OF UTOPIAS

The Unexpected Professor

An Oxford Life in Books

JOHN CAREY

FABER & FABER

First published in 2014
by Faber & Faber Ltd
Bloomsbury House
74–77 Great Russell Street
London WCIB 3DA

Typeset by Faber & Faber Ltd
Printed in England by CPI Group (UK) Ltd, Croydon, CRO 4YY

A CIP record for this book
is available from the British Library

ISBN 978–0–571–31092–0

2 4 6 8 10 9 7 5 3 1

For Gill

So good luck came, and on my roof did light,
Like noiseless snow; or as the dew of night:
Not all at once, but gently, as the trees
Are, by the sunbeams, tickled by degrees.

Robert Herrick

So good luck came, and on my roof did light
Like noiseless snow, or as the dew of night:
Not all at once, but gently, as the trees
Are, by the sunbeams, tickled by degrees.

ROBERT HERRICK (1591–1674), 'The Coming of
Good Luck'

Contents

Foreword

This book started life when a friend suggested I might write a history of English literature. It seemed an attractive idea at first, but I soon realised that it would mean a lot of donkey work, and that most of the facts would already be available on the internet. So I've written something more personal – a history of English literature and me, how we met, how we got on, what came of it.

You could read it as a short introduction to English literature – admittedly a selective and opinionated one. Or you could read it as a case study, showing how one kind of upbringing produces a preference for some books rather than others.

A lot of it is about Oxford, where I have spent my working life. Oxford has obviously changed greatly since I arrived there in the 1950s, and in many respects for the better. But I think even those who know the place well may be surprised to learn just how extreme the change has been.

One thing that has not changed is that Oxford – and Cambridge – still take vastly disproportionate numbers of public-school students. This is often blamed on Oxford and Cambridge. The blame, however, lies with those who destroyed the grammar schools. Selecting for merit, not money, the grammar schools, had they survived, would by now have all but eliminated the public-school contingent in Oxford and Cambridge, with far-reaching effects on our society. This book is, among other things, my tribute of gratitude to a grammar school.

Because my main subject is books, people get into the story only incidentally, and many friends and ex-students, who might reasonably expect to be mentioned, are not and may feel slighted. On the other hand, they may feel relieved to be left out. Either way, I'd like to thank them for the discussions about books we've had over the years.

Beginning

There can't really have been an elephant. But an elephant is what I remember. I was in a pushchair, and all around me were excited people shouting and waving flags. Away to the right I could see, coming up the road towards us, a kind of carnival procession, music and colours and an elephant leading the way. I now realise that these celebrations must have been for the Silver Jubilee of King George V on 6 May 1935, which means I was thirteen months old. The road, I'm pretty sure, was Castelnau, Barnes, a broad thoroughfare that crosses the top of Lonsdale Road, where we lived. As for the elephant, I suppose he must have strayed into my memory from some circus poster seen later in my childhood, and my brain, trying to make sense of things as the brain does, glued him onto that early scene of joy.

We were not a family much given to celebration, and I imagine we walked straight home once the procession had passed. Barnes is tucked into a loop of the Thames south-west of London, and Lonsdale Road runs beside the river. Our house looked out over broad, glinting sheets of water – reservoirs, belonging to the Metropolitan Water Board, surrounded by grassy banks. Beyond were trees, then the river, then, far in the distance, the tower of Chiswick church, sometimes with a flag on top.

One night my father carried me to an upstairs window to see a glare in the sky. It was, I was told later, the Crystal Palace burning down, which happened on 30 November 1936, so I must have been two and a half. It had originally been built in Hyde Park to house the 1851 Great Exhibition, and was relocated in Sydenham, where it became a popular resort for young office workers and their girlfriends, always packed with pleasure seekers on bank holidays. A hundred thousand people assembled to watch it burn, among them Winston Churchill, who said, 'This is the end of an age.' I suppose my father must have been feeling something like that too.

Apart from this chance glimpse of the outside world, my knowledge of my surroundings was confined to shopping expeditions with my mother, but these had their own excitements. At the top of the road, on a corner opposite where we had watched the Jubilee procession, was a branch of the United Dairies. A bell tinkled as you entered, and inside was a temple of immaculate whiteness, white marble counters, white-tiled walls, and the ladies who presided were all in white too including their gloves and hats. I was captivated by their dexterity. If my mother ordered a pound of butter one of the ladies would take up a pair of wooden butter pats, slice a wedge from a gleaming mound on the counter, beat it into a precise rectangular shape, drop it neatly onto a square of greaseproof paper on the scales, wrap it with a couple of deft flutters of the white gloves, and hand the completed artefact to my mother as if it was nothing remarkable.

Turning right out of the United Dairies we would approach Hammersmith Bridge, a magnificent Victorian iron structure, slung between imposing stone towers, which was one of the wonders of my childhood. It was a family legend that the dastardly IRA had once tried to blow it up but a brave policeman had foiled them by flinging the bomb into the river just in time. This was almost true, and happened in 1939. The rescuer, though, was not a policeman but a hairdresser from Chiswick called Maurice Childs, who spotted a suspiciously smouldering suitcase on his walk home and tipped it over the railings. The explosion sent up a jet of water sixty feet high.

For me the great pleasure of the bridge was that it shook when double-decker buses went across. My parents explained that it was a suspension bridge, and shaking made it safer. But it did not feel safe, it felt exhilarating. There I would be, far above the water, clutching my mother's hand, and the pavement would begin to spring up and down like a diving board. The bridge's other thrill was the seagulls. At Barnes the Thames is still tidal. On a good day you can smell the sea. At low tide gulls would crowd the mud flats and if you took a bag of crusts and tossed a few over the railings you would be surrounded by a swooping, screaming tornado of beaks and feathers.

Once across the bridge my mother and I were in Hammersmith, a quiet place in those days with no flyover and no motorway, and we would walk up towards Hammersmith Broadway and Palmers Stores, a grand emporium with, as old photographs show, an ornate four-storey Alhambra-style brick facade and sparkling white blinds at street level to protect shoppers from the weather. Palmers Stores was so big that you could walk through it from Hammersmith Bridge Road and come out on King Street the other side, but the only bit I remember was the fish department, which was the first you came to. The floor was covered in sawdust and the men in charge wore coarse blue aprons that shielded them from neck to ankles. Shoals of dead fish gaped on sloping stone slabs, and there were two-handled baskets of shellfish. I know almost nothing about my mother's likes and dislikes. She was too unselfish to consider them of any importance. But it was a family joke, perhaps a remnant from some seaside holiday before I was born, that she was fond of oysters and also winkles (which were considered lower-class and therefore comic). I wish I could remember her buying some in Palmers Stores but I don't think she ever did.

That was virtually the whole extent of my world up to the age of about five. There were six of us in the family, my father and mother, a brother, Bill, and two sisters, Marjorie and Rosemary. Bill, born in 1921, was thirteen years older than me; Marjorie, born three years later, was ten years older. So they belonged to another generation and seemed remote and adult to me as a child. Rosemary was only two years older than me but, being a girl, seemed rather remote too. As for my parents, it never occurred to me that they had ever been young. I knew almost nothing of their early lives. The past was never talked about. What I have been able to piece together was mostly discovered long after they were both dead.

My father, Charles William Carey, was born in 1887 in Sevenoaks. His father, described on his marriage certificate as a clerk and on his death certificate as a draper's assistant, died of TB when my father was eleven. His mother, the daughter of a solicitor called Samuel Magrath, died three years later of peritonitis, leaving four children, my father, Emily, Mollie and Arthur. Where the others were educated

I don't know, but my father was sent to the Royal Russell School in Purley, which had been founded in 1853 by a group of clerks in the textile trade to provide an education for the orphans of their fellow-workers. He became an accountant, and worked for a French firm, Les Successeurs d'Albert Godde, Bedin & Cie, which made beautiful and expensive fabrics. My sister Marjorie remembers him bringing silk ties back from France and lovely lengths of silk for my mother to have made up into dresses. His career with Godde, Bedin was interrupted by the Great War. I don't know when he joined up, but he was commissioned on 29 July 1916 as a second lieutenant in the Warwickshire Yeomanry. They were a cavalry regiment and took part in November 1917 in a famous cavalry charge at Huj, north of Gaza, cutting down the Turkish gunners and routing an enemy force ten times their number. By the time my father joined the first battalion, however, they had relinquished their horses and become a machine-gun battalion on the Western Front.

There is a photograph of him in uniform, looking very smart in service dress, Sam Browne, breeches and riding boots. With a magnifying glass you can pick out on his lapels and cap the bear and ragged staff that was the Earl of Warwick's crest and the Yeomanry's badge. Beside him stands his brother Arthur, easily identifiable as an Australian soldier by his slouch hat with the brim jauntily turned up on one side. I often pored over this photograph as a child, and I had been told that Arthur emigrated to Australia before the war, but it never occurred to me until recently to wonder how the photograph could possibly have been taken. I consulted Marjorie, who told me that Arthur had settled near Sydney, joined up when war came, and been sent to Europe to fight. Whether he was at Gallipoli I don't know, but it seems likely. The photograph was taken when the brothers happened both to be on leave in London. When my father rejoined his unit, Arthur took my father's girlfriend, later my mother, out once or twice. Perhaps they had tea at the Crystal Palace, with winkles. Then Arthur went back to the war and, when it was over, to Australia. The brothers never met again and I never saw my handsome uncle with the intriguing hat.

After the war my father returned to Godde, Bedin and made, Marjorie recalls, 'a great deal of money' – I have no idea how much. He furnished the house with antiques, *cloisonné* vases, fine prints and paintings (Marjorie still has two entrancing watercolours of eastern scenes by Noel Leaver) and they had a live-in maid. For Marjorie's sixth birthday he bought her a gold watch ('Mother was furious'). She and Bill were both privately educated. Bill went to Colet Court, the prep school for St Paul's, and Marjorie to St Paul's Girls' School. When cars were still quite rare my father bought one – a French model – from someone in Godde, Bedin. Later he bought a big brown Morris Oxford with curtains you could pull over the windows and a back part that folded down. Marjorie recalls that he had to go to Oxford to collect it ('you did in those days'), and she used to enjoy kneeling on the back seat and looking at the people behind. Its registration number was WL 4484. For holidays they would drive down to Devon and stop on the way to visit Stonehenge – you could wander quite freely among the monoliths – and at Taunton where they had buns hot from the oven. There were also seaside holidays in Kent at Westgate-on-Sea, not

Margate, which was considered common. There is a photograph of Rosemary and me (aged about four) on the sands at Westgate, mounted on donkeys. My donkey was called Pip, you can read it on his headband, and he was very pungent. Nowadays, as a beekeeper, I have a particular interest in oilseed rape, which is a big honey-crop, and Pip smelt exactly like a field of oilseed rape in full flower. It must have been on this holiday that I got lost on the sands and told the kind people who found me wandering, 'My mummy's got a bun,' meaning she wore her hair in a coil at the back. This, too, became a family joke, but it was accurate enough to get me restored to my relations.

A relic of my father's life in France is a watercolour I now have. It is a still life showing a plate of fruit – grapes, figs, a melon, a pomegranate. A label on the back identifies it as the work of Alberte Marie Ponchon of 3 Place des Victoires, Paris, and also supplies the information that it was shown at the Salon de l'Union des Femmes Peintres et Sculpteurs. The framer's label reads *Dorure, Encadrements. Le Michaux, 75 Rue St Jacques, Paris.* The Union of Women Painters and Sculptors was the first society of female artists in France, founded in 1881 by the sculptor Hélène Bertaux, and from 1882 it mounted annual exhibitions for women artists only. Whether my father knew Alberte, I have no idea.

The only other relic of his prosperous days that I have is the printed programme and menu for the Thirty-Sixth Annual Dinner and Dance of the Old Russellians, held on Saturday 9 February 1935 at the Criterion Restaurant in London. My father presided, and there is a smiling photograph of him on the front. Inside is the menu, all in French: *Hors d'œuvre Variés*, followed by *Consommé Brunoise* and *Crème Beau Rivage*, then *Barbue Duglèré*, then *Ris de Veau Milanaise* with *Petits Pois à l Étuvée*, then *Poularde Washington* with *Pommes Duchesse*, then *Bombe Pralinée* and *Arlésiennes*, and finally *Café*. On the facing page is the Toast List, with toasts to The King, The Old Russellians, The Old School, and The Chairman, all with the names of those who proposed and replied – my father replying to the last. On the back the entertainers are listed. Music during dinner and for the dancing was provided by The Sylvans Band. After dinner a contralto, Miss Miriam Benham, sang (she seems to have been quite well known and is cited in Sir Landon Ronald's 1937 *Who's Who in Music*). Clown Argo ('The Master Mimic') performed, and Mr George Piper was at the piano.

My mother must, I suppose, have attended this event, and I know a bit more about her early life than I do about my father's. She was ten years younger than him – born in 1897 – and was the daughter of a master blacksmith, James Cook, who had a forge off King Street, Hammersmith, employing several under-blacksmiths. As a child Marjorie used to go and watch them at work. I remember Grandpa Cook quite well. He was huge, as broad as a door, with drooping white moustaches and bear-paw hands. He had a specially made reclining chair, designed by himself. Improbably large, and upholstered in plum-coloured leather, it had various brass levers and pulleys that, properly operated, would lower its back until it lay flat like a bed and raise its adjustable footstool. This was not an invalid chair, it was just for comfort. Grandma Cook (née Walsgrove) was tiny, neat and gentle, with a sweet scrunched-up face.

The Cooks had three daughters. Dorothy (Dot) was the eldest, then came my mother, Winifred Ethel, and Eva. Dot married Reg Morgan, who was something high up in the Port of London Authority, and once, as a treat, Rosemary and I were taken on a tour of the London docks in a PLA launch. We were thrilled, and pretended we were looking for smugglers, as perhaps we were. Eva married Eddie Saxby, who was a partner in his family removals firm. Their two children, our cousins, were Barbara and Margaret, about the same age as Rosemary and me. Uncle Eddie had a Clark Gable moustache and was a bit of a card. One Christmas, it must have been 1938, we were all in the drawing room at Lonsdale Road when someone gave a shout and there, walking up the garden path, was Father Christmas. He came in through the conservatory with his sack and gave out presents. I was numb with shock. The whole room seemed suddenly different, as if in another reality. It was the only time in my life I have felt the presence of something otherworldly. A while after Father Christmas had left, Uncle Eddie came back. He had gone out earlier to get, he said, some cigarettes from the car. We all rushed at him shouting, 'You've missed Father Christmas.' He wouldn't believe us and said we were making it up. It was years before I realised what had happened.

Of my father's siblings Uncle Arthur went to Australia because he couldn't settle to any job in England. But he couldn't in Australia either, and lived in Newcastle, New South Wales, in a sort of shack. He sent us copies of an illustrated magazine called *Pix*, a kind of Australian *Picture Post*, which had matt, greyish pictures of life-saving teams on beaches and cheerfully racist cartoons depicting aboriginal families.

My father's younger sister, Mollie, married Tom Pockington, who made optical lenses, and they emigrated to Canada. I never saw them. They seem, though, to have been kind and generous. During the Second World War they sent us food parcels – chocolate, dried fruit, tinned ham. They were not wrapped in paper but stitched up in white cloth which someone said came from sugar bags.

Emily, the elder sister, was rather forbidding, and married Albert Jenkinson (Uncle Bert), who was a salesman in stationery. He used to give Bill and Marjorie pencils and paper when they were little. I have a photograph of Bert and Emily's wedding, which was evidently rather classy. The women are wearing fabulous hats and the men are dressed to the nines. My father – still a bachelor – is beautifully turned out, as always, in a jacket with braided lapels, a stiff white collar and a waistcoat with a gold watch chain looped across it. Uncle Bert was a conjuror on the side. He wore spats (neat little doeskin gaiters worn by gentlemen to cover the lacing of their shoes or boots), and would mystify Rosemary and me by putting his foot on a chair, inserting a penny under one side of his spat and taking it out the other side. He and Aunt Emmie had no children and he died young of TB.

While my mother was growing up the Cooks lived in Hammersmith at 44 Margravine Gardens, and she went to a London County Council School nearby. I know this because among my books now is a copy of *The Dog Crusoe* by R. M. Ballantyne, and pasted inside the front cover is a London County Council certificate which records that it was awarded to Winnie Cook of St Dunstan's Road School for General Progress in October 1908. *The Dog Crusoe*, subtitled *A Tale of the Western Prairies*, is a boys' adventure yarn, and seems an odd choice for an eleven-year-old girl. Still, it's a handsome volume, bound in blue with gold ornaments and a gold stamp proclaiming that it was a Prize Awarded by the London County Council.

The other book of my mother's I have is far more beautiful. It is called *Edmund Dulac's Picture Book for the French Red Cross*, and all profits from its sale went to help the sick and wounded in France. The contents are fairy stories, mostly from the Arabian Nights, and each is glowingly illustrated with a Dulac print, seventeen in all. When, in 2007, I went to the Dulwich Picture Gallery exhibition called 'The Age of Enchantment: Beardsley, Dulac and their Contemporaries', a copy of this book was on show. On my copy's flyleaf my father has written in a neat but rather dashing script 'To W E Cook from CWC Dec 1915'. So this was his present to my eighteen-year-old mother before he went to the war.

Apart from the two books, a remnant of my mother's youth I still have is a small oak chest which opens to reveal a glittering array of cutlery – large knives and small knives, all with ivory handles, large forks, dessert forks, dessert spoons, serving spoons, teaspoons, salt spoons, as well as carving knives and a steel for sharpening them, all fitting snugly into green-baize-lined lift-out shelves. Inside the lid the maker's name is stamped in silver, J. Rodgers & Sons, Cutler to His Majesty, 6 Norfolk Street, Sheffield. Screwed to the outside is an engraved silver plate which reads: 'Presented to Miss W. E. Cook on the occasion of her marriage, in recognition of her services with Les Successeurs D'Albert Godde, Bedin & Cie London during the years 1913–1919 and especially during the period of the Great War 1914–1919'. (We think of the war as ending in 1918, but it was in 1919 that the Treaty of Versailles was signed.)

After they married, on 23 August 1919, she and my father moved to 220 St Leonard's Road in East Sheen, which was where Bill and Marjorie were born. Then in 1928 my father bought the Lonsdale Road house and Grandma and Grandpa Cook moved into St Leonard's Road, which is where I remember them living. Grandpa Cook, having retired from blacksmithing, enjoyed collecting furniture and objets d'art, and used to go to sales, sometimes taking Marjorie with him when she was little. The drawing room at St Leonard's Road was a treasury of Victorian bric-a-brac – china ornaments, bronzes, and a ticking white-and-gold clock under a glass dome. There was a garden at the back, and to get to it you went through a small glassed-in conservatory where there was a wooden cabinet with a zinc-lined ice compartment – a kind of pre-refrigeration fridge for keeping butter and milk in. I used to be allowed to put my hand in, just for a moment, to feel the chill.

My mother's face in her wedding photo looks confidently at the camera from under a headdress of plaited summer flowers. Pretty, eager, excited, it is the face of a young woman blessed by chance. Her man has survived a war in which many thousands died. I saw this photo for the first time quite recently and I felt like an intruder, coming upon a happiness to which I did not belong. For the mother I knew never looked like this. Though brave and resolute, she was also anxious and careworn, and I now realise that by the time I was born, fifteen years after her wedding, her world had darkened. In the early 1930s Godde, Bedin went into liquidation and my father lost his job and a lot of money. When Rosemary and I were teenagers, we were shown, with a kind of wry amusement, bundles of worthless Godde, Bedin shares that were kept under the hinged seat of a wooden settle in the front hall. My father got another job as an accountant with the British radio manufacturer Cossor, and, Marjorie recalls, the live-in maid was kept on for quite a long time after the Godde, Bedin debacle. All the same, the future that had seemed secure had vanished, and the labour of caring for a growing family and a big house fell increasingly on my mother's shoulders.

Much more worrying was Bill. That there was something wrong with him was a fact I grew up with. I cannot remember a time when he seemed normal. Yet there is a photo of him in Colet Court uniform, taken a year or two before I was born, where he looks like an ordinary, jolly schoolboy, and Marjorie remembers how, on family holidays when they were children, the two of them would mischievously slip away from respectable Westgate and hang around the amusement arcades in downmarket Margate. She recalls, too, that at the age of eleven or twelve he had an astonishingly advanced vocabulary and would use difficult words she had never heard of. She thinks that perhaps he was on the edge of being very clever, until something went wrong. What that something was is a mystery. Our family GP told her much later that Bill never developed physically, so perhaps it was at puberty that abnormality began to appear. She says that Mother would never admit that there was anything wrong. Bill did not smoke or drink and was a fine brother, she would tell Marjorie. Perhaps in some unacknowledged way she resented Marjorie's being well when Bill was not, so treated her more severely. She was dosed once a week with California Syrup of Figs, which made her physically sick, so she had to stand in the bath before being given it, whereas Bill was given little chocolate pills. In itself this is trivial, of course. The middle classes were paranoid about constipation in the 1930s and California Syrup of Figs, though vile, was a popular remedy. Rosemary and I were also given it weekly when we were deemed old enough. All the same, my mother's severity to Marjorie, besides being a sign of her indomitable willpower, may have been connected in some oblique way with her anxiety about her firstborn son.

Bill's condition deteriorated over the years, so it is hard to describe it at any one time. I remember him as tall and painfully thin, with a shrunken chest, narrow shoulders that seemed to fold inwards, and long, lean hands which hung loosely in front of him. He would rub them together nervously and they trembled when he lifted things. He spoke very little and had almost no facial expression, just a pallid, blank, worried look. While conversation went on around him he would sit, seemingly abstracted, sometimes glowering, as if perplexed by a deep inner problem. Sometimes he seemed to take pleasure in aggravation. If, at mealtime, there was some small mishap, he would snicker with amusement, particularly if the mishap involved Marjorie or my father. This grew rarer as time went on, though, and he withdrew more. It strikes me now that autism may have been one of his troubles, but it was not a condition much known about in the 1930s.

On the other hand he was, in my early years, far from disabled. He could ride a bike, and had a job in the packing department of the Society for the Propagation of Christian Knowledge in Hammersmith. Within the family, his strangeness was never discussed. It was made clear that to refer to it or ask about it, or about what had happened in the past, was unacceptable. At that time mental illness was considered shameful, a thing to be hidden, so Bill's condition made it impossible for us to invite friends home or ask people to meals. However, this was probably less of a deprivation than it might seem now. Families at our class-level did not, I think, entertain much in those days. People kept themselves to themselves. At any rate, we did, and we never had meals out. We were a very enclosed family, and my mother was determined to keep it that way. Bill would clearly not marry, and the idea that the other three of us might, and leave home, was something she shut her mind to. In time this caused considerable unhappiness.

Quite apart from family worries, the late 1930s must have been an anxious time for my parents, as for most people in Europe. In August 1939 we were sent away to the little country town of Mere in Wiltshire for several weeks – my father stayed in London – and we were still in Mere on 3 September when Neville Chamberlain made his broadcast to the nation telling us that we were at war with Germany. When we got back to Lonsdale Road we found an air-raid shelter in the garden. I think Uncle Eddie's removal men had dug it, and they had done a thorough job. Where the lawn had been a huge mound of raw earth squatted like a tumulus, with a sandbagged entrance and a flight of wooden steps going down into the darkness. I was tremendously excited. I suppose I saw it as a new kind of adventure playground, and as we stood in the drawing room looking out at it through the French windows I glanced up at my mother expecting her to share my pleasure. She was in tears. It was the only time I ever saw her weep, and I couldn't understand why.

For a while the air-raid shelter did become a play-space for Rosemary and me. We used to buy Wall's Snow-Fruits, triangular water-ices in cardboard sleeves, from the corner shop opposite our garage, and lick them surreptitiously in the shelter's dark, rather smelly interior. But it palled after a while. Another memory from this waiting-time is of our family, all six of us, sitting solemnly in the drawing room at Lonsdale Road wearing our government-issue gas masks. I used to think we must have heard rumours of a poison gas attack, and decided to meet our fate in a dignified manner, like true Britons. But it's more likely we were obeying official instructions to get used to wearing our gas masks, so that we'd be less liable to panic in an emergency. Mine, I remember, made breathing difficult, and I could not see out of it because the transparent eyepiece misted up. Otherwise it was fine.

Then, one night in September 1940, my father took me to the upstairs window again and showed me another glare in the sky, not the Crystal Palace this time, but London's docks on fire – the start of the Blitz. In the weeks that followed the shelter briefly came into its own. I remember being carried to it, in pyjamas and dressing gown, across what was left of the garden, and looking up at a night sky busy with searchlights. However, it soon became clear that the threat to Barnes was small and the shelter rather horrible, so we took alternative precautions. Marjorie slept in the understairs cupboard, reckoned a safe place because staircases were strongly built. Rosemary and I slept on a mattress underneath my parents' big bed, which had been dismantled and reassembled downstairs in the drawing room. Bill slept under the dining-room table.

Nights were usually noisy. Once a bomb landed over by the reservoirs and blew in our front door. Marjorie, safe under the stairs, saw the parquet blocks on the hall floor rise in the air and fall back into place. Blast had odd effects. A nearby house lost its entire wall on the street side, exposing all its rooms with their furniture still in place, like a doll's house with the front lifted off. This became a common sight in the Blitz and must have kept Uncle Eddie's removal vans busy. Blackout regulations were strict. Rosemary and I were not allowed to have the light on in the drawing room for more than a few moments while we undressed. We used to crawl onto the mattress beneath our parents' bed in the dark and read by torchlight under the bedclothes. One night we were startled from sleep to find the drawing room full of light. 'You've left the light on,' Rosemary shouted, horrified. But I had not. An incendiary bomb had fallen in the garden and its furious glare was strong enough to penetrate the thick blackout curtains, making the room as bright as day. It was quickly put out by an ARP warden who clambered over the wall, and he gave my father the tail section as a trophy. I inspected it closely. It was about six inches long, with three fins enclosed at the base in a neat metal ring, and the little rivets that had held it to the bomb casing were still there, hanging twisted and wobbly in their holes. We kept it on the kitchen mantelpiece to hold spills for lighting the gas.

A more serious, high-explosive bomb fell near the railway line at the bottom of my grandparents' St Leonard's Road garden. It did not explode at once, and all the houses nearby were evacuated. My grandparents took refuge with us, and I have an image of neat little Grandma Cook standing at an upstairs window at Lonsdale Road, looking out. It occurs to me now she was waiting for the explosion that would tell her her house had been destroyed. But of course I didn't think of that at the time. I just wondered why she was looking so sad. She turned and saw me, and instantly smiled to show there was nothing wrong. In the event, the bomb was successfully defused, and my grandparents returned to their lovely curios and zinc-lined fridge.

I used to think that my father decided to take the family out of London towards the end of 1941 because the firm he worked for moved its offices. But I learned quite recently that in fact I was responsible. Apparently, after a particularly noisy night, I said to my father, 'Are we dead yet, Daddy?' This line, anticipating, I like to think, my later interest in Dickensian melodrama, so moved my tender-hearted father that he let the London house and moved us all out of danger to a Nottinghamshire village called Radcliffe-on-Trent.

2

Radcliffe

Radcliffe, my father told me, was in the Midlands. He was fond of quoting, somewhat sadly, Hilaire Belloc:

> When I am living in the Midlands,
> That are sodden and unkind,
> The great hills of the south country
> Come back into my mind.

I liked the sound of the great hills, but had no idea where they were meant to be, and could not remember any in Barnes. The nearest town to Radcliffe was Nottingham – also, I learned, in the Midlands – and my father got a job there as an accountant with a firm that made women's clothes. Bill and Marjorie both worked in Nottingham too, cycling the six miles there and back each day, whereas my father went on the bus. Bill's job was in the packing department at the *Nottingham Evening Post*, Marjorie's in Barclays Bank in Arkwright Street. It was freezing in winter, she told us, and she got terrible chilblains. But there was an open fire and Eric Wing, the man she later married, put a kettle on at eleven o'clock each morning and dissolved Oxo cubes in boiling water – which, with everything being rationed, was a luxury.

Radcliffe was just a village then. There was a crossroads with a few shops and a church. We lived in Walnut Grove, a stony track winding up from the crossroads. When it rained, little streams snaked down it, with gravel glinting through the water. At the top was a green gate and, beyond it, someone's enormous vegetable garden. We were forbidden to go there, and I thought of it as the garden where Peter Rabbit met Mr McGregor. Our house, Durham House, was halfway up on the left, a foursquare, detached, double-fronted brick house with laurel bushes in front and a long back garden. Next door, in a cottage, lived Miss Haslam, who was an ARCM and gave Rosemary piano lessons. Next door on the other side was a stable belonging to some people called the Greatorexes. Since there was no resident horse, they let Rosemary and me use the hayloft over it as a den. To get in you had to stand on an iron manger and clamber up through a trapdoor. It was a lovely place, smelling of straw and dust. Opposite us were the Richmonds, who had a bay tree in their front garden. When my mother prepared soused herrings for high tea on Saturdays I was sent to ask if we could please have some leaves from it for flavouring. Kind Mr Richmond would pick a sheaf and put them in my hand like a little pack of bright green cards. Apart from the Misses Bloodworth, who lived next door to Miss Haslam and were on bad terms with her and were known to be gossips, that was the entire population of Walnut Grove.

At the bottom of Walnut Grove was a long low shed housing Astell's, the newsagent's and confectioner's, where we bought our sweet ration. Mr Astell was a gaunt, square-jawed, wolfish-looking man, and all he usually had in stock were wine gums. They were shaped to look roughly like fruits, in various cloudy colours, and he kept them in a tall metal canister with a round lid which he would lever off, prior to pouring a meagre tinkling shower into the brass pan of his scales. The sweet ration was four ounces a week and if he went overweight his long fingers would select an errant gum from the scales, toss it back in the tin and clap the lid on, while we watched critically. He almost never had any chocolate in stock – not, anyway, for Rosemary and me – but luckily Marjorie had a boyfriend in the RAF called Chris who would send her bars of chocolate occasionally which we shared. At Astell's we also bought Erinmore Flake for my father's pipe and, using a fraction of our shilling-a-week pocket money, Rizla rolling papers for the cigarettes that Rosemary and I smoked secretly in our den. In the 1940s anyone who was the least bit stylish smoked, so we puffed away in solemn imitation.

The other shops were of less interest. Opposite the end of Walnut Grove was the Co-op where all the family's rations were measured out, and round the corner from Astell's was a baker's which sold cream buns. Up the village street was Smith's the chemist, a legendary shop because a previous Mr Smith had invented a hand cream called Cremolia and sold it to Boots for, it was whispered, unimaginable riches. You can still buy it and it is, so far as I know, the only famous thing to have come out of Radcliffe. But for Rosemary and me Radcliffe was heaven. The nights were so quiet, after Barnes and the bombs, that we found it hard to get to sleep, and the days were full of freedom. Radcliffe really does have red cliffs, as its name promises, and they were our playground. We would turn left out of Walnut Grove, walk up the road, climb a stile – the first stile we had seen in our lives – and cross a field to the cliff-top path. To clamber down the cliff face we clung to bushes and got footholds on tree roots and slipped and slithered the last bit, and there at the bottom was the River Trent with a weir stretching across it. It was a rather dank and gloomy place, with overhanging trees and lots of nettles, but the weir put everything else out of your head. The air was thick with the din of it, and you could stand on a concrete ledge, looking out over the foaming roar, so close that the shallow water by the bank, as clear as a plate of glass, was racing past just inches from your toes. Our cousins, Barbara and Margaret, Eva and Eddie's children, came to stay for a week and we tried to introduce them to the pleasures of cliff climbing. But they were terrified and we felt very superior. When Rosemary and I were grown up, and had children of our own, we wondered whatever our parents had been thinking of, allowing us such freedom. But I fancy that they, like the rest of us, just eased up, getting out of London, and were content to let things go.

Not that they relaxed, exactly. My father grew vegetables for us in the back garden, his part in the Dig for Victory campaign. The garden at Barnes had been small, and mainly lawn, or, later, mainly air-raid shelter. This one was huge by comparison and had extensive brick-built sheds and outhouses and fruit trees – a damson near the kitchen and several apples. I think my father was pleased and proud that he could grow so much. He had a cucumber frame, an adventurous thing for those days. I had never seen one and was fascinated by the idea of vegetables having a special room for themselves out of doors. He also joined the local Home Guard unit. They wore battle dress and had rifles and did manoeuvres down by the railway line. I remember watching them taking up a defensive position, a line of men, all, I suppose, ex-soldiers, sighting along their rifle barrels. It was serious, and the *Dad's Army* idea of the Home Guard popularised in the 1960s has always seemed to me insulting – a cheap laugh for a pampered, unthreatened generation.

My mother worked all the time – cooked, cleaned, catered. In the evenings she knitted sweaters and socks for Bill, me and my father. Until my late teens the only socks I wore were ones she had knitted, and usually darned as well. Buying socks in a shop would have seemed ridiculous, and it never occurred to me that anyone did. For darning she had a wooden toadstool, painted pink (though most of the paint was worn off), which she slipped under the place to be darned. She washed our clothes each Monday in the stone-paved scullery where there was a copper with a coke fire underneath and a wooden 'copper-stick', pale and worn from use, and wrinkled, like your hand when you've left it too long in water, which was for pushing the clothes down in the copper. For drying she used a mangle, a big iron frame, a bit like a printing press, with a screw at the top for adjusting the tension and two wooden rollers turned by an iron wheel at the side. The wet clothes were fed in at the back and came out from between the rollers flat as cardboard while water from them splashed down a wooden sluice at the front into a bucket. Ironing happened later in the week, in the afternoons, filling the kitchen with a lovely toasty smell. The house was kept spotless, every polishable surface polished. The dining-room sideboard had an array of silver objects on show – cake stands, salvers, fruit dishes – and they were always sparkling. Marjorie helped with this, but otherwise it was taken for granted by everyone, my mother included, that housework was her department. The idea that my father should help with the housework would have struck her as out of the course of nature.

She was a wonderful cook and provider, and eked out food so that despite rationing we never went hungry. Some of the best things were from leftovers, especially bubble and squeak and scraps of meat minced for shepherd's pie. The mincer was a big hand-cranked machine that had to be screwed to a table-edge before use. The meat went into the metal cup at the top and the little worms of mince wriggled out at the bottom. Then the mincer had to be taken apart and all its screws and cutters scrubbed clean. As a treat she would make toffee, using black treacle and pouring the mix into a greased baking tray. When it had hardened she broke it up with a hammer, and because of the greased tray you always got a slight taste of margarine when you first put a piece in your mouth. It was delicious. Rosemary and I had no memory of what food had been like before the war. We used to goggle at the old biscuit tins my mother kept knitting wool in, and the custard creams, rich teas or shortbreads pictured there seemed like other-world fantasies, not real food at all. I used to love Sunday breakfasts because she would make a kind of egg fritter out of reconstituted dried egg. Real eggs were pretty well unknown, but occasionally my mother would get one and boil it for my father. He always insisted on making soldiers out of bread and marge and dipping one into the yolk for Rosemary and one for me. My mother would plead, 'Don't, Will, don't. There'll be none for you.' But he did, and I never eat a boiled egg now without thinking of it.

Rosemary and I both had bikes. Mine was a BSA roadster with eighteen-inch wheels, a three-speed gear housed in its rear hub and, at first, wooden blocks screwed to its pedals because my legs were too short to reach them. Our regular ride was to Shelford, a village a couple of miles away. In the Middle Ages it had had a famous priory with a relic of the true cross and a phial of the Virgin's milk. But I knew nothing about this at the time and would not have cared if I had. For me the truly important thing about Shelford was the steep hill leading down to it. Once launched, you lost all control. The hedges zipped by, the wind rushed through your hair. The BSA, flying over the bumps, was a racehorse or a fighter plane, depending on which fantasy you were wrapped in. When it was over we trudged uphill for another go. Fortunately, as it was wartime, there were no cars.

Walnut Grove was a gentle slope by comparison, but even it could provide a thrill if you got up enough speed. One day I was pedalling furiously down it, crouched over the handlebars in proper racing pose, when a strange thing happened. I seemed to be waking up at home in bed, but the object in front of my eyes was unmistakably a bacon slicer, and I could not make out how it had got there. It turned out that the BSA had carried me across the Shelford Road, hit the kerb the other side and dumped me on the pavement outside the Co-op. Excited reports reached Durham House that eyewitnesses had seen me being carried lifeless into the shop. As I recall, my parents were very calm about it. In the middle of a world war a child falling off his bike was no great matter.

We all went to church every Sunday. People tended to during the war, but I think we would have anyway as my parents were rather religious. I don't mean they were preachy or given to discussing religion. That would never have entered their heads. But we always said grace before meals – 'For what we are about to receive may the Lord make us truly thankful. Amen' – and my father knelt by his bed and said his prayers every night, sometimes audibly. We were encouraged to do the same, though if it was cold I compromised by saying them when I had snuggled under the covers. I was an unquestioning believer and had evolved an elaborate personal prayer in which I asked God to protect all my relatives – aunts, uncles, cousins – each individually designated, as well as each of the stuffed animals I took to bed with me, which was quite a crowd.

Over the mantelpiece in my parents' bedroom hung a huge picture of the crucifixion in a black frame, showing the three victims on their crosses under dark clouds, and the gaggle of mourners and soldiers below. It must I think have been a print of some Renaissance painting but I have never been able to spot the original though I have kept an eye open in art galleries over the years. Looking back it seems a macabre ornament for a bedroom, but I thought it perfectly natural at the time. My mother's favourite hymns were 'There is a green hill far away' and 'When I survey the wondrous cross'. Perhaps that had something to do with the bedroom picture. I disliked hearing her sing, and when I was little I used to plead with her not to – 'Don't sing, Mum, don't sing,' which became a family joke. I think it was that the voice she put on for singing made her seem unfamiliar, and frightened me.

In Radcliffe, as soon as I was old enough, I joined the church choir. I didn't actually volunteer, but I agreed when my parents suggested it, partly because choirboys wore black cassocks and white surplices, which I thought rather dashing, and partly because they were paid half a crown (that is, two shillings and sixpence) each quarter. Being a choirboy, I heard the King James version of the Bible read in church every Sunday. I generally listened with half an ear, and just let the sounds drift over me, but that was, I suppose, when its exotic language and strange stories started to settle into my head and seem natural. Meanwhile, from singing hymns, I began to see what poetry was, though I wouldn't have put it like that. I especially liked the line about singing valleys – 'The valleys stand so thick with corn that even they are singing' – in William Dix's hymn 'To thee O Lord our hearts we raise'. It appealed to me because valleys obviously can't sing, yet I could see what it meant. It was a while before I realised Dix had taken his line from Psalm 65 – also part of a choirboy's repertoire – where it seemed even better because the valleys laughed as well as singing.

Reading in Radcliffe mostly meant comics. Rosemary and I got the *Dandy* and *Beano* every week and fought over who should read them first, and she bought *Sunny Stories*, the Enid Blyton weekly, which I read too, though it was a bit feminine for my taste. From time to time, if we could afford it, we got *Hotspur* and *Champion* as well, and for a while my hero was Rockfist Rogan of the RAF, a Spitfire pilot and boxing ace whose adventures *Champion* serialised. A comic we saw more rarely, *Film Fun*, had a kind of cross-genre piquancy for us, because at Radcliffe's small cinema ('The Rex') we screamed with laughter at Laurel and Hardy each Saturday at the children's matinees, and when we got *Film*

Fun there they were on the page, and it was like coming across a bad drawing of people we knew.

Though our staple was comics, there were a lot of books in the house. In the front room a large, shiny bookcase, with glass doors, displayed bound sets relating to the South African War, Living Animals of the World, and other serious topics, along with the *Encyclopædia Britannica* in green cloth. These books were furniture. No one, so far as I know, ever ventured to open the glass doors and disturb their austere calm. I still have that *Encyclopædia Britannica*. It always looks a little naked on my shelves, without its glass, and it is not much good for reference, being the eleventh edition (1910–11). But it is a time machine. Its pictures and descriptions of cities and countries show a world that two wars and modern communications have swept away. Here, preserved in photographs and tiny print, are Conrad's Africa and Proust's France and the Germany of Thomas Mann's *Buddenbrooks*.

But as a child I was immune to its appeal. The real books were upstairs – perhaps a couple of hundred of them, on some old varnished shelves in a room rather grandly called 'the study'. It also contained a big linen cupboard, in the top right-hand drawer of which were a box of revolver bullets and a policeman's truncheon. They belonged, I suppose, to my father – the bullets left over from the Great War, and the truncheon, I later surmised, from his brief period as a special constable during the General Strike. But I can't be sure, because I never discussed these magic relics with anybody, or disclosed that I knew of their whereabouts. I would just take them out, when alone, and finger them. The truncheon was new-looking and shiny, and disappointingly free of combat-marks. But some of the bullets had evidently been used – perhaps fired at Germans? – and the remainder rolled about and thudded importantly against the sides of their tough little cardboard box with its stoutly stapled corners.

Their spell filled the room with past time, and so did the books, for most of them dated from the 1920s and '30s when Bill was growing up. My favourite was a *Chums* annual for 1894. *Chums* was a boys' weekly started in 1892, and the 1894 volume must have belonged to my father when he was a boy, though oddly I never asked him about it. It was a huge book, in deeply embossed red and gold covers, inside which the weekly issues of *Chums* were bound together. They had no colour, just columns and columns of close-packed print, and greyish pictures showing schoolboys in Eton collars and knickerbockers and caps with stripes going round them. It had a distinct military tang. There were articles on the animal mascots adopted by British regiments, and pictures of army uniforms worn by different nations, including Austro-Hungary, which had ceased to exist by the time I read it. Each number had an instalment of a novel – 1894 started with Stevenson's *Treasure Island* – and there was a lot of rough-and-tumble humour based on class and race – tramps, beggars and foreigners all being automatically funny, which I thought hilarious. What I liked best were the column-fillers – jokes, fascinating facts, arresting anecdotes, each occupying its tiny paragraph. They were quite useless, but I would soak them up for hours, completely released from my own world, like an archaeologist at the bottom of a deep shaft.

Almost as strong a competitor for my attention was a *Hobbies Annual* from a more recent era – about 1933, I think, because one of its illustrations was an artist's impression of 'The Doomed R101 at its Mooring Mast'. In the accompanying article, describing the airship losing height as it crossed France, the writer referred to it as 'the crippled dirigible'. I was captivated by the phrase, and hoarded it in my memory for years like a line of poetry, hoping I might get an opportunity to use it myself, though it seemed unlikely. But in 1988, reviewing Michael Green's autobiography *The Boy Who Shot Down an Airship* for the *Sunday Times*, I came across Green's memory of seeing the R101 pass overhead, and in my review I was at last able to pass 'the crippled dirigible' off as my own. A small triumph, I know, but it's the kind of thing that makes a literary life feel rounded.

The main pleasure *Hobbies* offered, though, was not its literary style but its detailed directions about how to construct model steam yachts or electric motors or viaducts for Hornby layouts. These always carried the assurance that the necessary materials could be 'purchased for a few pence from any ironmongers'. I liked the opulence that evoked, though I knew of no likely ironmongers and, anyway, had no inclination to make the models. The pleasure they yielded was pure make-believe. I gloated over them rather, I suppose, as housewives, stinted by rationing, studied pre-war cookery books.

Most of the other stuff on the shelves seemed pretty unapproachable. There was a high proportion of John Buchan and G. A. Henty, and a quick look at these put me off. More manageable was *The Boy's Book of School Stories* by the intriguingly named Gunby Hadath. One story that impressed me indelibly was about a class studying Scott's 'Lay of the Last Minstrel' which contains the lines:

> O Caledonia! stern and wild;
> Meet nurse for a poetic child.

The master asks a not-very-bright boy what they mean and he is baffled. To him the lines sound 'like a telegram from a lunatic asylum to an employment agency'. (This was the story's best joke, and still seems funny to me.) In despair he blurts out, 'Sir, I don't quite understand who is to meet the nurse.' The class howl with laughter and the master is witheringly sarcastic. However, the boy gets his revenge. Climbing in the Alps in the summer holidays, he comes across a climber in difficulties, clinging to a narrow ledge. It is the same master! I remember the illustration. Stuck to the rock face like a starfish, in plus fours and long socks, he is staring downwards with the whites of his eyes enlarged to indicate terror. The boy, leaning out coolly from the rock below him, instructs him on which ledges to put his feet to reach safety. I suppose the story appealed to me as a triumph over the adult world – though the literary allusion also gave it a certain chic.

What the story was meant to teach me, of course, was that courage matters more than understanding poetry. Several other stories also promoted courage. The illustration for one showed an enormous rugby player in a striped shirt running full tilt towards the viewer with the ball tucked under his arm while a player in a different shirt watches him go past in dismay. The caption read 'He funked it', and the story was about how the dismayed player had meant to bring his gigantic opponent down with a diving tackle but lost heart at the last moment. I forget what he did to atone for his cowardice. Perhaps he found another climber in the Alps.

Contemporary writing was not represented on the shelves, so for that I had to depend on birthday and Christmas presents, and loans from friends. My favourite modern author was Captain W. E. Johns. I must have read nearly all his Biggles books (though not the cissy Worrals-of-the-WAAF series, of course). The Biggles adventures that most gripped me were the exotic ones. *Biggles in the Orient* was a marvel of deft plotting about a series of inexplicable crashes among the fighter planes operating against the Japanese from a certain Burmese airfield. Inspecting the wreckage of one plane Biggles finds a scrap of peppermint-scented silver paper. Chewing gum! All at once it dawns on him. Someone must be drugging the pilots' confectionery so that they pass out when flying over the jungle. Sure enough, back at base a 'moon-faced' Eurasian mess steward is found injecting the squadron's chewing gum with a hypodermic. Curtains for Moon-Face.

The scrap of pepperminty paper strikes me, even now, as a brilliant touch – like the chocolate paper William Golding's Pincher Martin finds in his pocket, with one agonisingly sweet crumb of chocolate still adhering to it. *Biggles in the South Seas* enthralled me even more. I forget the plot, but in one episode Biggles's friend Ginger becomes romantically attached to a young female South Sea Islander, and they have an adventure with a giant octopus, involving a lung-searing underwater swim. The girl is clad – scantily, one gathers – in something called a *pareu*. I had no idea what this garment was, but it lingered pleasantly in my mind, eventually getting mixed up with the brief costume worn by Jean Simmons in *The Blue Lagoon*.

In the cupboards under the glass-fronted bookcase that held the encyclopaedias I found eleven huge books, uniformly bound in thick, embossed red boards, and stacked on their sides like paving stones. They were too heavy to lift, so I dragged them out onto the floor, one by one, and opened them there. They were, I now know, bound annual sets of the French magazine *Figaro illustré* for the years 1890 to 1900. But to me at the time they were completely mysterious. I might as well have been exploring the remains of a dead civilisation. I don't think I even knew the language they were in was French. What kept me turning the pages were the pictures – huge, full-page colour plates on thick, glossy paper depicting scenes from late nineteenth-century French life. I especially liked the ones of beautiful young ladies in flowing robes, surrounded by flowers, which seemed different from the rest, partly because of the way the ladies and flowers had outlines round them which made them stand out. I now know that these were by the Czech artist Alfons Mucha, the inventor of what came to be called art nouveau. I know, too, that the other pictures I pored over in those ten years of *Figaro*s were by the most famous French illustrators of the time, including Toulouse-Lautrec. For an adult these sumptuous, decadent books (which I still have) mark a moment in cultural history. The last volume is devoted to the 1900 Paris International Exhibition, which spread the Mucha style worldwide. But at the age of nine or ten I was ignorant of all this. I could not connect the pictures with human life as I knew it, and did not want to. For me they were a fantastic world of otherness, endlessly absorbing. I would visit it surreptitiously, for I was not sure I was meant to touch or even know about these books, and I realised they must be valuable. I did not connect them with my father's wealthy French past, for at the time I knew nothing about that either.

But rummaging through the house, as children do, I found things that told me he had been rich, or at any rate richer than we seemed to be. A black tail coat, a dinner jacket, striped trousers and a white waistcoat hung in a wardrobe. In a drawer I found two beautiful diamond cravat pins, one in the shape of a fleur-de-lys, and gold cuff links engraved CWC. In a cupboard in the sideboard in the dining room were bottles of wine. Wine! No one drank anything alcoholic in our house of any sort at all. With the wine were two boxes of cigars, opened and still half full. I loved sniffing the fragrant wood and rolling the cigars – wrapped in tissue paper – between my fingers to hear them crackle. With the cuff links and pins I had found a strange little metal tube with a spring, which I now know was a silver cigar cutter. But I did not connect any of these rich remains with the *Figaro*s, or understand, as I now do, that my father must have brought them back from France, and perhaps sometimes leafed through them in suburban Barnes to remind him of his life in Paris, until the crash came and they were shut away in the cupboard out of sight.

These, then, were my education up to the age of about eleven – the King James Bible, *Hymns Ancient and Modern*, *Dandy*, *Beano*, *Hotspur*, *Champion*, Biggles, *Chums* for 1894,

Gunby Hadath, the 1933 *Hobbies* annual and *Figaro illustré* for 1890–1900. I can see they're not exactly what you would select nowadays as the ideal primary-school curriculum. All the same, they were what mattered to me, whereas nothing I read in school over the same period has stayed with me at all. I might as well not have been there. I am sure this was not the schools' fault but mine. Partly because of family circumstances, and partly just by temperament, I was, I think, an abnormally self-contained, self-absorbed little boy. The home, and what I discovered there, was real to me. What lay beyond was hardly real at all.

When we arrived in Radcliffe Rosemary and I were sent to the council primary school. It was a modern brick building with asphalt playgrounds and green railings and separate entrances for boys and girls. Rosemary and I were in different forms, of course, so I didn't see much of her. My form teacher was Miss Avison, who was fat, with glasses. I liked her and I think she found me amusing. She cast me as Herod in the school nativity play. I wore a gold paper crown and my mother supplied an opera cloak, black velvet with a shiny scarlet lining and white fur collar – another remnant, I suppose, of vanished prosperity. I also had a false beard which hooked over my ears. I thought I looked magnificently regal in these accoutrements. Seated on a chair centre stage, I had to open the play by telling the Wise Men to go off and follow the star to Bethlehem. As soon as the curtain rose – or, rather, was pulled aside, as it hung from a pole – the audience went into fits of laughter. I was astonished. I had no idea why they thought me funny and, as I recall, my Wise Men were similarly at a loss. Later Miss Avison did a watercolour painting of me as Herod in my autograph book, which my parents obviously found charming.

Everyone at the school had a third of a pint of free milk, mid-morning. It came in rattling metal crates, and the bottles were wider and thicker at the brim than modern milk bottles. They had cardboard tops with a circle stamped in the middle which you could press with your finger to make a hole for a straw. The milk had quite a thick layer of cream at the top, darker-coloured than the rest, as milk did in those days. Many years later, when I was studying seventeenth--century religious poetry, I came across 'The Weeper' by Richard Crashaw, a camp, and, I imagine, gay, English cleric, and the only English poet to write real baroque, counter-Reformation poetry, who fled to Rome and became a Catholic during the Civil War. In his poem he writes about the cream rising to the top in milk, and the text survives in two versions. In one it 'steals above, and is the cream', and in the other it 'crawls above, and is the cream'. 'Crawls' always seemed to me a better word for the sluggish infiltration of cream through milk, and I now realise that what I was recalling was those bottles with their soft, cream-covered cardboard tops at primary school.

The war was, of course, the only subject in news broadcasts at the time (I once asked my mother what they had put in the news before the war and she couldn't remember) and the only other incident I recall from primary school was war-linked. In November 1942, when news came of the British victory at El Alamein, there was countrywide rejoicing and, to celebrate the occasion, each child in our school was issued with a helping of trifle. It came in a sort of cardboard cup, white, with pleated sides, and consisted of custard, jelly and cream in about equal proportions. It was an unimaginable luxury in those sparse times. The trifles were handed round at teatime, with spoons, and before we tucked in the class stood up to thank God for victory and our trifles. In the middle of the prayer, I noticed something dreadful. My trifle was sliding down the sloping desk top. My hands were clasped in prayer, my head bowed, and to abandon this sacred posture merely to stop a sliding trifle was clearly unthinkable. So I did nothing, and it fell onto my shoe – or, rather, my boot, for in my early schooldays I wore, to my shame and embarrassment, boots, not shoes like everyone else, presumably because they were reach-me-downs from Bill's schooldays when polished black ankle boots were fashionable juvenile wear. When 'Amen' was pronounced and everyone started eating their trifles, I stooped down and ate mine from my boot. I managed pretty well, though there was a slight tang of Cherry Blossom shoe polish, and tiny portions of trifle that my spoon could not get to were left in the eyeholes. As I recall no one paid the least attention to what had happened. Perhaps they were simply too absorbed in their own trifles.

Rosemary and I must have passed the eleven-plus while we were still at Radcliffe primary, but I can only remember walking home afterwards and feeling glad it was over. Being older, she went to grammar school first, and I was sent for a year to a Catholic boys' school, Thomas à Becket, in West Bridgford. Maybe my parents thought it would be a good launching pad for grammar school, but if so they were mistaken. It was run by priests belonging to the

Order of the Augustinians of the Assumption. They wore ankle-length black cassocks with long leather straps knotted round their middles, with which they used to hit us on the palms of our hands – never, so far as I could make out, for any particular reason. It did not hurt much, but neither Rosemary nor I had ever been hit at home, so to be hit by the holy fathers and holy brothers seemed somehow indecent. I don't mean sexually, I had no thoughts of that kind, but socially – like spitting in someone's eye. I can see that this must seem a fastidious and uppish attitude for a child to have taken. Still, it's what I felt, as near as I can describe it, and I think children are often more fastidious than they are given credit for.

There was a school chapel, ablaze with the usual religious kitsch, but not being a Catholic I did not go to services there. I can't remember reading anything at all in my year at Thomas à Becket, but I was once sick over a history book, open at a page showing an illustration of the Venerable Bede, which has permanently tainted my feelings about that great polymath. Outside the school was the River Trent and a suspension bridge with a stall where an old woman sold hot orange squash in winter at a penny a glass, which was good for warming your hands on. The bridge was a battleground where the bigger boys fought the pupils of Mundella, a secondary modern across the river, shouting their war-song:

> Monkey Della
> Red and yeller

in allusion to the Mundella school colours.

After a year in the care of the Augustinians I followed Rosemary to West Bridgford Grammar School. She did well there, came top in her class and played the flute in the school orchestra. I idled. The staff were bright and well-meaning, but I had no interest in the things they wanted to teach – history, geography, mathematics – which seemed abstruse and far removed from any concern of mine. Naturally this annoyed them, and I was put on Daily Report. This meant that at the start of each week I collected a card – a white sheet with a black grid of little boxes, like a cage – and at the end of each lesson I had to walk up to the front of the class and ask the teacher to fill the appropriate box, reporting on my scholarly progress, or lack of it. It was shaming, and, I suppose, meant to be. I coped by retreating into a sort of numbness, sealing myself off, so far as I could, from everyone around. I was helped by a book that I got from the school library, which I think a sympathetic teacher must have chosen for me. It was Henry Williamson's *Tarka the Otter*, and I liked it because there were no people in it, or only incidentally, as enemies. With the very first sentence I was far away from West Bridgford: 'Twilight over meadow and water, the eve-star shining above the hill, and Old Nog the heron crying *kra-a-ark!* as his slow dark wings carried him down to the estuary.' I read it and reread it, not wanting to try any other book. Its fierce, cruel action made me feel secluded from everyday realities, and I realised that everything I had read before was trivial by comparison. I knew nothing about politics so I had no idea how lucky I was that Williamson's books had not been banned from the school library because of his membership, before the war, of Oswald Mosley's British Union of Fascists. It was many years before I found anything to match Williamson's masterpiece – not, in fact, until I read the poetry of his great admirer Ted Hughes.

I got the feeling that, because I was out of favour with the authorities, the weaker teachers picked on me. The art mistress, a prissy little woman importantly arrayed, as all the teachers were, in a long black academic gown, set us one day to paint the portrait of someone else in the class. I painted a boy called Bright, whom I had rather a crush on, though we had never spoken. I did his handsome profile and floppy straw-coloured hair and then, as background, I painted sloping scarlet dashes, to express what I took to be his eager approach to life, which was very unlike mine. I was rather pleased with it, but the art mistress took one look and said I had spoiled it with the 'silly background'. It's odd that I should have remembered such a tiny incident for so long, but I suppose it shows how raw I felt. I found some outlet for my frustrations in boxing. The school had a proper boxing ring set up in the gymnasium, and I knew from my reading of *Chums* and Gunby Hadath that boxing was a manly sport at which one should try to excel. I liked the leathery smell of the gloves and the tight, bouncy feel of the ropes and the neat, official-looking pads over the corner posts. Our bouts lasted for just three three-minute rounds and the gloves were so padded there was no danger of anyone getting hurt. But one day I did manage to knock down my opponent – a likeable boy called Jarvis who was rather a comic. He looked surprised and I felt elated – it was, after all, my only academic success at West Bridgford Grammar

School. The teachers, on the other hand, seemed disapproving, as if it confirmed their suspicion of my evil tendencies.

I did have one friend, a boy called Jack Worsdell. He was not a pupil at West Bridgford, so I think we must have met at primary school. Because of Bill, and the difficulty of bringing anyone home, we were not encouraged to make friends, and there was some amusement in the family that I had one. Jack and I both had collections of toy soldiers, mine were hand-me-downs from Bill, inappropriately dressed in scarlet tunics, but we engaged them in battles on the rockery in our garden. From Smith's the chemist we bought sulphur and potassium nitrate, which we said was for chemistry experiments at school, and mixing them together we made gunpowder, which could be enclosed in twists of lavatory paper to manufacture bombs or grenades. We could never get it to explode properly, but it flared and made an impressive whoosh and scorched the toy soldiers standing near it. Our other amusement was cricket. Nottinghamshire County Cricket Club offered cheap season tickets for youngsters and our parents forked out. So on Saturday mornings we would set off for Trent Bridge with meat-paste sandwiches and Robinson's Lemon Barley Water. The county had some famous players. Joe Hardstaff had been a test batsman before the war and scored a double century against India in 1946. Reg Simpson, an elegant opening bat, was just about to start his test career. But cricket, in pre-TV days, was not exciting to watch. The action happened very far away, and Notts lost their first wicket with about thirty runs on the board so regularly that I had a vague sense it was required by the laws of the game. All the same, Trent Bridge was a beautiful ground, and the atmosphere was peaceful and somnolent. Jack and I, both aged twelve, would sit side by side, like elderly bachelors, occasionally clapping a boundary, or a returning batsman doffing his cap to the crowd, while the shadows lengthened across the hallowed turf.

3

Grammar School

In 1947 we moved back to our house in Barnes. London was still in shock from the war. One day my father took me up to the City with him. Perhaps he thought it right that I should see it, and remember. From the top of the bus we watched gutted, boarded-up ruins go by, and patches of wilderness, with neatly piled rubble. I had no idea what it had been like before the war, so I felt nothing much except mild curiosity. What my father felt, I can't imagine. At St Paul's we stood on the cathedral steps and looked out. In front of us, no buildings remained, only a wasteland, pitted with deep square holes that had been cellars. Temporary brick walkways had been constructed across and around them. There was no traffic. Purple spikes of rosebay willow-herb wagged in the wind.

By comparison Barnes was lightly damaged, but it was grey and shabby. The big houses along Castelnau and the Hammersmith Bridge end of Lonsdale Road were divided up into flats and bedsits. Their front gardens had run wild, and the walls were crumbling where railings had been sawn off as scrap metal for armaments. Further down Lonsdale Road, Mortlake was a slum, dark and threatening. I used to be sent there on my bike to request free brewer's yeast from Watney's brewery – I think my father took it as a tonic. The cheerful brewer who ladled it into my pot was friendly enough. But I didn't linger on the way back. Revisiting Barnes and

Mortlake in the 1980s and '90s, I was astonished by the immaculate mansions and terraces, the garden urns and magnolias, the BMWs, Mercedes and 4 x 4s jamming the kerbs. It seemed like a foreign country, and not one I wanted to be in.

The school I was sent to was Richmond and East Sheen Grammar School for Boys. It was less pretentious than West Bridgford – no fancy add-ons, no school orchestra, no boxing ring, soccer instead of rugby. Architecturally it was undistinguished – plain two-storey, red-brick. Clothes, like many other things (bread, soap), were rationed, and though there was a school uniform (blue blazer and cap with a Tudor rose badge) we were a scruffy lot. The masters wore old sports jackets with leather patches on the elbows – the uniform of late-1940s intellectuals. But even if it was a bit basic, it was a wonderful school. (Having said that, it's probably needless to add that it has been abolished, swept away in the general vindictive extermination of grammar schools in the 1970s.) The headmaster, H. H. Shephard, a mathematician and First World War veteran, had been in charge since its foundation in 1927. He was a wise, quiet man, a music-lover and amateur botanist, and the masters he had appointed were the kind of people who change you for life. The senior English master, Dr W. H. Gardner, was the first editor of Gerard Manley Hopkins's poems and soon left to be professor of English at Pietermaritzburg University. In today's academic scene several of the other masters would be university professors, but their great gift, as teachers, was that they made you want to be like them – to know the things they knew and value the things they valued. The English masters were Mr White, Dr Copley and Mr Bryant, the French masters Mr Hyde and Mr McLaren, the Latin master Mr Brigden. Today I suppose I'd be able to trot off their Christian names. But, back then, using or even knowing a master's Christian name was virtually unthinkable. (To be honest, I did know Mr Brigden was called Reg, but it was a thought I suppressed.) There was also an art master, Mr Fairhurst, an ARCA, who was fiery and bohemian and wore a cravat, like a real artist, and a patient, sagacious woodwork master, Mr Shackell, who taught us how to make mortise and tenon and dovetail joints, or tried to.

It was a small school, about four hundred boys, with an average class size of thirty, and we were divided into A and B streams. I was put in the B stream, no doubt due to the dire reports emanating from West Bridgford, but was moved up to the A stream after a couple of weeks. That was because I had started to work. I'm not sure why. Maybe it was the teaching, or the chance to make a new start, or just being able to see things (my mother took me to St Bartholomew's Hospital, shortly after we got to London, where an optician tested my eyes and prescribed glasses – I remember him saying, 'You've been missing rather a lot, young man'). But I suspect what weighed with me most was competitiveness. I had never felt it before, and perhaps it was related to the onset of puberty. At the end of each week, in all forms in the school, a list was pinned to the green baize notice board at the front of the classroom, showing each boy's name, in order of merit, based on the marks given for written work and tests during the week. I imagine anything so discriminatory would be illegal nowadays, but it was certainly a stimulus to me. The boys who regularly came top enjoyed a kind of legendary status – people whispered how brilliant they were – and I think the same ingrained scepticism that had made me resist the well-meaning teachers at West Bridgford now made me feel that I could surely knock these local heroes off their perches if I worked. So I worked.

Of course, working to come top would have been barren if it hadn't developed into working because I enjoyed it – but it soon did, and I soon discovered that what I really liked was poetry, which – apart from hymns and the Bible – had rather passed me by till then. A turning point was reading G. K. Chesterton's 'Lepanto', with its battering rhythms and dazzling historical vistas:

> White founts falling in the courts of the sun,
> And the Soldan of Byzantium is smiling as they run;
> There is laughter like the fountains in that face of all men feared,
> It stirs the forest darkness, the darkness of his beard,
> It curls the blood-red crescent, the crescent of his lips,
> For the inmost sea of all the earth is shaken with his ships.
> They have dared the white republics up the capes of Italy,
> They have dashed the Adriatic round the Lion of the Sea,
> And the Pope has cast his arms abroad for agony and loss,
> And called the kings of Christendom for swords about the Cross.
> The cold Queen of England is looking in the glass;
> The shadow of the Valois is yawning at the Mass;
> From evening isles fantastical rings faint the Spanish gun,
> And the Lord upon the Golden Horn is laughing in the sun.
>
> Dim drums throbbing in the hills half heard,
> Where only on a nameless throne a crownless prince has stirred,
> Where, risen from a doubtful seat, and half attainted stall,
> The last knight of Europe takes weapons from the wall,
> The last and lingering troubadour to whom the bird has sung,

That once went singing southward when all the world was young,
In that enormous silence, tiny and unafraid,
Comes up along a winding road the noise of the Crusade.
Strong gongs groaning as the guns boom far,
Don John of Austria is going to the war,
Stiff flags straining in the night-blasts cold
In the gloom black-purple, in the glint old-gold,
Torchlight crimson on the copper kettle-drums,
Then the tuckets, then the trumpets, then the cannon, and he
 comes.
Don John laughing in the brave beard curled,
Spurning of his stirrups like the thrones of all the world,
Holding his head up for a flag of all the free.
Love-light of Spain – hurrah!
Death-light of Africa!
Don John of Austria
Is riding to the sea . . .

'Lepanto' is a poem glorifying a crusade against Islam, so you couldn't read it in school nowadays. But I thought it grand stuff, and still do, despite its politics.

We used an anthology in class called, not very invitingly, *Longer Narrative Poems*, edited by E. E. Hale, and it was there I found Matthew Arnold's 'Sohrab and Rustum'. Based on a story from Persian history, it tells of a heroic warrior who kills an unknown challenger in single combat, only to discover that it is his son. I found it deeply moving, even the parts that sophisticates might consider sentimental – as when Rustum's famous warhorse, Ruksh, is overcome with grief at Sohrab's death:

> . . . and from his dark, compassionate eyes,
> The big warm tears rolled down, and caked the sand.

But best of all I liked the splendours of the eastern setting. A favourite bit was the simile comparing the Persian soldiers, breathless with suspense, to a troop of pedlars crossing the Hindu Kush:

> That vast sky-neighbouring mountain of milk snow;
> Crossing so high, that, as they mount, they pass
> Long flocks of travelling birds dead on the snow,
> Choked by the air, and scarce can they themselves
> Slake their parched throats with sugared mulberries –
> In single file they move, and stop their breath,
> For fear they should dislodge the o'erhanging snows.

In the same book I found Keats's 'The Eve of St Agnes', and fell for it instantly – not just the glamorous historical setting and the sexual titillation, but the low temperatures. In those days, before central heating, nearly everyone was cold most of the time. We used to press warmed pennies against the windows to make spy-holes in the ice. Keats's poem struck a chord because it was cold right through, from the hare limping through the frozen grass at the start to the beadsman sleeping among cold ashes in the last line. When I came to the bit about Madeline shivering between her chilly bedsheets I knew just how she felt. No one in the 1940s and '50s ever thought of heating a bedroom, and getting into bed in winter was like diving through ice. I had doubts, though, whether the fruits Porphyro brings along for his strangely inopportune midnight feast – 'candied apple, quince, and plum, and gourd' – would really fill the room with perfume, as the poem claims, given the cold. My closest friend at the time was a boy called Dennis Keene, later a professor of English in Tokyo, a published poet and a prize-winning translator from Japanese into English, and we used to discuss such questions eagerly, Dennis laughing as he recalled how Keats used to chew peppercorns before drinking chilled wine, to make the sensation more acute. I thought of 'The Eve of St Agnes' as a sort of gorgeous animated tapestry rather than a poem, and resolved to write something in a similarly high romantic vein myself. So for several afternoons I sat in solemn isolation at our kitchen table, composing a Gothic tale, in heroic couplets, about a beauteous young maiden (named Geraldine) who, by ill chance, wakes from supposed death to find herself in a morgue – rather as Juliet does in the tomb of the Capulets. Writing poetry like Keats proved surprisingly difficult, however, and I got no further than an introductory catalogue of Geraldine's charms.

I suppose the exoticism of these poems appealed because it contrasted with the sombreness of post-war Barnes where sugared mulberries, for instance, were hard to come by. Perhaps most people form their aesthetic preferences very early, or maybe they are partly inbred. I don't know. But I do know that I wanted poems to supply vivid, sensuous images, and I still prefer ones that do. Another poem that became a touchstone was Tennyson's 'The Lotos-Eaters', which tells how Odysseus and his men make landfall on a strange, sleepy island, where time stops:

> In the afternoon they came unto a land
> In which it seemed always afternoon.

The islanders feed them magic fruit, so that they fall into a coma, forgetting their homes and families. The poem is famed for its dreamy cadences, but what I liked best were the waterfalls the sailors see as they approach the island:

> . . . some, like a downward smoke,
> Slow-dropping veils of thinnest lawn, did go;
> And some through wavering lights and shadows broke,
> Rolling a slumbrous sheet of foam below.

That 'downward smoke', vivid as a film, was exactly what I wanted poems to be like.

The novels among our set books were George Eliot's *Silas Marner* and Thomas Hardy's *The Mayor of Casterbridge*. They were the first grown-up books I had read, and they were intimidating because I could see they were the start of something huge – an unexplored continent of literature I was just nibbling at the edge of. I had the same feeling, only worse, when I joined Hammersmith Public Library and saw the English literature shelves. How could anyone ever read so many books? However, I read a few of Hardy's novels, choosing what seemed the shorter ones – *Two on a Tower* and *A Pair of Blue Eyes* – and started to recognise his voice and feel at home, for the first time, inside someone else's world. I found my mind lingering rather fondly around the scene in *A Pair of Blue Eyes* where the heroine, Elfride, rescues her lover, who is trapped on a cliff face, by slipping off her underclothes, making a rope of them, and lowering it to him. Years later I learned from Brian Aldiss that *A Pair of Blue Eyes* had been Marcel Proust's favourite Hardy novel, so perhaps he was similarly stirred by the concurrence of lingerie and life-saving.

The set book that most bowled me over, though, was Shaw's *Saint Joan* – both the preface and the play. I'd never read anything so clever and self-confident. I knew nothing about Shaw, but I could see he enjoyed annoying people, and I guessed the holy fathers at Becket School would have been enraged by his presentation of the Catholic Church. I thought it must be wonderful to write like that, and I admired the way he said big things very briefly and simply – for example, in the exchange between Robert de Baudricourt and Joan, when Joan insists the voices she hears come from God.

Robert: They come from your imagination.
Joan: Of course. That is how the messages of God come to us.

Unanswerable. And it was not just the brilliant point-scoring that etched the play in my memory. Its greatest scene comes after Joan has been burned at the stake. A bigoted English chaplain, who has been avid, all along, to see her executed, staggers in from the courtyard, howling and sobbing.

I did not know what I was doing . . . If I had known I would have torn her from their hands. You don't know, you haven't seen; it is so easy to talk when you don't know. You madden yourself with words, you damn yourself because it feels grand to throw oil on the flaming hell of your own temper. But when it is brought home to you, when you see the thing you have done, when it is blinding your eyes, stifling your nostrils, tearing your heart, then – then –

I imagine no one who has read or seen *Saint Joan* ever forgets that speech. Remembered in a moment of all-but-ungovernable rage, it might just save someone from committing murder – perhaps it has – and there are few texts outside of scripture you can say that for.

Another A-level text was *Samson Agonistes*, which was a different kind of revelation for me. The language that blind

Milton invents for his blind hero seemed to be steeped in anguish but also majestic.

> O dark, dark, dark, amid the blaze of noon,
> Irrecoverably dark, total eclipse
> Without all hope of day . . .
> The sun to me is dark
> And silent as the moon
> When she deserts the night,
> Hid in her vacant, interlunar cave . . .

I thought it was how great statues would speak if they could get their marble jaws to move.

Our Shakespeare set texts were *Twelfth Night*, *Antony and Cleopatra* and *The Winter's Tale*, and the problem for me was what to say about them – or about any of Shakespeare's plays for that matter. With most writers I found I could make up some sort of criticism or comment that would pass muster. But with Shakespeare there seemed nothing to say. Criticism seemed ridiculous. The only adequate response was to learn the best bits by heart, which I did. My favourite was Othello's suicide speech ('Soft you, a word or two before you go . . .'), which I would intone haughtily in front of my bedroom wardrobe mirror, wearing my red dressing gown, the nearest thing I had to Moorish garb, and plunging an imaginary dagger into my stomach at the end. It was a moving performance, and, I thought, compared favourably with Laurence Olivier's and Vivien Leigh's *Antony and Cleopatra*, which we were taken to see at the St James's Theatre in 1951 when we were in the sixth form – my first visit to a theatre. Not that Olivier and Leigh were particularly bad. It was just that, as often with Shakespeare, when actors start to waddle around and gesticulate it seems absurdly inferior to what your imagination has created from the words on the page.

A bonus derived from learning those set plays so thoroughly is that nowadays bits of them keep floating into my mind, often for no evident reason – Feste's 'The rain it raineth every day', for example, or Orsino's 'The spinsters and the knitters in the sun', or Antony's 'Sometimes we see a cloud that's dragonish', or Leontes, on how his little son's company cheers him up ('And with his varying childness cures in me/Thoughts that would thick my blood'), or the old shepherd on what a nuisance young males are, and what a good idea it would be if they were put to sleep between the ages of ten and twenty-three, instead of 'getting wenches with child, wronging the ancientry' and stealing and fighting. As an industrious sixth-former I had no idea I was laying up for myself in later life this daily inner buzz of Shakespeare, but I think it's the best thing I got from school – which is saying a lot.

For relaxation, in spare moments, Mr White would read to us from A. G. Macdonell's *England, Their England*, a satire on Englishness as seen through the eyes of a young Scot, Donald Cameron. Its account of a village cricket match is often anthologised as a masterpiece of English comic writing. But a part I liked better, because the humour was slyer, was when Donald, walking down the King's Road, is alarmed by the headlines on newsvendors' placards: ENGLAND OVERWHELMED WITH DISASTER (the *Evening News*); IS ENGLAND DOOMED? (the *Star*). The subject, he discovers, is the collapse of England's batting in the second test against Australia in Melbourne (Hobbs out first ball, Hearne 9,

Woolley o). He watches men digging into their pockets for coins, snatching papers, then staggering away with ashen faces and quivering lips.

In the Underground at Sloane Square Station an elderly man in a top-hat and black, velvet-collared overcoat, with an elegant long white moustache, and carrying a rolled-up silk umbrella, said fiercely to Donald, 'It all comes of treating it as a game. We don't take things seriously enough in this country, sir, damnation take it all,' and he stepped heavily upon the toes of a humble, clerkly-looking person behind him.

Macdonell makes fun of modern art and literature which – though I laughed with the rest – I knew nothing about. So out of curiosity I borrowed T. S. Eliot's *Collected Poems* from the school library, and was immediately won over. I had no idea what most of it meant, but the phrases sounded terrific, and the world-weary tones – 'I have known them all already, known them all', 'I have measured out my life with coffee spoons', 'To prepare a face to meet the faces that you meet'– were irresistible to a fifteen-year-old. Converted, I gave a talk on Eliot to the Sixth Form Literary and Debating Society, which I copied, almost word for word, from F. O. Matthiessen's book on Eliot, also on loan from the library.

Like many teenagers I felt sure, with the arrival of puberty, that my destiny was to be a poet, and Prufrock's melancholy reflections figured importantly among my early inspirations, combined with Ginger's girl and her *pareu* from *Biggles in the South Seas*. I wrote some wistful elderly recollections, in free verse, of my youth among the islanders, tapping out my poems one-fingered on my father's huge old Underwood – its keys arranged like a miniature auditorium – which lurked under a sort of tarpaulin shroud on his desk in the front room. This took a long time, as I had no way of correcting typing errors, and as soon as I made one my authorial pride obliged me to start the whole page again. At last I produced perfect copies, however, and sent them off to the *Listener* for publication. Why I chose the *Listener* escapes me, but I realise now that the then literary editor was J. R. Ackerley, later famous for his love affair with his Alsatian bitch Queenie, which he wrote up in *My Dog Tulip*. However, my tasteful blend of Biggles and T. S. Eliot must have seemed unusual, even to someone of his wide experience.

My poems were some time coming back, as I had omitted to enclose a stamped addressed envelope. This was pointed out (in the great Ackerley's hand?) on the rejection slip, which was decorated with the BBC's crest in pastel blue. I was not as pained as I had expected. Being a rejected poet seemed somehow even finer than being published. Dennis Keene, on the other hand, was a real poet, and I still remember what convinced me of this. Hiroshima and Nagasaki were quite recent, and everyone was terrified of nuclear warfare – which curiously we seem less worried about nowadays. Dennis wrote a poem about the bomb which had the line, 'Who took the sun and hung it in the trees?' The idea of phrasing it as a question, as if asked by an angry God, seemed – still seems – majestic, and I knew I could never write a line like it.

In French our set books were Molière's *L'Avare* and Balzac's *Eugénie Grandet* (both, like *Silas Marner*, about miserliness, and chosen, I think, to encourage us to compare them), Edmond Rostand's *Cyrano de Bergerac* and Racine's *Phèdre*.

I knew that Racine was one of the greats, reputedly on a level with Shakespeare, whereas I gathered that informed critical opinion dismissed *Cyrano de Bergerac* as a swashbuckling romp concocted by Rostand to cheer the French up after their defeat in the Franco-Prussian war (which we were studying in history – another bit of good syllabus planning). So I felt guilty, when I read them, to find I thought exactly the opposite. *Cyrano*, with its heartbreaking balcony scene and dashing versified sword-fight, seemed a marvel, whereas Racine's rhymed alexandrines were like walking on stilts. When I voiced these doubts in class Mr McLaren, without exactly disagreeing, explained how deeply traditional French theatre was, and went on to tell us about the riot that had broken out on the first night of Victor Hugo's *Hernani* in 1830, when Hugo had packed the stalls with his supporters, and classicists and Romantics came to blows because Hugo flouted the rules by using enjambement – running the sense over from one line to the next. It was a brilliant bit of teaching – typical of the way he aroused our interest by anecdotes – and it has stuck in my mind much more vividly than anything in *Phèdre*. I didn't feel I'd found a version of the story worthy of Euripides' original until I saw Jules Dassin's film *Phaedra* in the 1960s.

The French set book I liked best, though, even more than *Cyrano*, was Alphonse Daudet's *Lettres de mon moulin*. The southern sun seemed to shine from its pages, and I felt I knew just what it would be like to wander through vineyards and olive groves serenaded by cicadas. Rereading it years later I was surprised to find how many of its stories are sad. The ones I remembered were stylish comic fantasies, like 'L'Élixir du Père Gaucher', about a monk who concocts an exquisite new liqueur, so glowingly described by Daudet that you can almost taste it, or 'La Mule du pape', which is set in Avignon long ago, and is about a beautiful mule who becomes the Pope's favourite. Besotted, he takes a bowl of spiced wine to her stable every night, though his cardinals strongly disapprove. But then a handsome young ne'er-do-well called Tistet Védène worms his way into the Pope's favour, and is entrusted with giving the mule her wine. Instead, he shares it out among his cronies and, out of pure malice, drives the mule up the bell-tower stairway so she is left trembling high above the marketplace and has to be lowered down with block and tackle. She naturally thirsts for revenge. But Tistet, whom no one suspects, is honoured by being sent away for seven years to the court of Naples. He returns, jaunty and unrepentant, with a huge ibis feather in his cap, and gets himself appointed the Pope's head mustard-maker. But on the way to the ceremony he makes the mistake of stopping to give the mule a friendly pat, and she lets fly with a tremendous kick – so tremendous that the dust from it is seen miles away, and all that is left of Tistet is a mustard-coloured cloud and a fluttering ibis feather.

Reading Daudet taught me that he had to be read in French. In translation the vocabulary and rhythms seemed all wrong. So I began to realise that learning a foreign language teaches you the limits of your own. Not that any of us were any good at speaking French. We learned it as a language to be read. That was common in those days, partly because foreign travel was more or less impossible. When we were in the sixth form Mr Hyde encouraged us to go along with him to a group called Le Cercle Français which met monthly in the Café de Paris in Richmond. It was run by French expats, and we would stand around, tongue-tied, listening to their impossibly fast chatter, and hoping none of them would speak to us.

From that point of view Latin was preferable, because no one spoke it any more, so we were on equal terms with other Latinists. Mr Brigden was a down-to-earth teacher. He did not descant about the glories of Latin literature, which would have been lost on us anyway. Instead he made sure we memorised the principal parts of irregular verbs, page after page, until they were second nature, and taught us useful versified mnemonics (which I still know by heart) to distinguish the gender of third-declension nouns – always tricky because you can't tell the gender just by the ending. The Romans, he told us, were a practical race, and wrote about People Doing Things. That is, they avoided abstractions and preferred active verbs to passives. He made us see that when we translated English into Latin we had to break down and rearrange the English sentences first so as to get the word order and sentence structure a Roman might use. I thought of it as like Meccano (I had inherited a slightly battered Meccano set from Bill, along with the 1930s schoolbooks). You separated the various bits and pieces, and then decided how to bolt them together. In this way Latin became a sort of game. Latin grammar was the rules of the game, and learning vocabulary by rote (which I did on every possible occasion – in bus queues, at mealtimes, during sermons in church) was acquiring ammunition for the next time you played. To make it easier I imagined sensory qualities for the Latin words – *aestas*, meaning summer, for example, I thought of as sounding like a blast from a furnace, and *hiems*, meaning winter, was thin like a bare twig, and *daps*, meaning a feast, sizzled like cooking fat. But I knew these imaginings had nothing to do with the way Romans would have heard the words. It was the same with our Latin set books, which were Virgil's *Aeneid*, Books 4 and 6, and Horace's *Odes*, Book 3. I drilled myself till I could translate them at sight, but I didn't believe anyone could tell what they had meant to their first readers. I tended to like them if they reminded me of English poetry I knew – so I liked Horace's ode about a fountain (*O fons Bandusiae*) because it reminded me of the white founts falling in 'Lepanto'.

So those were the things – in English, French and Latin – that occupied my mind most of the time between the ages of thirteen and seventeen. For relaxation I read Richmal Crompton's William books – matchlessly witty – and the complete series of Arthur Ransome's Swallows and Amazons adventures, which I loved so much that I used to read them crouched in the dark space behind the sofa in the empty drawing room, so that I could feel there was just me and the story, and the rest of the world didn't exist.

Life outside books was fairly humdrum. We played football and cricket against other Surrey grammar schools. I was no good at either, but as ours was a small school it was easy to get a place in the side. The big shock, every Saturday morning, was our first sight of the opposing team. They can't really have been much bigger than us, but they always looked enormous, slouching up the school drive with their colossal school sports bags stuffed with equipment. Away matches were even worse, because then you first saw them out on their school field, bowling whizzing deliveries at each other in the nets, or hoofing thunderous practice shots at goal. It has made me understand better that bit in the Book of Numbers, where the Israelites send out spies to size up the opposition, in this case the Sons of Anak, and the spies come back aghast to report that they are giants, and 'we were in our own sight as grasshoppers'. I'd guess the Sons of Anak weren't that big really; they were just visiting-team size. We must have won some games, I suppose, but we usually lost, unlike the Israelites.

Still, I did win one sporting event – the only one I ever have. At the end of the summer term every year the whole school, except those with medical certificates, had to take part in a cross-country run in Richmond Park. The course was not long by today's standards, probably not much more than five miles. This meant you had to go all out right from the start, particularly as there was a narrow track with a wall on one side soon after the start, where overtaking was impossible, and if you weren't ahead there you might as well give up. I very much wanted to win in my last year at school, and practised by running the whole course several times a week. On the great day we gathered in a pack, and there was a lot of sweaty pushing and shoving at the start, but at the end of the first mile, where the course left the road and climbed up a cinder track, I looked back and there was no other runner in sight – just boys following the race on bikes. It was a marvellous feeling, like having wings on your heels. At the finish the headmaster, Mr Shephard, seldom seen out of doors, was standing by the tape and murmured,

'Well done, Carey.' My mother, when I got home and told her I had won, said, 'Well, that's what you wanted, wasn't it?' I felt let down at the time. But my parents' lack of interest in what I did was an advantage in a way, because I never felt pressured. Besides, they had other things to worry about. Bill's condition was getting worse. His glowering silences were more glowering and silent, his hands shook more, and he lost his job. Compared to that, having a son who had won a race can't have seemed important. Anyway, I wasn't much good really. A few weeks later a school team, with me in it, took part in a county junior cross-country event, and none of us came anywhere. The first three places were taken by Sons of Anak.

Because I was staying on at school in the sixth form I was expected to get jobs in the holidays to earn some money. Dennis Keene and I worked for one summer as sweepers in the Chrysler factory at Kew. The car workers were an interesting bunch. One of them knew whole swathes of Shakespeare by heart, and would act out Shylock's 'Hath not a Jew eyes?' speech for his admiring workmates. Dennis and I made the mistake, though, of continuing to sweep for a few moments after the hooter had gone for the mid-morning break, and a union official ticked us off, accusing us of being in cahoots with the management. After that we rather lost interest in sweeping. Instead we discovered a sort of hangar stacked with huge piles of Dunlopillo for car seats. It made a marvellous trampoline, and we used to leap around, trying to hover weightless in the air like astronauts. A job I had two winters running was in Orton's, a shop in King Street, Hammersmith. It was an outfitter's and linen draper's, and

I worked in the soft furnishing department, measuring out yards of curtain material against a brass rule screwed to the counter and advising old ladies on cushion covers. When you made a sale you had to write out a bill, put it and the customer's money in a canister, and click the canister into a holder attached to an overhead wire. Then you pulled a lever and the canister would zip along the wire to an elevated glass-fronted cubicle where the lady cashier sat. She would check the bill, count out the customer's change, put it all in the canister and send it back down the wire. I suppose this system dated from the time when people who served in shops could not be trusted with money, but no one seemed to resent it. For a time the young H. G. Wells was a draper's assistant, and when I read books like *The History of Mr Polly* I felt things had not changed all that much. My employers were kind, though. They were two brothers, a tall one and a tubby one, and the tubby one's son was a school friend of mine. So I really was in cahoots with the management, and on Saturday evenings I would be invited into a snuggery on the top floor for a cup of tea, with the twinkling lights of King Street far below.

I had joined Barnes parish church choir as soon as we moved to London. When my voice broke I became an altar boy for a while, and then joined the men's section singing a sort of baritone. My father and sisters – and my mother, if she was not at home doing the cooking – were also regulars at this church. But Bill became increasingly religious as his condition worsened and he worshipped at Holy Trinity church, which was 'higher'. He came to think of himself as a kind of minor ecclesiastic, purchased a biretta, genuflected a lot, and was sometimes, I gathered, allowed to swing the incense pot during services. The embarrassment my parents suffered must have been acute, but they never showed it, and perhaps they managed to persuade themselves that Bill's devotions were not so abnormal after all. My own religious faith petered out in the sixth form as a result of thinking and questioning in the way adolescents do. The headmaster, who was, I imagine, an agnostic, set us as an essay subject, 'What is the Significance of Human Beings?' The more I thought about it the more it seemed obvious that human beings were of no significance at all from a cosmic viewpoint, and had invented a human-style God to hide this from themselves. I could tell from the headmaster's wan smile as he handed my essay back that I had given the right answer. So I told my mother I had lost my faith, and she said I should talk to my father, as he was 'a good man', which was certainly true. He didn't seem very surprised when I broke my news, and didn't blame or cajole. He just said, 'It's a dark road you are going down,' and we never discussed the matter again.

Though faithless, I continued to sing in the choir, and Rosemary and I belonged to the Church Youth Club, which held talks and discussions and went on country rambles in the summer to places like Henley or Maidenhead. It was at the Youth Club that I met my first girlfriend. She was called Heather – well she wasn't, but I shall call her that – and she worked as a trainee librarian. We both still lived with our families, so it was hard to be alone together, as we found we wanted to be. However, we managed as best we could. I had been brought up to believe that women were pure, and would engage in sexual activity unwillingly, if at all, and it was a great relief to learn from Heather that I had been mis-informed on this point. My mother was furious when she heard of the relationship, and delivered a passionate tirade – I was too young to have a girlfriend, I should be work-ing for my exams not messing around with women, besides, her family were 'not of our class'. I think all this was mainly panic about Bill, and the possibility of having him seen by strangers. But the result was that Heather never set foot in our house, whereas I was welcomed by her family, who were, in terms of class, indistinguishable from mine. As it seemed likely I'd be going away soon, she had two studio photos taken, showing her in 1950s-style soft-focus profile, with some gauzy stuff around her bare shoulders. They fitted into a double leather frame which opened like a book, so that it could stand on a bedside table. For three years, while I was away from her, they were the most precious things in my life.

I also met, at the Church Youth Club, a boy called Peter who was a doctor's son, and had access to medicines normally available only on prescription. I was working for an Oxford scholarship – Mr Hyde, the French master, had called on my parents and persuaded them that I should have a try, and that it would cost them nothing. So I read late each evening trying to catch up on areas of English literature I was still ignorant of. I was particularly worried about Dryden and Pope, who were a blank to me and might, I imagined, be highly prized at Oxford. But I found I could not stay awake much after midnight, so I asked Peter to get something that would help. The next week he turned up with two bottles of pills called Benzedrine and Dexedrine. I now know that Benzedrine was widely used during the war by RAF bomber crews to help them keep awake on night flights, and that it's the chemical base of the recreational drug Ecstasy. But this was years before the era of recreational drugs, and I had never heard of amphetamines or what they might do to you. Besides, I wasn't interested in recreation: I simply wanted to get an Oxford scholarship. So I took one of Peter's pills each evening, and the results were phenomenal. I read and read until dawn came and birds started singing, and I discovered that Pope was a great poet and Dryden much less boring than I'd supposed. I loved the neat way he delivered insults when he was describing people in his satires – 'Stiff in opinions, always in the wrong', for example, or 'For every inch that is not fool is rogue'. It seemed such a beautifully high-handed way of disposing of people – almost as good as George Bernard Shaw.

I went to Oxford for the scholarship exam just before Christmas in 1951. People had told me it was important to apply to the right college, but I didn't even know what a college was, or how colleges differed from the university. In the end I chose St John's because it had been Mr Shephard's college. Nowadays entrance candidates are greeted by swarms of friendly undergraduate assistants, and every kind of back-up, from male and female chaplains to paramedics, is in reserve in case of emergencies. There are even coloured placards saying 'Welcome', and balloons (I am not making this up) strung up over college entrances. In 1951 it was different. The night was freezing and the college in darkness. I pushed open the creaking wicket door in the huge, iron-studded front gate, like something out of a Gothic novel, and found the porter in his snug, brightly lit lodge. He asked my name, consulted a list, and seemed surprised when he found me on it. Then he handed me a key, told me the number of my room, and bade me good night. As I stumbled off across the dark quadrangle it occurred to me that I probably did not belong in Oxford.

I was roused next morning by a white-jacketed man-servant (a 'scout' in Oxford parlance), who called me 'sir' and had lit a fire in the grate. Breakfast was in the college hall which looked to me a bit like a medieval abbey – not that I had ever seen one. There were long tables and benches, full of excitedly chattering candidates, all of whom seemed to know each other, while more white-jacketed servants took round coffee, toast and cereals. We sat our exam papers in a lecture room. A don – or anyway an elderly man in an academic gown whom I took to be a don – came in to dis-tribute them, and returned to collect our scripts when time was up. Apart from that we were left alone. No one super-vised or invigilated – perhaps because we were regarded as gentlemen and gentlemen didn't cheat, or perhaps because it was a competitive exam so we could be trusted not to help each other. No one did: a tomblike silence reigned. Apart from the English literature essay papers there were French translation and translation into and out of Latin. The Eng-lish into Latin was the hardest. I wasn't absolutely sure what some of the words meant in English, let alone knowing the Latin for them. But I applied my trusty Meccano technique, and thanked heaven for Mr Brigden's third-declension noun mnemonics.

Interviews were on the evening of the second day. Six of us sat, waiting to be summoned, in a don's room that contained, besides us, wrapped Christmas presents, presumably for his family, among them a beautiful white rocking horse, too big to wrap. I remember thinking that this festive cheer was a bit thick, given how wretched and nervous we felt. When my turn came a black-coated servant, whom I now know to have been the senior common room butler, led me to a room where about a dozen elderly men sat round a long polished table. There was an empty chair at the end, in which I was asked to sit. Their questions did not seem to relate to English literature much. The only one I clearly remember was whether I thought Horace or Virgil the greater poet. I answered instantly, 'Oh, Horace,' and they all laughed, except one who seemed to be asleep. I realised I had spoken too impetuously, and felt foolish. Pursuing the point my questioner asked why I liked Horace. I could hardly tell him it was because one of his poems reminded me of G. K. Chesterton's 'Lepanto', so I said it was because I found it interesting how he adapted Greek lyric metres to Latin. This lie was accepted with grave approval, and I was told I could go.

Two days after I got home, a letter arrived telling me I had won the William Lambe Open Scholarship to St John's College, Oxford. It was passed round reverently, but I don't think any of us understood, at the time, quite what it would mean. Perhaps my parents had an inkling, though. Their expressions of pleasure were subdued, as if they foresaw this would take me away from them to somewhere they felt they did not belong. It was the same with Heather. She kissed me and said how delighted she was, but there was something like terror in her eyes.

The letter from St John's also said that I was expected to do national service before coming up, which was usual then, and that if I liked I could read classics rather than English. This surprised me because, though I'd had one-to-one Greek lessons from Mr Brigden in the sixth form, my Greek wasn't good, and I'd confessed as much at the interview. So I'd guess it was his solid, no-nonsense, grammar-school Latin teaching that got me into Oxford. As for national service, my family assumed I would be exempt because I was short-sighted. But they were wrong. I turned up at Hammersmith town hall for my medical, with a bunch of other seventeen-year-olds, and we stripped off to be weighed and measured, and a doctor told us to cough while he held our testicles. I never discovered what your testicles were meant to do when you coughed, but it was at the time a universal qualification for getting into the British armed forces. Mine reacted properly, and I was passed A1. My parents were alarmed and anxious, but I felt glad. It meant I would get away.

Rosemary had started a BA in history at King's, London, the previous year – though she still lived at home for cheapness's sake – and just before my army service began we went for a week's holiday in Paris with two of her boyfriends from college. None of us had ever been abroad before and we were thrilled by everything we saw. Shopfronts with French names on them seemed unreal, like theatre sets. Even the pervasive smell of drains and the lavatories that were just a hole in the floor were transfigured by their romantic foreignness. We saw Notre-Dame and the Sainte-Chapelle and the Louvre and the impressionist paintings in the Jeu de Paume.

We went to the Opéra and saw the Ride of the Valkyries. Our cheap box – all we could afford – was squashed high up at the side of the auditorium, so only one of us could see the stage at any one time. However, we found Wagner so boring that we slept contentedly on the nice red carpet at the back of the box for most of the performance. Rosemary and I sought out the current whereabouts of Godde, Bedin & Cie, the firm that had swallowed our family's wealth. It was a drab building, with faded gold lettering, and we stood before it astonished it was real, not just a name.

We were staying at the Cité Universitaire, a group of student houses near the Parc Montsouris. If you got off the Métro at Denfert-Rochereau and changed to the RER line, Cité Universitaire was the next stop. The houses were more like hotels in size, and had been funded by different nations and built in national styles. Ours was the Maison Franco--Britannique – but there was an International House too, where students from all over the world could meet and chatter. It was a lovely place with big lawns and gardens and, if you were a student, residence cost almost nothing. For dinner each night the four of us went to a little restaurant down by the Métro station. It was foggy with cigarette smoke and thunderous with young voices, but it seemed to us the last word in sophistication. The food was better than anything we had ever tasted. As *hors d'œuvres* there were *filet de hareng*, *œuf dur mayonnaise*, *salade de tomates* and *salade de crudités* – the standard ones in every cheap restaurant, but exotic to us – and then we always ordered *steak frites* and red wine. The lady who owned it sat in a cubicle by the door and took your money when you left, making out the bill by hand. She always seemed to undercharge us, partly, I think, because we were English, and partly because she saw we hadn't much. On our last night we stopped on our way back from dinner, lay on the sweet, dry grass – a bit drunk, I suppose – and talked dreamily of all the things we had seen. I gazed up at a sky full of stars and thought that life was unfathomably wonderful.

4

Playing at Soldiers

So one summer morning in 1952 I took a bus to Kingston barracks, the depot of the East Surrey Regiment, and joined the army. We queued up to be issued with our kit, everything from underpants (khaki) to greatcoats, and our first job was to get it all ready for inspection. Old soldiers who hung around the barracks gave us tips. To get a crease in battle-dress trousers, they explained, you have to shave the fuzzy trouser leg very gently with a razor blade before you iron it. To make boots shine you have to heat the handle of a teaspoon in a candle flame and put the polish on hot. You should be careful, because if you nick the trouser leg or scorch the boot you'll be on a charge for maliciously damaging the Queen's equipment. No one dared to ask what sort of penalty that would incur.

Then there was webbing. Each of us had a big pack, a small pack, two cartridge pouches and a belt. These had to be coated in buff-coloured Blanco, bought at the NAAFI and applied with a brush dipped in water. The brass buckles and fittings had to be cleaned with Brasso. Getting Brasso on the webbing or Blanco on the brass were other offences it was wise to avoid.

On the second evening we had our first inspection. We stood to attention beside our beds in two long lines down each side of the barrack room. By every bed was a tall steel locker, and on top of the locker was our webbing kit. We had been shown how it was meant to look, a cubic arrangement, neat as a pile of bricks, with the big pack folded at the bottom, the small pack on top, the cartridge pouches at the side, and your steel helmet on the summit like a little dome.

Having a house-proud mother I felt I knew about this sort of thing, and had taken special care, stuffing the packs and pouches with newspaper and stiffening up the corners with cardboard. Glancing round I thought some of the other efforts looked rather slouchy, but I reckoned advice might be resented, and anyway it was too late. A sergeant strode into the room. He was a picture of regimental elegance, buttons, badges and toecaps dazzling, battle dress glove-tight, and he surveyed our pathetic efforts to look military with undisguised contempt. It occurred to me later that this must have been his favourite moment in the whole working week, but the air was far too doom-laden for any such irreverence to surface at the time.

Stopping by each recruit in turn, he looked him up and down, and slowly raised his eyes to the webbing piled on top of the locker. Then, allowing himself a few moments to cull suitable epithets from his ample vocabulary, he shouted, with his lips perhaps six inches from the defaulter's ear, an explanation of why his efforts fell short of the required standard. To make his disapproval unmistakable, he swept the offending equipment to the floor with his beautifully polished brass-bound regimental pace-stick, and passed on to the next victim.

Everyone remained rigidly to attention as he made his devastating progress down the row. At last he came to me, halted, and raised his eyes to my webbing pile. I held my breath. 'Whose is that kit?' he roared. 'Mine, sergeant,' I quavered. He scanned me with some disdain, regretting, I think, that I was not a more soldier-like specimen. Then he strode to the centre of the room. 'That man's kit', he thundered, pointing at me, 'is how it's meant to look. Yours will all look like it by tomorrow night.' Then he strode out, and we sank quaking onto our beds.

Surprisingly I was not taken out, there and then, and dropped from a tall building. One or two shattered souls sidled up to ask for advice, and I magnanimously lent them some bits of cardboard. But everyone else just got on with retrieving and reassembling their kit.

Basic Training, as it was called, turned out to consist, to an unexpectedly large extent, of undressing and dressing very quickly and often. It was rather like rehearsing for a French farce, only more serious, of course. We changed from battle dress to sports gear to denim fatigues to full marching order – and back again – a dozen times a day, dashing from one assembly point to another as we did up the last buttons or fastened the final clip. Everything had to be done at breakneck speed. We marched and drilled and paraded, we tripped and blundered our way through assault courses with instructors yapping at our heels, we bolted our meals, we rushed through the evenings in a haze of cleaning fluids, we dropped thankfully into bed when the bugle sounded Lights Out at ten, and we snored through the night till it sounded Reveille at six.

We were not allowed out of barracks for four weeks, on the principle that it would be a disgrace to the British army to let us be seen before that. On the Saturday morning of our first weekend leave, two hawk-eyed NCOs scrutinised us, from cap badge to boots, before reluctantly giving us permission to step through the barrack gate. But when we did, it felt marvellous. We were young, fit and strong, and we looked with disbelief at the dowdy, hag-ridden civilians creeping along the pavements. They seemed to belong to a different species. The first thing I did, of course, was to go and see Heather. We found that we had a lot that needed doing rather urgently. But that meant I was late getting home and could not explain why, since my mother had made it clear her name was not to be mentioned in the house. So the usual miasma of unspoken truths and guilty silences settled on us, with Bill's hunched, mournful, innocent presence at its centre.

Back in Kingston a number of us were identified as Potential Leaders – on the grounds, I worked out, that we had passed some A-levels – and we were sent to join other scholarly types at a barracks in Canterbury. It was really a continuation of Basic Training, except that it had a competitive edge, because if you turned out not to be a Potential Leader you were sent back to your unit. The best part was the weapons training. I had never even heard a .303 rifle fired before I joined the army, and I was flabbergasted, the first time, by the deafening noise it made. Learning to shoot – to line up the rear sight and the fore sight, to lock yourself in stillness, to squeeze the trigger gently – was beautiful and precise, and the pleasure was intensified by the ranges we went to for firing practice. They were on the Kent coast at Lydd – a vast expanse of dunes and sandy scrubland, with the sea glittering in the distance, and huge skies, like Dutch landscape paintings. There always seemed to be skylarks, singing high and shrill in the electric blue, and there was usually a NAAFI van, so you could stroll over for tea and buns.

The Officer Cadet School I went to was at Eaton Hall in Cheshire. The Hall itself was a grotesque Victorian folly, bristling with turrets and pinnacles, and now happily demolished. But we lived in huts in the grounds. As officer cadets we wore white facings on our battle-dress collars, and we had to buy white riding macs and trilby hats to wear when in civvies. The hats were needed so we could raise them if we met an officer. It was at Eaton Hall that I first came across the English class system. Most of the cadets were from public schools. They talked in public-school voices, and tended to have unbelievable names. In our squad alone there was a Fitzherbert-Brockholes and a Fearnley-Whittingstall. Thanks to TV, names like that are commonplace now. But in post-war socialist Britain they seemed comic and offensive, and their harmless proprietors filled my mind with tumbrils and guillotines.

We were drilled every day by apoplectic sergeant majors from the Brigade of Guards, and we went to battle camp at Trawsfynydd in Wales, a romantic spot, where we launched ferocious platoon attacks against inoffensive corrugated iron shacks, riddling them with Bren-gun fire and pounding them with two-inch mortars. The NCO in charge was Corporal Recton, a tough infantryman with a neat row of medal ribbons over his breast pocket. Once, during training, we had to jump off a brick hut. It was eight or nine feet high and we lined up on the roof. We were more encumbered than you would normally choose to be for jumping off a roof

– wearing backpacks and steel helmets and carrying rifles. But it was no ordeal, and one by one we duly thudded to the earth. Suddenly, though, there was a halt. The next man to jump stood shuddering at the roof's edge, his face twisted in terror. (I want to say that he was one of the toffee-nosed public-school types, and I truly believe he was, but that may just be my prejudice.) Some sniggering broke out among those of us on the ground, but Corporal Recton rounded on us in fury. 'Stop that,' he yelled. 'It's more difficult for him than it is for you.' He talked quietly to the frightened man, who eventually jumped, and we returned to camp, having learned something more important than how to jump off a roof.

Cadets were weeded out and sent back to their units from Eaton Hall pretty regularly, and I felt extremely bucked to have finished the course. At our Passing-Out Parade the adjutant was grandly mounted on a horse – never seen before, and perhaps borrowed for the occasion – and the sergeant major, unusually cheerful, roared encouragement as we marched past – 'Swing those arms. Bags of swank.' My orders were to join the First Battalion of the East Surrey Regiment in Egypt, and within a couple of weeks I was boarding a troopship at Southampton. Carefully stowed in my luggage was a highly polished leather belt and shoulder strap. This was my father's Sam Browne, which had been through the Great War with him, and was now coming to Egypt with me.

The East Surreys were stationed at Tel el-Kebir, which was not a part of Egypt you would recommend to tourists. Essentially it was a stretch of barren desert, about a hundred kilometres north-east of Cairo, where, during the Second World War, the 8th Army had created an enormous depot of ordnance and vehicles, surrounded by a perimeter fence and a minefield. An infantry brigade, of which the Surreys were a part, was responsible for guarding it. The political situation was tense, since the anti-British 'Officers' Movement', under General Naguib and Colonel Nasser, had recently ousted King Farouk and seized power. Not that these headline developments were of primary concern to me in Tel el-Kebir, where the chief enemies were heat, flies and boredom.

The Surreys lived in a tented camp – not bivouacs, but big tents, like fair-sized rooms, with sloping roofs. The company lines were pitched on three sides of a wide tract of sand, which was the parade ground. The CO's and adjutant's offices and the guard room occupied the other side, and the officers' tents were in a wattled enclosure beyond A Company's lines. The officers' mess was several tents joined together, and outside was a patch of grass, watered twice daily to keep it alive, and a rather windswept-looking banana tree.

That was all there was – no cinemas, no shops, and British troops were not allowed into Egyptian cities, even those in the Canal Zone like Suez and Port Said. There were, of course, no women either. Around us stretched the desert, offering nothing of interest except, a short distance from the camp, some shallow trenches snaking across the sand. These marked the site of the Battle of Tel el-Kebir where, in 1882, Lieutenant General Sir Garnet Wolseley had put the Egyptian army to flight, massacring two thousand of them. You were said to be able still to dig up cartridge cases and bayonets.

Junior officers shared a tent, and also a batman, and I shared with another second lieutenant called Dorey, who was soon going back to England. When he went he generously left me his radio, made of cream-coloured Bakelite with a plastic-covered wire at the back that acted as aerial. It strikes me, now, that, apart from my clothes, it was my only possession. That did not seem odd at the time, because we were used to austerity and shortages, and people did not possess things very much – or not the people I knew. But the contrast with today is striking. Though I was proud of my radio, it was not, strictly, useful, since for the most part no sound came from it except an atmospheric hum. However, if you were lonely that was better than nothing.

Things did not go well at first. When I reported for duty to the adjutant, a thin, acidic-looking man, he remarked that I was wearing the wrong sort of hat. It was, in fact, a normal officer's service dress hat, recently bought from Gieves in Piccadilly. However, the adjutant insisted that mine was made of barathea whereas East Surrey hats were made of some other fabric. (I may have got this wrong – possibly the Surreys' hats were barathea and mine was something different – but at all events the mismatch was obviously profoundly upsetting to the adjutant, though to the naked eye his hat and mine appeared identical.)

Looking back it seems surprising I didn't just get another hat sent out from England. But in those days that would have cost a lot and taken a long time, and even the adjutant did not suggest so extreme a measure. Instead, I was reprimanded for insubordination in the matter of hats, and told that I would have to serve as orderly officer for several successive days. Being orderly officer was an unpopular chore because it meant you had to wear uniform all day, even in the mess, and perform various duties such as guard-mounting. Normally an officer would expect to do it once every few weeks. As the orderly officer's name was posted daily in battalion orders, it was clear to everyone, if your name appeared for several days consecutively – as mine did – that you were in some sort of trouble.

Of course it was not a severe punishment, and in some respects it was enjoyable, especially the nightly guard-mounting. I would meet up with the orderly sergeant at about five to eleven – he wearing his scarlet orderly sergeant's sash, I my father's Sam Browne and the offending hat – and we would march up together to the guard room. Outside, under the star-crammed Egyptian sky, the guard would be lined up, and behind them a disgruntled row of defaulters who were currently serving time in the guard room. At one side stood a bugler. The sergeant called the parade to attention, and it was my job to inspect them, and give the command – 'Duty drummer, sound off!' Then the bugler played the Last Post, and everyone was free to go to bed, except the guard. This little ceremony, with its strangely worded command and its plangent bugle call, always seemed to me like something out of musical theatre, and I never got over feeling how bizarre it was that I should be taking part in it.

We spent most of our time training or being trained, and one morning I was taken by a gigantic young officer called Hugh – a full lieutenant and a regular soldier, not a national serviceman – to teach some recruits how to throw hand grenades. The grenade range was just a stretch of sand, sited well away from any tents or buildings. In it a deep L-shaped trench had been dug, with wooden steps for getting in and out. The recruits lined up in the leg of the L pointing away from the range; Hugh and I were in the front part; and at the intersection was a sergeant with a box of grenades and a box of detonators. The drill was simple. The sergeant put a detonator into a grenade and handed it to the first man in the queue, who came into the front trench. There he gripped the grenade in his throwing hand, making sure that he was holding down the safety lever with his thumb. With his other hand he pulled out the split pin that held the safety lever in place. The pin had a ring attached, to make it easier to pull. Then he threw the grenade out to the front of the trench as far as he could.

As soon as a grenade leaves the thrower's hand its safety lever flies off, igniting the fuse which burns down to the detonator. It takes about four seconds, after which the grenade explodes with a shattering roar and shrapnel whizzes in all directions. Everything went smoothly for a while, and the number of grenades in the sergeant's box gradually diminished. The soldier who had just thrown made his way to the back of the queue, and the next soldier took his place, grasped his grenade correctly, and threw it high and far. As usual, everyone ducked and held their ears. But nothing happened. We waited. Still nothing happened.

This was a quandary. The grenade might explode at any moment, and while it was still unexploded it would be unsafe for us to try to get the recruits back to camp. On the other hand, we could not remain where we were for ever. Hugh took a decision. 'You stay here,' he said, and climbed out of the trench. I said, without thinking, 'No, I'll come too,' and followed him.

It had been cool in the shadows of the trench. Up in the open the sun was scalding, and the light dazzled. The grenade lay peacefully on the sand about twenty yards away, and we walked towards it. I knew we might hear a click, and if we did we'd probably have four seconds before it exploded. I also knew that a grenade was supposed to kill anyone within five yards' radius. We were less than five yards away when Hugh suddenly burst out laughing, strode forward, picked up the grenade and showed it to me. The pin was still in it.

Back in the trench he handed the grenade to the man who had thrown it, and explained, with not the slightest trace of temper, what had gone wrong. The man took the grenade, pulled the pin out, and threw it. It exploded correctly, and the rest of the morning's training passed without incident. Then we marched back to camp. I was not sure what would happen. I had, after all, disobeyed an order in following Hugh, and I had followed him not out of any courageous impulse but because I was afraid of seeming cowardly if I stayed behind. Following him had been foolish and useless, and risked two officers being killed rather than just one. In the event nothing was ever said to me about it, by Hugh or anyone else. But I think a favourable view must have been taken at some level, and I did not have to do any more ex-tended spells as orderly officer.

I was appointed Battalion Intelligence Officer, in charge of the Intelligence Section, which occupied a tent up near the guard room. Our job was to keep the battalion's maps up to date, so that they showed recent Egyptian troop movements in the delta. We also went on patrol to surrounding villages and joined infantry detachments on road blocks, searching cars and buses for weapons. The gulf between rich and poor was like nothing I had ever seen. The men and women in the cars that we stopped oozed wealth, but in the villages mothers brought us their half-starved children, dressed in rags, with horrible sores on their faces, and we rummaged through our first-aid kits looking for something that might help. We were all upstanding young 1950s egalitarians, and concluded that Egypt was a disgusting country. We would have been incredulous if anyone had told us that this rich–poor gap would be the pattern for the future worldwide, as now seems increasingly likely.

Back in camp we tried to make the Intelligence Office into an islet of civilisation, a place to read books and preserve cultural values – the *quartier Latin* of Tel el-Kebir, as it were. I suspect it went by a less fanciful name in the battalion at large. My NCO, Sergeant Roberts, was in the Education Corps, and organised the various courses that soldiers were taking to secure qualifications. So he, at any rate, did an important job. I also had an artist in the section, John Gillard, who founded the School of Communication Arts after he was demobbed. I still have a sketch he did from Tel el-Kebir's main gate. They were patient with my attempts to impose order, and tolerant of my mistakes. One night we were investigating a report of suspicious activity in a remote sector of the perimeter. We were creeping forward in the dark, armed with Sten guns, when I was aware of Sergeant Roberts, directly behind me, tugging at my shirt. 'Ssh!' I ordered, turning fiercely. His face was a mask of horror. 'We're in the minefield, sir,' he croaked.

He was right. Slowly and jerkily, like sufferers from acute arthritis, we retreated, placing our feet precisely in the footprints we had made on the way out.

Almost blowing up the entire Intelligence Section was probably my finest hour. But others came close. A couple of months later we were on detachment with C Company guarding a filtration plant near the Sweetwater Canal that runs from Cairo to Suez. It was a pleasant spot, surrounded by eucalyptus trees, and the civilian engineer, manning his lonely outpost, might have come from a novel by Conrad. I used to chat with him in the evenings, while the eucalyptus trees rustled in the breeze. The company were living in tents, but the officers were housed in a low brick building adjoining the plant. I was sharing a room with a new officer called Bobby, just out from England. My early-warning system had instantly diagnosed him as public-school, but on the other hand he was very nice – polite, fresh-faced and boyish. One night we were discussing guns, and Bobby admitted that he had never actually fired a .38 revolver of the kind officers carried. He had heard, he said, that there were two pressures on the trigger, but did not understand what that meant. Eager to demonstrate my superior skills with weaponry I drew my own revolver and pointed it at the door. 'Oh, it's quite easy,' I explained. 'You take the first pressure like this' – tightening my trigger finger a little – 'and then you take the second like this.' At that moment several things happened simultaneously. There was a sharp crack, a neat hole appeared in the door, I turned to stone, and Bobby's eyes opened wider than I had ever seen eyes open before. As the blood gradually seeped back into my brain I realised he was wondering if this

was a perfectly usual way of teaching the use of small arms
in the East Surreys, or whether, alternatively, he was shut in
a room with a madman who might easily shoot him next.
However, a far more pressing concern thrust itself on my
attention. Outside the door were the tents containing the
sleeping soldiery of the East Surreys, one of them possibly
with a .38 bullet lodged in him.

Stumbling round tents at night, waking up soldiers to ask
if they are still alive, is not a task that earns you universal pop-
ularity. But Bobby and I stuck to it until we were quite sure
the company would not be one man short when it lined up
for inspection next morning. By this time a sleep-befuddled
Major Reed, commander of C Company, had arrived, asked
a couple of questions, told me curtly to report to him first
thing next morning, and gone back to bed. I did not spend
a peaceful night. What the penalty was for discharging a
weapon in the company lines I had no idea, but I was clear
it must exceed by many orders of magnitude that incurred
for wearing the wrong sort of hat. As it turned out, I was
lucky. Major Reed, like all the battalion's senior officers, was a
war veteran, and my misdemeanour must have seemed small
beer after what he had been through. All the same, he let rip.
Standing to attention before his desk I was forced to admire,
with a small, detached, literary-critical portion of my mind,
the colour, variety, cogency, rhetorical incisiveness and dramatic force of his language, even though its purport was far
from complimentary to me. That evening we dined together
as usual and both behaved as if nothing had happened.

Readers may conclude that I was unfit to handle weapons,
and they may be right, but I would plead that not all the

bad moments were my fault. Back in camp after the filtration plant debacle, I was awoken one night by the sound of someone in my tent. At that point I was not sharing the tent with anyone – the officer I'd been sharing with had gone back to England – so I was alone, or should have been. But as I lay in the pitch dark I could hear unmistakable sounds of stealthy movement no more than a few feet away. I recalled that a NAAFI manager had recently been murdered during the night. Maybe this was another attack. Obviously I must investigate, but that was difficult. We slept under mosquito nets, I had no torch, and the light switch was attached to the tent pole at the foot of my bed. I strained my ears. The stealthy sounds continued. A cautious, shuffling noise – then silence – then another shuffle. As silently as I could I withdrew my revolver from under my pillow and gently eased the edge of the mosquito net from under the side of the mattress. Then, in what I hoped would be the kind of athletic leap executed by heroes of adventure stories, I jumped out of bed and snapped on the light. There was a frantic scrabbling and my would-be assailant fled through the tent door. It was a cat. On the table in the middle of the tent lay a packet of sandwiches that had been prepared for me as I had to leave before breakfast next morning to go on a course. The cat had been trying, as quietly as possible, to unwrap the sandwiches, while I had been trying, as quietly as possible, to plan its assassination.

The course I was going on was in Christian Leadership, which did not seem very appropriate as I was not a Christian. But we were sent on courses on a rota system because, as there was no chance of home leave, they were as near as we got to having a holiday, and it was correctly estimated that any course would be in a more attractive location than Tel el-Kebir. The Christian Leadership course was actually quite a prize because it was in Ismailia – the nearest thing to civilisation the Canal Zone offered. I sunbathed and swam in Lake Timsah and made friends with the course leader, a delightful, bookish chaplain. When I left he presented me with a copy of Fielding's *Tom Jones*, rather reproachfully rubber-stamped, on its flyleaf, 'From the Library of the Christian Leadership Centre, Middle East Land Forces'. I still have it.

The other course I went on was more serious and its subject was Desert Navigation. We were flown to Benghazi and taken by jeep to Adjedabiya, where a brisk Royal Signals major taught us how to ascertain our position anywhere on the globe by means of a sun compass – provided, of course, that the sun was shining, which in Egypt it usually was. The calculations we had to make involved books of nautical tables and, I think, logarithms, which I had learned to use at school. After three days' instruction we left Adjedabiya and headed south into the desert in two jeeps. The Royal Signals major waved goodbye with what I construed as a rather ironic smile.

We felt very intrepid. This was the real Sahara, not the scrubby wasteland around Tel el-Kebir. There were deep wadis, which were difficult to get the jeeps across, and hills of sand, smooth and sculpted by the wind, like enormously elongated suntanned limbs. We travelled in the early mornings and evenings, and in the blazing middays we sheltered from the sun and tried to calculate our position. My calculations usually suggested that we were somewhere in the Mediterranean, but luckily our group contained other mathematicians who were more adept. The silence and emptiness when the jeeps' engines were switched off were so intense that we found ourselves speaking in hushed voices. It seemed we had penetrated to where no human foot had ever trod. Then, four days out, we met a bus. Well, not an ordinary bus – it had big wheels like a tractor, to manage the sand. But it was a bus all right, and packed with Arabs who laughed and waved and shouted greetings as they went past. I suppose they were on their weekly shopping trip to Adjedabiya from whatever oasis they lived in. We waved back, abjectly.

My only other escape from Tel el-Kebir was to the Sinai. I had made friends with another second lieutenant called Derek. Like Bobby he was unmistakably public-school, but like Bobby he had compensatory qualities, among them skill at fencing. He had fenced in the public-school championships and had brought foils, masks and jackets out to Egypt in case he could find anyone to fence with. He couldn't, so he taught me. In the torrid Egyptian afternoons we panted up and down a strip of sand between the officers' mess tents, lunging and parrying. I tried to make up in aggression for what I lacked in skill. I recall a dapper major, one of the less approachable senior officers, pausing to watch us one day as I made an energetic sally. 'Vicious little bastard,' he murmured, as he strolled off.

Apart from fencing, Derek and I talked about ways of getting out of Tel el-Kebir and we hit on the idea of a trip to the monastery of St Catherine in the Sinai. Officially it was to be an armed reconnaissance by the Intelligence

Section, with Derek as escort. But really it was a holiday. We took two Land Rovers, whose drivers were glad of the break, and loaded into them everything we'd want for a week away. Sinai in those days was virtually unvisited. There were no roads, just sand tracks between gaunt, jagged mountains that looked just as they must have when Moses led the Israelites across this peninsula to the Promised Land. Patches of soft sand were a hazard, but we had brought spades and rolls of steel mesh to rescue our Land Rovers when they started to sink. In all the barren miles we covered we met only two people, young Bedouin men who indicated, in sign language, that they were goatherds, though we saw no goats about. They grinned broadly for photographs which we took with the Intelligence Section camera.

The monastery, as we first saw it, coming over the final rocky ridge, was a never-to-be-forgotten wonder. I had not known it was a fortress as well as a monastery. Its granite walls shot up sheer from the desert, with no window or aperture. In the evening light they looked rosy, and smooth enough to stroke. We could glimpse the roofs of huddled buildings inside the fortifications, and a couple of domes, and tall cypress trees. Above it loomed the craggy, boulder-strewn mass of Mount Sinai, where God gave Moses the ten commandments.

We were not very welcome. It took a while before we managed to attract anyone's attention. At length a monk appeared. He was robed in black, with a flat-topped black hat as worn by Greek Orthodox clergy, and had a grizzled beard. Eyeing our armaments, he expressed regret that the monastery did not receive overnight guests, but said he would show us round next day. So we unrolled our sleeping bags on the warm sand, and took turns on guard duty till dawn. He came to see us after breakfast, and took us inside. It was like a little town, and utterly deserted. Not another soul appeared. Perhaps the other monks were at prayers, or hiding in their cells. After the glaring light outside, the basilica was too dark for us to see anything, so we had to take it on trust when our monk extolled its rare and splendid icons. We declined his offer to show us the charnel house, and he declined our request to see the library. In 1844 a German visitor called von Tischendorf, to whom the monks showed their treasures, took away with him a large portion of the oldest surviving manuscript of the Bible, the Codex Sinaiticus, which has never been returned, and is now in the British Library. Memory of his theft evidently lingered, so we had to make do with a peep through the library door. However, we were shown the Burning Bush, and photographed it for reconnaissance purposes. It did not look a healthy shrub. Perhaps it has never quite recovered from its miraculous ignition. The monastery garden, on the other hand, enclosed in its own fortified wall, was lush and fragrant. Date palms, lemon trees, olives and figs spread their grateful shade. There were beds of herbs – thyme, rosemary, juniper. Jasmine scrambled everywhere. On leaving we presented our monk with some packets of cigarettes, which he accepted eagerly. In those days no one knew that smoking killed you, so we all smoked, and felt no guilt handing him our lethal packages. I came away thinking perhaps an Oxford college would be quite like this monastery – the seclusion, the scholarly calm, the garden. It was not a very accurate prediction.

Really the officers' mess was a better preparation for college life. Being on the left in politics, and rather austerely brought up, I should have been superior to the pleasures the mess offered. But in fact I found them completely captivating. I was deeply impressed by the sophistication of some of the older, regular-army lieutenants. One, known as 'Pips', had seen action with the Trucial Oman Levies. Another had once owned a pet cheetah. These majestic beings did not, of course, address second lieutenants, apart from the odd bit of chaff, but I listened to them with care, noting their haughty preference of Marsala to port, for example, and admiring the graceful turn of the wrist with which, at dinner, they would pour half the contents of their sherry glass into their clear soup. I practised it back in my tent, using an egg cup.

Once a week there was a dinner night, at which attendance was obligatory. We wore white monkey jackets with miniature regimental badges on the lapels, dress shirts, black bow ties, maroon cummerbunds and No. 1 dress trousers, dark blue with a broad red stripe. All this peacockery might seem pointless, given that no women were present. But it was like nothing I had ever known, and I was enthralled. The regimental silver would be on display – elaborate centrepieces depicting camels and palm trees and pagodas that related, I suppose, to lands where the regiment had served. The regimental band played on the lawn outside during dinner, ending with the regimental march ('A southerly wind and a cloudy sky'), after which the bandmaster would come into the mess to have a glass of port (or Marsala) with the colonel. Much alcohol was consumed, of course, on these and other evenings, which helped to atone for the lack of women. The chic drink at the time was gin and lime.

Apart from *Tom Jones*, I did not get much reading done during my army service. My father kindly sent out, at my request, novels by Sir Walter Scott, about whom I felt ignorant, and I tried to read them, but it was difficult to relate them to Tel el-Kebir. Letters were another matter. Heather and I wrote to each other every week, sometimes more often, and whenever I heard the bugle call for mail I hoped there would be a letter from her when I got back to the mess. We wrote on flimsy, pale blue air-letter forms, with gummed edges which you licked and folded down to make an envelope. Over the year and a half I was in the Canal Zone her letters gradually piled up in my bedside locker, like scraps of blue sky.

We were flown home in an RAF Dakota, and before we crossed the Egyptian coast the pilot came up on the intercom saying he would take us on a sweep across the delta first to see the pyramids. I prepared to be awed. But as I looked down at them under the tilting wing I found I was thinking of the thousands of people who had slaved and died to erect these blank-looking monuments to tyranny and stupid self-aggrandisement. Then I thought of the village children we had seen with sores on their faces, and of the rich, fat slobs who had got out of their flash cars at our checkpoints, and it seemed to me that Egypt had been going on in the same way for thousands of years, and the pyramids, so famed and fabled, were just another shameful manifestation of it. As we flew on, and I thought a bit more, I realised that what I was hating had nothing specifically to do with Egypt but was far more widespread and stretched through human history. Then I thought of the padre who had given me *Tom Jones*, and how much I had admired him, and it came to me that, though I thought of myself as an agnostic, I was really a Christian who just did not happen to believe in God. As a choirboy I had sung the Magnificat hundreds of times, praising God for putting down the mighty from their seat and sending the rich empty away, and my belief that this was right, and that the mighty and the rich deserved to be humbled and to go hungry, had outlasted my belief in God.

The other thing that struck me forcibly, after the Dakota touched down in England, was that the neatly uniformed member of the Women's Royal Air Force who came tripping across the tarmac to greet us was a very nice shape, and that living without a woman as I had for a year and a half was a mistake. Armed with this admittedly rather random set of critical convictions, I looked forward to getting my teeth into English literature when I went up to Oxford.

5

Undergraduate

I had enjoyed the army a lot – more, I was pretty certain, than the army had enjoyed me – and I wondered whether going back to a life of books and study might not seem dull by comparison. Besides, I didn't feel I belonged in Oxford. For the first week or so I slunk around like an intruder, quite prepared to be detained and ejected if spotted. I think this would have been worse if I hadn't been in the army beforehand. In the army I'd learned to pretend – pretend to be a soldier, pretend to be an officer – and it had worked, more or less. So I found it relatively easy to pretend to be like the other St John's freshmen, with the same background and interests, and they accepted unquestioningly that I was. I suppose a lot of them were pretending too.

All the same St John's is, simply from a physical angle, an awesome place to find yourself resident in. I'd had no chance to explore it when I came up for the entrance exam, but now I did. It stretches along almost the whole length of St Giles, the great tree-lined highway that leaves Oxford to the north. Going in through the castellated gateway tower, the first thing you come to is the front quadrangle, which even I could see was very old. In fact it is constructed from the remains of a fifteenth-century Cistercian monastery. Through a narrow passage at the far side you step, by contrast, into what looks like an illustration from a book on Renaissance art – a piazza in Florence or Rome, perhaps. This is Canterbury Quadrangle, the first Renaissance quadrangle in Oxford. Built in 1636 by Charles I's Archbishop of Canterbury, William Laud, it is a perfectly proportioned square, with delicately columned cloisters and carved, pillared porticoes festooning the gates at each end. The statues niched in the porticoes are flattering likenesses of Charles and his queen, Henrietta Maria.

Walk through the gate at the far end, under Charles's statue, and you come to an Alice-in-Wonderland vista. A huge garden opens before you – the biggest in Oxford. The main lawn stretches far into the distance, surrounded by groves of trees, and away to your left are two other lawns, one with a famous rock garden and a weeping beech, its branches sweeping the ground so that, in summer, you can push through them and sit inside, hidden from the world in a leafy tent.

My rooms in my first year were in North Quadrangle, a rather higgledy-piggledy collection of buildings – kitchens, workshops and staircases for undergraduates – which you got to through a passage between the dining hall and the chapel. My name, I was thrilled to find, was hand-painted, in italic letters, white on black, over the door. Admittedly, all the other doors had similar painted signs, but it made me feel distinguished all the same. My scout was called Arthur, a veteran retainer who knew everything there was to know about undergraduate life, and told me as much as he thought was good for me. I had two rooms, a bedroom, looking out on St Giles, and a sitting room-cum-study. The outer door was stout and studded, and you could lock it to show you didn't want to be disturbed (this was called 'sporting your oak'). My Bakelite wireless had come with me, and I now had a second possession – a Russell Hobbs electric coffee pot, donated by my parents. On my first day in Oxford I went to Woolworths in the Cornmarket and bought sensible plain white plates, cups and saucers that I knew my mother would approve of. As I arranged them on the empty shelves in a cupboard I felt I was creating a home base in a possibly hostile land.

Nowadays St John's is a top college academically, but in my time it was rather second-rate. I think I was lucky in this respect, because I might have felt discouraged if everyone had been brainier than me. As it was, my conversations with a number of other freshmen assured me that they were not among the masterminds of the western world. How one or two of them had got into Oxford at all puzzled me. One possible answer, I discovered, was that St John's had been founded by Sir Thomas White, a London merchant, who also founded Merchant Taylors' School, and the school had 'closed' scholarships to St John's that only its pupils could compete for. Open scholarships, of course, carried more prestige, and I suppose the school put its bright boys in for those and entered the cerebrally challenged for closed scholarships, which they were virtually bound to get. Hence their presence in St John's.

To today's undergraduates college life in the 1950s would seem prehistoric, and even at the time I thought some aspects of it a trifle antiquated. There were no women, of course. Women were segregated in five heavily fortified colleges on the outskirts of town. All the other colleges were men only. We wore our black academic gowns almost all the time –

for meals, for lectures, for tutorials, and even on the streets of Oxford. This was so we could be identified as members of the university by the proctors (youngish dons taking a turn as university disciplinary officers) who patrolled the city at night with their bowler-hatted Bulldogs (university police), arresting undergraduates for offences like going into pubs. Scholars' gowns reached to the ankles and had big, billowing sleeves, but non-scholars (known as 'commoners') wore flimsy little waist-length affairs with a couple of tapes dangling from the shoulders. As a scholar, I considered this distinction entirely appropriate.

I also approved of the fact that, at dinner in hall, scholars sat grandly at a separate table. In return for this privilege one of us had to read the Latin grace before dinner each night. (It was best to learn it by heart because a favourite practical joke among commoners was to remove the printed text from the reading stand.) Another ritual in hall was sconcing. The sconce-pots were silver tankards, gorgeously ornate, and often dating from the late seventeenth and eighteenth centuries. Each held several pints of beer. If, during dinner, you mentioned a lady's name or 'talked shop' (that is, alluded to your academic work) or committed any other ungentlemanly indiscretion, anyone at the table who took offence could sconce you. He had to fill in a special slip, beginning *Sconsam posco tibi quod* . . . (I demand a sconce from you because . . .), and add the reason. The permitted languages were Latin, Greek and Hebrew. A scout would take the slip to high table, where the presiding don would check the Latin, Greek or Hebrew, and judge whether the offence justified a sconce. If he approved he wrote *Stet* ('It stands') on the slip, and the scout would deliver it to the offending diner, who then had a choice. He could either pay for a sconce-pot full of beer which the sconcer would share with his cronies, or he could try to drink the sconce himself. If he chose this alternative, he had to stand up, lift the brimming pot to his lips, and start drinking. He could pause for a rest, provided he did not take the pot from his lips until it was drained. The procedure was evidently more difficult than you might suppose, because attempts were liable to end prematurely in spectacular cascades of vomit.

Presumably the authorities took the view that this was all part of the rough-and-tumble of a gentleman's education, and a similarly tolerant attitude was adopted in academic arrangements. At the end of term there was a ceremony called Collections, when each undergraduate appeared before the head of the college and his tutors, who delivered a report on his work. Nowadays, out of consideration for the sensibilities of the young, these meetings are conducted in cloistered privacy. But in the 1950s they took place in public. The dons would assemble at high table in hall, and the undergraduates gathered in a mob at the far end. As each name was called its possessor walked up the hall and took his seat at the table. His reports were read out, the presiding don added his comments, and any other don who cared to could chip in with advice or raillery as the mood took him – all this clearly audible to the assembled undergraduates at the back of the hall. Some of the exchanges that took place became legendary. Once, a third-year classicist called Bott, who had received a poor report on his work in Latin, informed the assembled fellows that he considered Latin 'a barbaric language'. The presiding don huffed and puffed and there was general consternation. But one of the classics tutors tactfully interposed, 'I'm sure Mr Bott meant "barbaric" in its original Greek sense of "non-Greek".' Bott looked mighty pleased with himself as he clumped back down the hall.

My tutor, J. B. Leishman, did not have a room in the college, so we cycled up to his flat in Bardwell Road for our tutorials. He was a disconcerting figure, tall and gaunt, with a thatch of grizzled hair and the profile of an angry hawk. This appearance was misleading, for he was a kind man. He kept open house on Thursday evenings, when his pupils could bring their friends for coffee and chat, and he would play choice items from his big collection of gramophone records. It was on one of these evenings that I first heard W. B. Yeats's quavering, singsong rendition of 'The Lake Isle of Innisfree'.

Leishman's room exactly fitted my idea of a scholar's sanctum. It was lined with books from floor to ceiling and overlooked a garden. For tutorials he would sit in a chair by the window, and I and my tutorial partner would sit opposite and read out our essays, one after the other. He puffed at his pipe as he listened, and if it was a morning tutorial he would pour himself an occasional cup of coffee from a Thermos flask. If it was evening, the table in the middle of the room would have been laid for his supper by his housekeeper before she left – for he lived alone. There would be a white cloth with cutlery and a glass and a bottle of Woodpecker cider.

Leishman was a 'lecturer' at St John's, not a fellow, which was why he did not have a college room, and dined alone at home, and had to teach round the clock to earn enough to live on. I was told he was considered 'too eccentric' to be a fellow, but so far as I could see he was a more distinguished scholar than many of those deemed normal enough to be fellows of St John's. A classicist by training, he had a wide and precise knowledge of modern European literatures, especially German and Italian. His great love was the German poet Rilke, and the first of his translations of Rilke, the *Sonnets to Orpheus*, had been published by the Hogarth Press back in 1936, so I suppose he must have known Virginia and Leonard Woolf. Other Rilke translations followed, including the *Duino Elegies*, in collaboration with Stephen Spender. He also translated poems by Hölderlin and selected odes of Horace. He published a pioneering study of John Donne, called *The Monarch of Wit*, and one of the earliest studies of Andrew Marvell's poetry, and a work of dazzling erudition on Shakespeare's sonnets. As for his being 'too eccentric', it was nonsense. He was an old-world scholarly gentleman, naturally courteous and without affectation. Usually he wore a baggy tweed jacket and tweed plus fours, with long socks. A keen cyclist, he had two bikes – a 'winter machine', hung with panniers to accommodate provisions for excursions into the Oxfordshire countryside, and a 'summer machine' that was more sporty. Cycling gave him time for meditation. Once, after I had graduated, I cycled with him to Woodstock and round Blenheim Park, and I asked him how he had decided which odes of Horace he would translate. He replied that they were the ones that he found he could retain in his memory while out walking or cycling.

As a tutor he was stimulating because he treated us like

grown-ups. He seldom said anything about our essays – he had, after all, heard the same sort of thing countless times before. Instead, after an expressive silence, he would allude to some passage in Shakespeare or Virgil or Dante that seemed to him apposite, and that he assumed we knew, and follow it with a string of interrogative bleats – 'Eh? Eh? Eh?' – that invited us to comment on it. Occasionally he would venture an aphorism. Marlowe, he said (scornfully), 'made little men feel big'; Milton (admiringly) was 'fiercely simple'. These sallies were accompanied by a harsh, abrupt laugh that resembled a cough and sometimes developed into one. Without quite realising it I imitated both his way of talking and his laugh until my friends begged me to shut up.

Though I envied his learning, and wanted to be like him, I now think he was perhaps a sad and lonely man. I envisage him, sitting in that room, giving endless tutorials to the callow bunch of idiots that we must have seemed to him, and then I think of Rilke's heartrending poem about the panther in the Jardin des Plantes in Paris, plodding endlessly round its cage – which Leishman translates:

> His gaze those bars keep passing is so misted
> With tiredness, it can take in nothing more.
> He feels as though a thousand bars existed,
> And no more world beyond them or before . . .

I have wondered whether, like so many of his generation, he was one of those who yearned for male love, but was inhibited by upbringing and convention. I have wondered, too, whether that was what 'too eccentric' meant, and it makes me think of another of Rilke's poems that Leishman translated:

I'd like above all to be one of those
Who drive with wild black horses through the night
Torches like hair uplifted in affright
When the great wind of their wild hunting blows.
I'd like to stand in the front, as in a boat,
Tall, like a long floating flag unrolled,
And dark, but with a helmet made of gold
Restlessly flashing . . .

I hope I am wrong about his being sad. He died in 1963, falling from a mountain path in Germany, and there was some talk of suicide. But others said he was trying to pluck a flower – an edelweiss – which he could not quite reach. I owe him a great deal, not least that, partly in memory of him, I went to evening classes and learned German when I was in my thirties so that I could read Rilke in the original – or, at any rate, try to.

I did not see much of the college fellows, but that was usual in those days when the idea that everyone should live in universal chumminess had not yet taken hold. The college president, Lane Poole, was an invalid, so the job of entertaining undergraduates devolved on the vice-president, John Mabbott, a prim, fidgety philosopher, with the most humourless laugh I have ever heard. He produced it by simultaneously baring his teeth and making an urgent lowing sound. Clearly he could not stand the thought of having lunch or dinner with a bunch of freshmen undergraduates so we were asked, in batches, to 'dessert', with an unambiguous directive, inscribed on the invitation, that this festivity would commence promptly at eight thirty and cease an hour later. We arrived in a gaggle at the president's lodgings and were shown up to a dark, candle-lit room which contained a large, shiny table and Mabbott. There were bowls of fruit on the table and an empty plate in front of each chair, surrounded by gleaming silver cutlery. None of us had ever been invited to dessert before, and we had no idea what to do. The silence was terrifying. We scarcely dared breathe, let alone talk. Those of us who ventured to consume a fruit felt that every munch and swallow echoed through the room, and when you replaced a knife or fork on the table it clanged like a dropped bucket. Mabbott did his best to engage us in conversation, and tried out his laugh several times, baring his teeth desperately, but it was a forlorn endeavour. On the stroke of nine thirty we all scrambled for the exit, and no one, I feel sure, was more relieved than Mabbott.

The Oxford English syllabus in the 1950s was a scandal or a joke, depending on your sense of humour. Its cut-off point was 1832 – that is, it omitted all Victorian and twentieth--century literature. The unspoken assumption seemed to be that any gentleman would acquaint himself with the Victorian poets and novelists, without needing to study them, and modern writing was not worth serious attention anyway. Anglo-Saxon and early (that is, pre-1300) Middle English, on the other hand, featured weightily in the syllabus, on the grounds, I suppose, that since no one could conceivably read them for pleasure they suited the rigorous demands of an academic discipline. I could see that Anglo-Saxon must be fascinating for philologists. As the written remains are so scanty, reconstructing what the language was actually like provides endless opportunity for conjecture and controversy. But the same factors make it unappealing to undergraduates.

Learning it is a chore, and by comparison with the literatures that learning Greek or Latin or any modern language gives you access to, Anglo-Saxon literature is almost non-existent. Apart from *Beowulf* only three or four poems are worth reading, and *Beowulf*, for all its fame, is fragmentary and full of insoluble linguistic tangles. The best bits, about Grendel and his mother, are, it's true, strange and haunting like nothing else in English literature, partly because of the mystery that age invests them with, and it's also true that no translation can do them justice. Grendel, for example, is called a *mearcstapa*, that is, a 'mark-stepper', or one who walks on the borders or boundaries ('marks'), and the word conjures up a whole way of thinking about territory, and the need to keep safe within it, and what horrors might lie beyond it, that no modern word can represent. This kind of occasional excitement kept me working at Anglo-Saxon, but I could sympathise with those who found it repugnant and they, for their part, pointed out that W. H. Auden had famously got a third-class degree because he couldn't stomach *Beowulf*, so disdain for it was virtually a guarantee of superior literary sensibility.

We were sent out for Anglo-Saxon tuition to a don in Wadham called Alan Ward. He was a small, nervous man who lived in a kind of burrow beneath the level of Wadham's front quadrangle. We went to him in a bunch of half a dozen or so, and could scarcely fit into his tiny room. I think this made him jumpier than he would otherwise have been, and regularly, halfway through each tutorial, he would murmur an inaudible apology and leave the room, returning some fifteen minutes later. There was much speculation about this. Some held he must suffer from urinary trouble, others that he went to put money on a horse. The mystery was never solved. Knowing that none of us wanted to learn the stuff he had to teach, Ward was painfully anxious to please. A member of our group was my school friend Dennis Keene, who had come up to Oxford with me. He, like many others, had no intention of wasting time on Anglo-Saxon, and when Ward requested us, with effusive apologies, to hand in a piece of written work midway through term, Dennis omitted to do so. A couple of weeks later Ward asked politely when he might expect 'Mr Keene's' written work. Dennis replied unblinkingly that he had handed it in the previous week, adding, 'I hope you haven't lost it, sir, because I'd like it back to use for revision.' The rest of us were struck dumb with admiration, but poor Ward went into convulsions of self-blame, assuring Dennis that he could indeed remember receiving his work and must have carelessly mislaid it and would make a determined search.

Some years later I got to know Alan Ward and found him a learned and loveable man, with a passion I'd never have guessed for amateur dramatics. The fact that he was a hopeless teacher meant I had to grind away at Anglo-Saxon by myself. But then, giving you time to work by yourself was what, so far as I was concerned, university was for. It was a luxury to get up each morning and know you could spend the whole day just reading. Alone with a book, I could stop pretending and just be myself. I felt guilty about it at first. Could it be right, I wondered, to have so much spare time? What about all those people out in the real world, slogging away at their dull jobs from nine to five? What about Heather, now an assistant librarian in the Fulham Public Library, and studying at night for her librarianship exams?

My undergraduate life seemed pretty easy compared to hers.

However, I did not allow these worthy thoughts to spoil the pleasure I got from my undisturbed hours of reading. Week after week I felt ignorance slipping away, and writers who had been just names before became more real to me than the half-recognised faces I tried to keep up conversation with at meals. Chaucer was the first writer this happened with. His Prologue to the *Canterbury Tales* had been a set text at school, but when I went through his complete works the big revelation was his epic poem *Troilus and Criseyde*, about two lovers torn apart by war. It astonished me because it already has everything that the modern novel is supposed to have introduced – depth psychology, a shifty, sophisticated narrator, serious, tender, graphic sex. The high point comes in Book 2 where Troilus and Criseyde fall in love. It is dangerous for her because he is the king's son and she is alone and unprotected. As she lies awake one night a nightingale sings in the white moonlight outside her window. Then she goes to sleep and dreams that an eagle, 'feathered white as bone', rips out her heart with his talons. But it doesn't hurt, and she isn't afraid, and the eagle flies off with her heart leaving his heart in its place. Then, when the lovers are at last in bed together Troilus – stroking and kissing her nakedness – jokingly commands her to 'yield', and she, joking too, or maybe reminding him who's really in charge, replies that if she hadn't yielded before this she wouldn't be here.

You couldn't, it seemed to me, find a scene like that, as liberated, as psychologically acute, anywhere in English literature until modern times. I also got very fond of Pandarus, ostensibly the wicked schemer of the poem. When he's trying to lower Criseyde's defences by making her laugh, he begins, Chaucer says, cracking his best jokes ('beste japes'), which makes him sound modern too, like someone polishing up his funny stories before a party. So my previous ideas about how English literature developed (i.e. starting virtually unreadable and getting gradually more readable until it arrived at the twentieth century) had to be adjusted.

I knew Elizabeth's reign was supposed to be a great age for literature, so I looked forward to getting on to it. However, it was a blow to find how dull a lot of it was. Had the critics who glorified Good Queen Bess's time ever actually tried *reading* Lyly's *Euphues* or Sidney's *Arcadia* or Sidney Lee's two tomes of instantly forgettable Elizabethan sonnet sequences? It seemed to me that if you took Shakespeare and three or four other authors out of the reckoning, Elizabethan literature would be strictly for antiquarians. The biggest disappointment was Spenser's *Faerie Queene*. I read it in an old Macmillan's Globe edition from Blackwell's second-hand department, and a previous owner had, rather curiously, crossed out with a single bold pencil stroke all the sexy passages. I often wondered whether perhaps he was going to read it aloud in the family circle, and pencilled out these portions to remind him to omit them, or whether he had found them so inflaming first time round that he wished to avoid them in future for chastity's sake. At all events, he had inadvertently highlighted the best moments in the poem – the Bower of Bliss with its two naked damsels jumping around in a fountain; Jupiter, disguised as a swan, 'ruffing' his feathers as he prepares to mount an all too willing Leda; Serena, naked and trembling in the 'glims' of starlight as the cannibals close in with their knives, and all the other famous stripteases that spice up Spenser's moral truisms. But it wasn't just the mix of prurience and preaching that I disliked. What *The Faerie Queene* does is mythicise political power, attributing supernatural status to a dictatorial regime, and this makes it, at heart, crass and false – just like the pyramids. (Reading my essay to Leishman I missed out this last bit as I feared that, not necessarily sharing my view of the pyramids, he might be startled.)

Admittedly, I could see that Spenser's decorative effects were exquisite. One of my favourites came in 'Prothalamion' where he is describing two swans on the Thames:

> The snow, which doth the top of Pindus strew,
> Did never whiter shew,
> Nor Jove himself, when he a swan would be
> For love of Leda, whiter did appear,
> Yet Leda was (they say) as white as he,
> Yet not so white as these, nor nothing neare,
> So purely white they were.

That reminded me of the United Dairies ladies in Barnes – an association they might not have been too happy with. But it was still (I told myself) just decorative writing, an ornamental cover for Spenser's trite allegories, not something that came from the heart. In the whole *Faerie Queene* (if you omit the so-called 'Mutability Cantos', which are admittedly better than the rest) there seemed to me only one stanza of deep personal feeling, and it came at the start of Book 2, Canto 8:

> And is there care in heaven? And is there love
> In heavenly spirits to these creatures base,
> That may compassion of their evilles move?

> There is, else much more wretched were the case
> Of men than beasts. But O! th'exceeding grace
> Of highest God, that loves his creatures so,
> And all his workes with mercy doth embrace.
> That blessed Angels he sends to and fro,
> To serve to wicked man, to serve his wicked foe.

You don't have to be a Christian to find the idea of man as God's 'wicked foe' alerting. No other stanza so clearly contradicts W. B. Yeats's jibe that Spenser's religion was just 'undelighted obedience'.

All the same, it was a relief to move on from Spenser to John Donne:

> All kings and all their favourites,
>   All glory of honours, beauties, wits,
> The sun itself, which makes times as they pass,
> Is elder by a year now than it was
> When thou and I first one another saw;
> All other things to their destruction draw,
>   Only our love hath no decay,
> This no tomorrow hath, nor yesterday,
> Running, it never runs from us away,
> But truly keeps his first, last, everlasting day.

Everything about this is light years away from Spenser. The language is direct and modern, as against Spenser's fake-archaic poeticisms, and instead of Spenser's craven power-worship Donne relegates kings and their pomp to insignificance, excluding them from the charmed circle of himself and his love. Spenser kowtows to Elizabeth even in the love sonnets he wrote to his future wife, undertaking to praise his betrothed, but only moderately ('let her praises yet be low and mean/Fit for the handmaid of the Fairy Queen'). Imagine Donne writing anything so abject! I knew from reading Donne's satires that he had dared to criticise Elizabeth's persecution of England's Catholic minority, to which his own family belonged, and I learned that he had ruined his career by marrying for love – all of which earned him extra points in my assessment.

I linked him with Ben Jonson because Jonson had the same inner strength and the same defiant rejection of everything around him.

> False world, good night! since thou hast brought
> > That hour upon my morn of age;
> Henceforth I quit thee from my thought,
> > My part is ended on thy stage . . .
> Nor for my peace will I go far,
> > As wanderers do, that still do roam,
> But make my strengths, such as they are,
> > Here in my bosom, and at home.

I loved 'such as they are' – the modest disclaimer coming like a second thought, as if it's just ordinary speech, not poetry, and he's making it up as he goes along. Donne does this too – starting a poem 'So, so, break off this last lamenting kiss . . .', as if he has just pulled his lips away from her mouth to speak the line. I felt like applauding the magnificence of Jonson's contempt when he resolves to give up writing for the theatre and:

> . . . sing high and aloof,
> Safe from the wolf's black jaw, and the dull ass's hoof.

The glimpse of dark gums, not pink as in a human mouth, that 'black jaw' gives you, and the hollow thud of 'dull', like a kick, both seemed to me richly physical, and I thought it was wonderful to be able to dismiss your critics, almost casually, as asses. It reminded me of the self-confidence I'd so envied in Shaw when I read his Preface to *Saint Joan* at school.

But what I liked most fiercely was Jonson's exposure of rampaging luxury through his sinister consumerist buffoon Sir Epicure Mammon in *The Alchemist*. Believing he's soon to possess boundless wealth, Mammon imagines what he'll be able to buy – countless wives and concubines, sex aids, top-quality pornography, fabulous bathrooms so dense with perfume that he and his women will lose themselves in it, as if in a mist, and mirrors, faceted like diamonds, so they'll see their naked bodies multiplied over and over, and baths 'like pits/To fall into', and gossamer and roses for them to roll themselves dry in. Slaves will fan him with ostrich tails, he'll eat off gold plates studded with emeralds, sapphires and rubies, his food will be cruelly invasive delicacies – the tongues of dormice, 'the swelling unctuous paps/Of a fat pregnant sow, newly cut off'. And so on. Through Mammon, Jonson shows that luxury is obscene, mad and sad, an endless chase after ever-elusive phantoms. Since I'd been brought up in wartime to think that frugality and austerity were virtues, that was exactly what I wanted to believe.

The great opposite to Spenser, though, was not, for me, Donne or Jonson but Milton. We'd studied *Samson Agonistes* at school, but I hadn't read *Paradise Lost* and I wondered how it could be of any importance, given that it was based on the Book of Genesis and other biblical stories no one believed in any more. This not very subtle objection was quelled by reading it. In some ways it seemed more like a theorem than a story, exposing hard-edged issues of power, justice, authority and free will that matter to any human being, Christian or not. It's a more uncomfortable poem for Christians than non-Christians because Satan gets all the best lines, and because Milton puts God in the dock, introducing the Almighty as a character and making him defend his own conduct – with, it's generally agreed, mixed success. (That, I realised, was what Leishman had meant by calling Milton 'fiercely simple'.) I was a bit disconcerted to find that Milton had admired Spenser, but then, you can't get everything right even if you're Milton. That he had defended the beheading of Charles I in a great, defiant Latin work addressed to the shocked monarchies of Europe naturally put me on his side.

I could see that his characters weren't human in the way Shakespeare's are, partly because they speak that statuesque language I'd noticed in *Samson Agonistes*, and partly because, like characters in science fiction, they lack the realistic surroundings that make people seem real. Satan seemed the most human character (an irony I assumed Milton was well aware of) and the grandeur of his hatred made him talk like the hero of a tragedy Shakespeare never got round to writing. I especially liked him in *Paradise Regained*. This was partly a private thing, because I couldn't find anyone among my contemporaries who had read *Paradise Regained*, so I felt possessive about it. But it was also because the Satan of *Paradise Regained* is defeated and puzzled and tries to be winning – so I was won. He tries to tempt Jesus in the wilderness, and when Jesus warns there's some terrible fate in store for him Satan, very humanly, can't bear the suspense, and wants the worst to happen straight away. (Perhaps, though it only occurs to me now, I was thinking of the restless night I spent after I nearly shot Bobby.)

> I would be at the worst, worst is my port,
> My harbour and my ultimate repose,
> The end I would attain, my final good.
> My error was my error, and my crime
> My crime, whatever for itself condemned,
> And will alike be punished, whether thou
> Reign or reign not; though to that gentle brow
> Willingly I could fly, and hope thy reign,
> From that placid aspect and meek regard,
> Rather than aggravate my evil state,
> Would stand between me and thy father's ire,
> (Whose ire I dread more than the fire of hell)
> A shelter and a kind of shading cool
> Interposition, as a summer's cloud.

That long, lingering 'Interposition', which mimics the cloud's slow passing, was typical of the audio effects that made Milton's verse irresistible. Much later I learned that some critics consider this speech to be Satan's most cunning temptation – tempting Jesus to have mercy. But that never occurred to me as an undergraduate. The speech seemed heartfelt, and I could see that the lines about the 'port' and 'harbour' echoed Othello's grand finale, as declaimed by me in front of my bedroom mirror.

> Here is my journey's end, here is my butt
> And very sea-mark of my utmost sail . . .

I felt smug about noticing that, and thought it justified learning Shakespeare by heart, because otherwise you would miss how much there is of him in all the poetry that comes afterwards. Leishman, who had read *Paradise Regained*, and knew – it seemed probable – most of Shakespeare by heart, seemed unimpressed.

At its simplest level Milton's poetry in *Paradise Lost* worked for me because the noise it made was matchlessly grand. Like a Latin poet, he brings in exotic proper names for his sound effects – a line like 'Nor where Abassin kings their issue guard', for example, or 'Jousted in Aspramont or Montalban' – and he combines this with verse-movement so expressive that you can almost see what's happening – this, for example, about one of the evil angels, Satan's followers, being thrown out of heaven:

> . . . and in Ausonian land
> Men called him Mulciber, and how he fell
> From heaven they fabled, thrown by angry Jove
> Sheer o'er the crystal battlements, from morn
> To noon he fell, from noon to dewy eve,
> A summer's day, and with the setting sun
> Dropp'd from the zenith like a falling star
> On Lemnos th'Aegean isle . . .

That slow, slow fall, as if seen from far away, stops abruptly as he hits the earth, and the words are squashed – 'th'Aegean' – by the impact. It's like a film made out of sounds.

When we got on to the eighteenth century I had another surprise, rather like discovering that Elizabethan literature is not so glorious after all. I had been told that the eighteenth century was the age of reason. But it seemed to me to be the age of fury, madness and terror. Swift was the great revelation. I suppose I'd read *Gulliver's Travels* at some point, probably in a bowdlerised children's version. Now I could read it uncensored, and his other works as well. I could hear the black laughter in *A Modest Proposal*, where he expounds his plan to serve up the flesh of Irish children on English dining tables, and so provide 'a most delicious, nourishing and wholesome food, whether stewed, roasted, baked or boiled'. I realised it was 'irony', of course. But it was like seeing someone smile, and then noticing a fang at the corner of his mouth.

How much Swift really cared about the Irish or their poverty I was never sure. He hated Dublin and referred to it as a 'dirty dog-hole and prison', which doesn't suggest they were exactly his favourite people. No doubt England's Irish policy did stir his indignation. But the fury he felt about how humans behave went far beyond local political issues. In Book 4 of *Gulliver's Travels* the Yahoos, a filthy, apelike race, represent human beings, and perform disgusting imitations of human customs. The royal Yahoo, for example, has a favourite courtier whose duty is 'to lick his master's feet and posteriors, and drive the female Yahoos to his kennel'. When the favourite is eventually disgraced or dismissed, his successor and all the other Yahoos of the district 'come in a body and discharge their excrements upon him from head to foot'. However distasteful we might find these imaginings, they are, give or take a detail or two, perfectly recognisable depictions of human life. Swift seems simply to have realised – more than a century before Darwin – that humans are animals, and animals of a uniquely vicious and quarrelsome kind. I was reminded, reading him, of the essay on the significance of human beings our headmaster had ironically suggested we write. But Swift didn't just think humans insignificant (absurdly self-important midgets like his Lilliputians), he thought them contemptible. The reasons for this, I supposed, were buried deep in his psychology, but the reason he himself gave was that he was a Christian. In his *Letter to a Young Clergyman* he says that it is 'the duty of a divine to preach and practise the contempt of human things'. It was an aim I found exciting and realistic – which is odd, since I was young, happy, not a Christian, and there were quite a few humans I liked.

With Johnson, that other eighteenth-century giant, it was terror, not rage, that displaced reason, so far as I could see. The idea of eternal damnation so horrified him that he would not allow anyone to discuss it, angrily cutting Boswell short when he tried. He was terrified of going mad too – Mrs Thrale is said to have kept a straitjacket in the house – and he thought imagination was a kind of madness. 'There is no man whose imagination does not sometimes predominate over his reason . . . All power of fancy over reason is a degree of insanity'. Distrusting the imagination is not a good start for a literary critic, and Johnson's religious terrors were a handicap in that respect too because they made him feel that poetry was too trivial to deal with the most important things. 'Man, admitted to implore the mercy of his Creator, and plead the merits of his Redeemer, is already in a higher state than poetry can confer.' His disparagement of Milton flowed naturally from this prejudice.

He thought that the terrors that agitated him agitated everyone. He once told Boswell that when he first visited the pleasure gardens at Ranelagh, 'it went to my heart to consider that there was not one in all that brilliant circle who was not afraid to go home and think'. It followed that happiness (for Johnson) was a mirage: 'We are long before we are convinced that happiness is never to be found, and each believes it possessed by others to keep alive the hope of obtaining it for himself.'

This dark, haunted, half-mad Johnson seemed to me, as an undergraduate, much more interesting than the kindly old codger beloved of Johnsonians who fed his cat on oysters and made an ex-slave from Jamaica his son and heir. (Strangely, with the passage of time, the kindly old codger has come to seem more appealing.) It was a disappointment to find his famous *Lives of the Poets* was so boring, and that most of the poets he chose are now forgotten. I slogged through it of course, because my aim was to learn, not to have fun, and I knew that those two aims seldom coincide (a truth that might, I feel, be made clearer nowadays to those starting out on education). I thought Johnson's best moment as a critic was not in the *Lives* but in his Shakespeare criticism, when he says that Falstaff illustrates 'the pain of deformity'. It was such a relief after all the sentimentalising of Falstaff I'd had to read.

Alexander Pope, the third most interesting person in the eighteenth century, on my count, was not, I was prepared to grant, as mad as the other two, but to imagine that he had anything to do with reason was absurd. When he tried to be reasonable he came up with the proposition (in *An Essay on Man*) that 'Whatever is, is right' – which is what Voltaire's idiotic optimist Pangloss believes. Pope was a satirist to his toenails, and a satirist must believe that whatever is is wrong. Pope did, and he makes the wrongness surreal and grotesque, which is what his poetry springs from. So Sporus (poor Lord Hervey, who suffered from epilepsy and really did drink ass's milk as part of his diet) is 'the mere white curd of ass's milk' and a 'bug with gilded wings' and a 'painted child of dirt that stinks and sings'. Timon, dwarfed by his colossal country house, is 'a puny insect shiv'ring at a breeze'. The statues that decorate Timon's gardens give Pope a chance to revel in the absurdities that he loves – 'swallows roost in Nilus' dusty urn', 'gladiators fight, or die, in flowers'. On Belinda's dressing table in 'The Rape of the Lock' great beasts of sea and land assemble:

> The tortoise here and elephant unite,
> Transform'd to combs, the speckled and the white.

Pope produces these marvels inexhaustibly, pulling reality to pieces and putting it together again in ways that are rich and strange – 'Heavy harvests nod beneath the snow', 'Whales sport in woods and dolphins in the skies', 'Other planets circle other suns'.

When, for once, he didn't use couplets, I found that he gave himself a new, poignant music – in 'A Hymn Written in Windsor Forest', for instance.

> All hail once pleasing, once inspiring shade,
>   Scene of my youthful loves, and happier hours,
> Where the kind Muses met me as I strayed,
>   And gently pressed my hand, and said, Be ours –
> Take all thou e'er shalt have, a constant Muse,
>   At court thou may'st be liked, but nothing gain,
> Stocks thou may'st buy and sell, but always lose;
>   And love the brightest eyes, but love in vain.

It seemed surprising to me that he should include losing money on the stock exchange among all the poetic wistfulness. But it sharpens the poem's realism, and behind the last line you hear his bitterness about being a cripple. As a child he had suffered from tuberculosis of the spine, so he was stunted, and had to be laced into a corset in order to stand upright – all of which his enemies mocked.

When I quoted those lines in an essay for Leishman he quoted, out of the blue, some lines of Wordsworth:

> Thus, while the sun sinks down to rest,
> Far in the regions of the west,
> Though to the vale no parting beam
> Be given, not one memorial gleam,
> A lingering light he fondly throws
> On the dear hills where first he rose.

I was surprised, because it didn't seem exactly top-class Wordsworth to me. But I could see it fitted in with Pope looking back on his youth, and it clearly meant a lot to Leishman. I can still hear how he spoke – or almost sang – the plangent final line.

Wordsworth was the last poet I studied with him. We ran out of syllabus after that. It's easy to pretend you have read Wordsworth when you haven't – you can hold forth about nature-worship or his curious relations with his sister Dorothy – and I had done that and now felt ashamed of it. So as a kind of atonement I read him right through in the microscopically-printed single-volume Oxford edition. It was not exactly an On-First-Looking-into-Chapman's-Homer experience. But then, nor is first looking into Chapman's Homer unless you happen to be John Keats. A lot of Wordsworth, I found, was ponderous in a distinctively Wordsworthian way. But you can't know that unless you've read him, and when you do you find that even the stickiest passages yield unforgettable phrases.

My life had not been at all like Wordsworth's, but he made me feel it had. I think that's a common experience. It's part of his greatness that he can make you recognise something in yourself that answers to his feelings. When he wrote:

> The sounding cataract
> Haunted me like a passion . . .

I was back beside the weir at Radcliffe-on-Trent, deafened by the din. When he wrote about tree climbing as a boy:

> . . . the sky seemed not a sky
> Of earth – and with what motion moved the clouds . . .

I felt the tree sway under me. Those lines are very character-istic because he doesn't tell you what the sky *did* seem like or how the clouds *did* move. He leaves you to imagine it, and the effect is that you write the poem for yourself. Some of his greatest lines are like that. He says that his brain:

> Worked with a dim and undetermined sense
> Of unknown modes of being;

or that his soul,

> Remembering how she felt, but what she felt
> Remembering not, retains an obscure sense
> Of possible sublimity . . .

and you feel that he has told you something marvellous, though really he has told you it can't be told. It's strange this should be so powerful, but it is. Maybe it's because we are so used to finding that we can't put our deepest feelings into words that when Wordsworth says he can't either we are stirred to our depths.

> To me the meanest flower that blows can give
> Thoughts that do often lie too deep for tears.

He is the only poet who can point so unerringly to the aching gulfs in ourselves that lie beyond poetry, beyond expression, beyond help. He remembers quite ordinary things that have, for him, enormous significance, though he can't explain why – a girl, carrying a pitcher on her head across a windswept waste, for example:

> I should need
> Colours and words that are unknown to man
> To paint the visionary dreariness.

Sometimes he can open these inexpressible depths just by adding the negative prefix 'un' to a word. In *The Prelude* he remembers seeing a father in a London slum who had carried his sick child out onto a sunlit patch of grass and 'Eyed the poor babe with love unutterable'. Or he writes about how ancient, ruined buildings have been known to collapse at the least tremor:

> . . . drop like the tower sublime
> Of yesterday, which royally did wear
> His crown of weeds, but could not even sustain
> Some casual shout that broke the silent air,
> Or the unimaginable touch of Time.

That last line is the only memorable moment in all the 132

Ecclesiastical Sonnets, but that, it seemed to me, made it all the more worth finding. The bit about the tower's crown of weeds shows Wordsworth remembering mad *King Lear*:

> Crowned with rank fumiter and furrow weeds,
> With burdocks, hemlock, nettles, cuckoo-flowers,
> Darnel, and all the idle weeds that grow
> In our sustaining corn . . .

but I refrained from pointing this out to Leishman since he had seemed so unimpressed by my noticing Shakespeare in *Paradise Regained*.

People who spend a lot of their lives reading books, as I was doing, find, after a time, that they prefer reading about things to actually seeing them. Reading about them surrounds them with imaginative allure, but when you actually see them they seem bald and ordinary. Wordsworth was the first author I'd come across who described this. In his case it happened with Mont Blanc. He'd read about Mont Blanc and looked forward to seeing it, but when he did it was just a mountain, and he:

> . . . grieved
> To have a soulless image on the eye
> That had usurped upon a living thought
> That never more could be.

So living your truest life in books may deaden the real world for you as well as enliven it.

In addition to Leishman's tutorials I went to university lectures which were, on the whole, a waste of time. J. R. R. Tolkien, lecturing on *Beowulf*, was mostly inaudible and, when audible, incomprehensible. He seemed immemorially aged, and green mildew grew on his gown, as if he had recently emerged from a wood. Helen Gardner, prim and stately, delivered what were not so much lectures as reverential sermons on John Donne. In our first term we were lucky to hear Humphry House lecturing on Aristotle's *Poetics* – one of our set texts for Prelims, the university exam we took after our first two terms, and for which we also read (in translation) Aeschylus' *Agamemnon*, Sophocles' *Oedipus Rex* and Euripides' *Hippolytus*. House was the star of the Oxford English school. He had been Elizabeth Bowen's lover, wrote landmark books on Dickens and Coleridge, and inaugurated the great Pilgrim edition of Dickens's letters, completed half a century after his death. He died suddenly, in his forties, a few months after I heard him lecture.

The lectures I learned most from, though, were given by F. P. Wilson, then Merton Professor of English literature. Wilson did not have, so far as I could discover, any ideas of his own. But he read to us passages from seventeenth-century prose writers – Francis Bacon, Sir Thomas Browne, John Bunyan, George Fox – of whom I was completely ignorant. He read dramatically, and it was breathtaking. Here, for example, is a passage from Bunyan's spiritual autobiography *Grace Abounding to the Chief of Sinners*, which relates how Bunyan struggles to withstand the temptations Satan casts in his way. Satan for Bunyan was so real that he could feel him pulling at his clothes when he tried to pray, and one of his temptations was bellringing, which Bunyan had enjoyed before his conversion, but came to think wicked. So for a time he just went to watch the ringers but did not ring himself.

But quickly after I began to think, How if one of the bells should fall? Then I chose to stand under a main beam, which lay overthwart the steeple from side to side, thinking there I might stand sure. But then I should think again, should the bell fall with a swing it might first hit the wall and then rebounding upon me might kill me for all this beam. This made me stand in the steeple door, and now, thought I, I am safe enough, for if a bell should then fall I can slip out behind these thick walls and so be preserved notwithstanding.

So after this I would yet go to see them ring, but would not go farther than the steeple door. But then it came into my head, How if the steeple itself should fall? And this thought, it may fall for all I know, when I stood and looked on did continually so shake my mind that I durst not stand at the steeple door any longer, but was forced to flee for fear the steeple should fall upon my head.

Bunyan was clearly what we should now call mad. But his belief and the way he expressed it seemed to me compelling and magnificent. Reading him and other writers – like George Herbert and, of course, Milton – I came to feel that studying seventeenth-century English literature was really the same as studying Christianity. That was all they seriously cared about, and they cared enough, at a pinch, to kill or be killed for their own particular brand of it. I was excited by this. As a lapsed Christian I felt I could imagine – just – how it would be to believe as they believed. At heart I knew this was a delusion. I was simply substituting aesthetic admiration for belief, and a real believer would probably tell me there was a special department in hell reserved for people who did that. All the same, it was the nearest I could get. When I read Henry Vaughan, for example, describing his experience of God:

> O joys! Infinite sweetness! With what flowers
> And shoots of glory my soul breaks and buds!

It seemed to me that no one in the post-God era ever feels joy like that. The death of God has meant the death of joy – if joy means absolute certainty of eternal life. If a modern poet wrote those lines they would be about having sex, which doesn't seem a very adequate substitute. Anyway, I resolved that, if I did well enough in my final exams and stayed on in Oxford to do research, it was this century of mystics and religious maniacs who fought a civil war and chopped a king's head off that I wanted to study. In my pious atheism I even started turning up, with one or two other oddballs, at the late-night service called Compline in the college chapel. It was restful after a day's reading, and the chaplain, a lean, intellectual type called Kenneth Woollcombe, who later became bishop of Oxford, didn't seem to mind whether you believed in anything or not.

I spent as little time as I could in the world outside books, and for the most part it bumped along satisfactorily without me. Though I had saved up my army pay, and had a scholarship, I was short of money, so I got vacation jobs. I delivered mail at Christmas, and while sorting letters in the Barnes and Mortlake sorting office I stood two or three positions away from Christopher Ricks, who was a year ahead of me at Balliol. He was reading an eighteenth-century novel, Richardson's *Clarissa* I think, and seemed able to keep turning the pages while sorting mail. We did not speak, though we became friends later.

During several vacations I worked as a barman in Liverpool Street station. People who drink at station bars are in a hurry and accustomed to swift service, so it was a bit hectic at first. But the food was good. You had to climb up to the staff dining room among the roof girders. It was packed and noisy and smelt deliciously of meat and veg and gravy and steamed puddings, and the nice ladies wielding their big scoops at the serving counter kept a motherly eye on us students and made sure we got full plates. Customers liked us less. I am afraid we were a bit uppish, and it must have been annoying, if you were frantic for a Mackeson's milk stout or a double G and T before your train left, to hear snatches of arty conversation wafting across from the catering staff. 'Why don't you get a better job if you're so clever?' snarled one exasperated client. I hope I didn't reply, 'Actually, we're students,' but I fear I may have done.

Our boss was a thin bespectacled man called Alf who wore a brown packing coat and was chronically uncommunicative. The only thing he ever said was, 'Want a wet?' – which meant, did we want a drink. We always said yes, of course, and would follow him down rickety metal stairways and along gantries into the bowels of Liverpool Street station where gigantic kegs of various beers lay on their sides with thin metal pipes leading up from them to the pumps in the bars above. Alf had discovered some – I suppose illicit – way of tapping these monsters, and he silently handed round brim-full pint glasses. The cellar was chill and bare, and we sat on the stone floor, leaning against the walls, while we drank, so it was not what you would call festive. Still, it was free alcohol. I was working there when my twenty-first birthday came round, and as the Carey family did not go in for parties Alf's bootlegged beer was as near as I got to a celebration. My parents, though, gave me a Rolex Oyster watch, which must have cost them a lot, and which I still have.

Heather gave me a chess set. I still have that, too, but fairly soon I no longer had Heather. She had been up to see me in Oxford several times and kind Arthur had turned a blind eye to her staying the night. Then one day at the start of my second year, at a lecture by Leishman in St John's Hall on the subject of Milton's minor poems, I caught sight of a girl sitting on a bench on the far side of the hall. She had her back to me, but was turning towards the lecturer, so I saw her in profile. She was petite and demure-looking and very pretty, and after the lecture I walked back to my room in a daze. For the next seven days I could think of nothing else. Books were no help. Next week she was there again, and I followed her out of the hall afterwards, and made some cringe-making attempt at a chat-up line. (Actually I remember exactly what I said, but was concealing it out of shame – I said, 'I see you're persevering with Leishman's lectures' – perfectly judged to be at once condescending and intrusive and to suggest I was some special kind of sinister academic stalker.) She seemed surprised, but not offended, and when we got to where her bike was parked I asked her to tea. She made an excuse, as I'd expected she would, but I discovered she was called Gill and that she was reading English at St Anne's.

That was the start of a long campaign of attrition on my part, during which she gradually became resigned to her importunate wooer. As a second-year scholar I had a beautiful white-panelled room, overlooking the front quad, and I was proud to be able to ask her there when she did agree to come to tea. I laid out my possessions to impress her – the Bakelite radio, the coffee pot and (I'm ashamed to say) Heather's chess pieces set up as if for a game. The first time I took her out was to a performance of *The Nutcracker* at Oxford's New Theatre. I remember glancing sideways at her during the first act and feeling astonished that I had something so precious in my care, even for an evening. Years later she told me she was wondering what drink she ought to ask for in the interval, supposing I offered her one.

Heather had to be told what had happened, which was horrible. She didn't cry, and I was grateful for that. But I felt base and treacherous. Of course, it never occurred to me that she might not consider me such a terrible loss, and I was a bit surprised to learn, not long after, that she had married someone else and started a family and was happy. So perhaps I need not have felt such a worm. When my sister told my mother that I had broken up with Heather, she exclaimed, 'That poor girl!' Given that she had set herself adamantly against the relationship right from the start, it seemed a bit disingenuous. But I expect she meant it.

Gill and I worked together for our final exams (called 'Schools' in Oxford). My strategy was to learn enormous swathes of English literature by heart, and she had to put up with me reciting them to see if I'd got them right, which must have been a trial. But she was kind, and realised how desperate I was to succeed. What I remember most about the actual exams is the heat. It was a blazing June and the sheets of paper on the desks flared up at you like arc lamps. It seemed risky to touch them, let alone start writing on them. People quickly abandoned their jackets, ties and gowns. Heaps of them littered the floor, along with other trash brought in by candidates – teddy bears, smelling salts, wilting carnations – so you had to wade through a sort of flea market to get to your place. Finding the right desk on the first morning was the major trauma. Exams in Oxford are held in a gaunt, echoing pile, resembling in size and decor one of the larger London railway stations, its gigantic rooms filled with rows of inky little wooden desks, each with a glued label bearing someone's name. During the half hour or so before an exam a mob of candidates, several hundred strong, crushes itself into the entrance hall of this building – a few pathetic stragglers still trying to memorise crumpled fistfuls of notes. Then, at a given signal, the entrance hall's iron gates are flung open, and the crowd surges along the corridors, debouching dazzled and bewildered into the exam rooms, where the search for desks begins. Of course, the names are arranged alphabetically, but at this pitch of nervousness you tend to forget the alphabet, and quite possibly your name as well. Candidates could be seen darting around among the desks, emitting little animal noises of panic, until they were caught and taken away for sedation.

Once this hazard was past I can't say I remember any great sense of strain. I got busy writing out all the passages I had learned, with brief bits of explanation in between to make them seem relevant to the questions asked. True, there were some distractions – the invigilators, for instance. Shuffling along between the rows they looked immensely ancient, so it was strange to see them sloping off to the back of the hall for coffee and a smoke, rather as if the British Museum mummies were taking a break for refreshment. It's a bit alarming to think they must all have been younger than I am now. The girl undergraduates were another source of slight disturbance. At Oxford you wear subfusc for exams, which means dark suits, white shirts and white ties for men, and, for girls, white blouses, black ties, black skirts and black stockings. I imagine this severe costume was originally designed to quell all thoughts of sex, but being surrounded by neat, black-stockinged creatures had, as I recall, rather the opposite effect.

My only other distinct memory is of tiredness. In those days Schools were a bit of a marathon. You could not, as now, do some of the papers at leisure beforehand, looking stuff up in books. You were expected actually to know things. There were nine three-hour papers – two papers, morning and afternoon, on the Thursday and Friday at the start of the exam, one on the Saturday morning, then two on the Monday and Tuesday. By the end my writing hand was almost dropping off. Starting the last question on the last afternoon was the hardest bit. The tempter whispered 'Why bother? The bright world is only an hour away.' The evening we finished the weather broke. Torrential rain caught Gill and me and some friends in a punt on the river. We didn't mind, of course. After Schools, you don't mind anything.

Except that there was one last ordeal in store – the vivas. In those days every candidate had to attend for a viva voce examination, and they happened about a month after the written papers. You turned up on a given day and were told what time your viva would be. You could calculate from the list of times whether you were in for a long or a short one. Long ones, which could last up to an hour, were for candidates on the borderline between classes, who might go up or down depending on what happened in the viva.

As Oxford is divided up into colleges, you know more or less how you compare with people in your own college, but have no idea – until a university exam happens – how you measure up to all the other undergraduates in your year. This worried me, and getting to know Gill made the worry worse, partly because she was obviously very bright, and partly because her account of the super-efficient regime of teaching at St Anne's, masterminded by a terrifyingly switched-on tutor called Dorothy Bednarowska, made my high-minded exchanges with Leishman seem rather amateurish. Another worry was the fact that I had mentioned in one of my papers an obscure Middle English poem called Layamon's *Brut* which I had not actually read. I felt sure I would be quizzed on this at my viva, so I secured a copy from Hammersmith Public Library (who got it from Westminster Public Library – the central depot for English literature) and slogged through all sixteen thousand lines of it. It was unspeakably boring, but at least I felt I'd closed a loophole.

Vivas were nervy things. You walked into a large, echoing room in the Examination Schools, and there, sitting in a row, in full academic rig – subfusc, gowns, hoods – were all your examiners, about a dozen of them, with a green-baize-topped table in front of them and, on it, piles of candidates' exam scripts, including yours. I sat down in a chair on the near side of the table, as requested, and my mind froze. The chairman, F. P. Wilson, smiled and said something, I could not tell what. Then the examiner on his right said something, and then the next one along. It dawned on me that they weren't asking questions but saying they had enjoyed my papers. Dorothy Whitelock, the grande dame of

Anglo-Saxon studies, said she hoped I would maintain my keen interest in Anglo-Saxon in later life. I was bewildered. Was it some kind of joke? Had I done so badly they were just being kind? Wilson could see I was in shock, and at the end he leaned forward and said, 'You realise we are congratulating you.' Then I got up and stumbled out.

Gill got a first too. So did her friend Gillian Thomas (later Gillian Beer, Regius Professor at Cambridge) and Gillian's American boyfriend Del Kolve (later a professor at UCLA), who shared the top first with me. There were nine firsts that year (nowadays there are always about forty) so the four of us accounted for almost half the list.

6

Research Student

A few weeks after my viva I found myself, late one August evening, playing bowls with the fellows of Merton College, Oxford. As I did not know how to play bowls, and had never been inside Merton College before, this was not something I could have foreseen, and the train of events that led to it was rather contorted.

In my last term at St John's I decided to take the civil service exams. Not that I relished being a civil servant. The prospect of kowtowing to a gaggle of politicians and being rewarded on retirement with some daft title wasn't one I found alluring. I could imagine how Swift would have sneered at such an ambition. For that matter, Leishman made it clear he thought it pretty contemptible too. All the same, it would be a safety net if my hopes of an academic career came to nothing. In the 1950s there were two ways of getting into the civil service. One was by examination, the other, commonly known as the 'country-house weekend method', concentrated (I gathered) on social graces. I suspected I lacked these, so I chose the exams, and sat the papers shortly before my viva, mostly replicating stuff I had written in Schools – though there was also a précis test where you had to summarise something like a complete sheet of newsprint in a thousand words.

I was called for an interview at the Civil Service Commission in Burlington Gardens, where there were four interviewers. The two older ones were polite, the two younger ones clever and impolite. I remember thinking it might be fun to work with people like that. The only question I recall was 'Would it be a good idea to make it a legal requirement that all clocks exhibited in public places should show the right time?' After thinking for about half a minute – while the clock exhibited on the wall ticked impatiently – I said no, because it would be impossible, or at any rate expensive and endlessly contentious, to enforce. As with the other questions, my interrogators gave no indication – not so much an eyebrow-twitch – whether that was the right answer or not.

A few days later I got a letter from the Commission saying I'd come out best of the Method I bunch (whether the country-house set had bagged all the top places, or limped in as also-rans, wasn't divulged) and asking which branch of the civil service I'd like to join. I was a bit surprised that a knowledge of English literature was reckoned so desirable as a qualification for the civil service. Looking back, though, it strikes me that the Commissioners may have valued it because they believed literature trains you in ways of thought outside your own place and time. If so, I think they had a point. But as it was I just felt bucked, and I chose the Treasury as my branch because it sounded important. I explained, though, that I'd like to apply for deferment to do graduate work at Oxford. In reply I received an elegant letter in italic script and brown ink from a Mrs Olga Collett, an Assistant Commissioner, asking for clarification. She explained she was sending a handwritten letter 'to save typing time' as she wanted an immediate reply. Presumably the typists had knocked off for the night. I replied by return, and two days later she wrote again – typed this time – saying that the First

Commissioner had discussed my request with the Treasury and decided to grant it. She stressed it was 'an exceptional decision, made possible only by the fact that you are head of the Method I successful list', and she signed off 'Best wishes for the D.Phil.' It seemed to me (still does) very generous, and I felt relieved. So did my parents, to whom my talk of 'staying on at Oxford' sounded vague and precarious.

In those days there were State Studentships for graduate research in the arts, and I had been given one. But several colleges advertised research posts which were a better deal, offering board and lodging as well as paying fees, so I put in for one – a Harmsworth Senior Scholarship at Merton College. I had only the dimmest ideas about Merton. I thought of it as a gloomy, damp, medieval place on Oxford's southern edge, a good ten minutes' walk from St John's – which, as I seldom ventured further than the Bodleian Library, seemed like another country. So when I arrived there early for my Harmsworth interview and looked around, I was taken aback. Merton is ancient and glorious, and dominated by a cathedral-scale chapel, glimmering with early fourteenth-century stained glass. Tucked under the shelter of its great tower is a tiny fourteenth-century quadrangle called (no one knows why) Mob Quad, which hoards the sun in its Cotswold stones and releases it as the day cools, so that I was folded in warmth the moment I stepped through Mob's narrow entrance that first evening. It's always warmer there than anywhere else in the college, and the bees who have – for centuries, I suppose – been building their honeycombs in cavities high in the chapel masonry always settle in great swags on Mob's sunny west wall when they swarm each spring. I didn't know about that at the time, of course, and I managed to fit in only two or three more Merton highlights on my quick tour – the intricate web of medieval ironwork that fortifies the massive Hall door, and the garden with its acre of lawn bounded by the old city wall, and the path on top where sentries used to pace to and fro, looking out over the meadows to the river.

My interview was mostly conducted by Hugo Dyson, an Oxford 'character', known for his wit. I always found him alarming. He was like a hyperactive gnome, and stumped around on a walking stick which, when he was seized by one of his paroxysms of laughter, he would beat up and down as if trying to drive it through the floor. It brought to mind Rumpelstiltskin driving his leg into the ground in the fairy tale. He had been one of the 'Inklings' – the group of dons, including Tolkien and C. S. Lewis, who met during the 1930s in the Bird and Baby pub opposite St John's. It was he and Tolkien who, one summer night in 1931, had converted Lewis to Christianity during a stroll along Addison's Walk. So he was, at least in part, responsible for the Narnia books. I never asked him if he liked them. But it was well known that Tolkien's *Lord of the Rings* was not to his taste. Tolkien had been in the habit of favouring the Inklings with readings from it, but one day Dyson, driven to exasperation, interjected, 'Oh not another fucking elf!' and after that the readings stopped. On a good day he was the funniest man I ever met – or maybe the second funniest. Peter Ustinov, whom I met only once on a Melvyn Bragg *Start the Week* programme, was marginally funnier because he could do mimicry, which was not Dyson's thing. On the other hand, with Ustinov you felt it had all been done before, whereas Dyson was famous for his spontaneity. It was said that, one evening in Merton when there was duck on the menu, and the bird served was not duck but pheasant, he remarked, 'Ah, *le mallard imaginaire*.'

My interview was brief. This was chiefly because Dyson had been one of my Schools examiners and, having read my papers, already knew all I knew. But it was also because he was an old-style don who did not really believe in literary 'research'. Literature was for enjoyment and it was misguided to turn it into something arcane and scholarly. That was a common view in Oxford at the time, and one I was keen to discredit, not least because part of me sympathised with it.

Before dinner I was introduced to the other fellows – there were no more than twenty, among them Tolkien and F. P. Wilson. As it was out of term we dined not in Hall but in Merton's most beautiful room, which has seventeenth-century pear-wood panelling and, over the fireplace, a portrait of Henrietta Maria, Charles I's queen, who had her court in the college during the Civil War. Bowls followed. It was taken for granted everyone would play, and we trooped out into the gloaming and onto the immaculate turf of Fellows' Quad. I wondered vaguely whether this might be part of the Harmsworth competition, and, if so, would it be better to win, and risk appearing uppish, or lose and seem a failure? But I was slightly drunk by this time and didn't much care. Besides, as soon as I rolled my first bowl (or 'wood', as I was told they were called) I realised the course it chose to follow was entirely beyond my control. Watching it, I remembered Pope writing about bowls (or woods) 'obliquely waddling to the mark in view', except that mine obliquely waddled away from it. We played till the mark was no longer in view. Then my hosts said goodnight and faded into the dark, and I walked back to St John's.

Next morning I got a note from Merton's wispy, husky-voiced classicist, Robert Levens, who was what other colleges call the Dean but Merton calls Principal of Postmasters, to say I had been elected to a Harmsworth and could move in when I liked.

I was given rooms in an enormous bow-fronted Victorian mansion opposite the college known as the Old Warden's Lodgings. It had been built for a former Warden (that is, head of college) who, though a bachelor, had insisted that, for the sake of his more prolific successors, the new house must have, in addition to state rooms for entertainment, ample accommodation for a large family and the nursemaids, governesses and upper and lower servants large families require. In obedience to these directives a grotesque five-storey palace arose on the far side of Merton Street, which the college has ever since been trying to find a use for. My rooms were in the servants' quarters on the lower ground floor at the back. I think my study must have been the butler's parlour, because it had superior brass door knobs, and looked out on a rose garden (now a car park).

Gill arrived back in Oxford at the start of the new term. She had decided to read for a Diploma in Education, which took a year, not a research degree, because, she said, she felt guilty about 'sponging off her parents' any longer. We were both hard up and used to seek out cheap places to eat, finding a splendid one up a flight of stairs from the High Street, called the Stowaway, where you could get sausages, baked beans, fried egg and mashed potato for almost nothing. Years later a fashionable Thai restaurant opened in the same location and, taken there by a generous friend, we goggled at the grandeur our old greasy spoon had aspired to.

I took Gill, as one did, to see Merton's oldest inhabitant, Professor H. W. Garrod, who was the last fellow of Merton (or, I believe, any Oxford college) to be allowed to retain his college rooms on retirement. They were lovely rooms, looking south over the meadows, and full of the scent of wisteria in spring. A spiral staircase in the corner led to his sleeping quarters. When I arrived in Merton he was seventy-nine, and meeting him gave you a sense of the courtesy and irony that had been in the air of Oxford before the First World War – the Oxford of Max Beerbohm, who was born six years before Garrod.

He enjoyed entertaining students and their girlfriends to tea, but it was tea with a competitive edge. The walls of his room were festooned with picture postcards – sets of the English poets, the English cathedrals, English cricketers and old master paintings pinned to the bookshelves – and before you had tea you had to identify as many as you could, while Garrod at your elbow chuckled delightedly at your mistakes. When you did get to the table you found – besides cakes and sandwiches – an array of tiny clockwork toys that you were invited to wind up and set going, with Garrod bubbling joyfully as the little dogs wagged their tails, the miniature drummers drummed and the scooting policeman scooted with his single mobile leg. The toys were gifts from affectionate ex-students, and new arrivals kept appearing.

Garrod was keen on chess, or, rather, keen on winning

at chess, and since he found it hard to sleep at night Senior Scholars were recruited to play with him once or twice a week on a rota system. As he was very short-sighted he had a special board made, measuring about a yard each way, and the pieces were the size of half-pint milk bottles. The board rested on a rickety trestle structure, and it was said that Garrod's dog Chips, an elderly cocker spaniel, was trained to blunder into it and upset the board if his master was losing. I never saw this happen, possibly because I seldom won, or perhaps when I did Garrod did not see it coming and failed to give Chips the necessary signal. He did his best to befuddle his opponent by pouring him glass after glass of port, while not drinking himself. Stumbling back to the Old Warden's Lodgings at two or three in the morning I often wished I had resisted his generous libations.

Another duty of Senior Scholars was to de-flea Chips. You had to stand him on a folded-out copy of the *Times* newspaper and rub flea powder into his shaggy black-and-white coat. Garrod, who cared about Chips's *amour propre*, would peer at the paper and deny that any fleas had come out, though in fact they were perfectly visible. He was very fond of dogs, and for years had favoured Sealyhams. There is a drawing of him by Muirhead Bone in Merton's senior common room showing him in his battered trilby, which he tended to wear indoors as well as out, with a Sealyham by his side. It is this Sealyham he wrote about in his essay 'Dogs', published in the volume *Genius Loci*, of which he gave me a copy. With advancing age the much-loved little creature had grown blind and deaf, but still:

He went where he would, and he did what he liked, however feebly.

Until, one winter morning, going where he would, but not knowing where, he walked, in the uncertain dawn, into one of those static-water-ponds with which the War studded our Gardens; and the half-frozen waters closed over the loveliest of old heads that ever wanted brains – for he had no cleverness.

After that, I suppose, the sight of a Sealyham caused unbearable heartache, so he got Chips instead.

His tastes were admittedly narrow. He once shocked the Royal Society of Literature with a flippant and dismissive lecture about Jane Austen, and he could not tolerate literary modernism. T. S. Eliot had been a student at Merton in 1914 and when, later, there seemed to be a chance some Eliot manuscripts might come Merton's way, Garrod, who was librarian, is said to have refused them. His parody of a Wordsworth sonnet runs:

> Milton! Thou should'st be living at this hour,
> England hath need of thee, and not
> Of Leavis and of Eliot . . .

His fun could border on cruelty. If, at dinner, some callow junior fellow made the mistake of greeting him from the far end of the table with a good-natured platitude – 'Lovely evening, Professor Garrod', or some such – he would feign deafness, cup his ear, lean forward eagerly and beg for the remark to be repeated, again and again, louder and louder, until his luckless victim was bellowing it and the rest of the table fell silent. But these were rare lapses. I treasure a letter I got from him, dated 29 December 1958, because it's so old-Oxford in its tone and manner. I'd sent him an addition to his contingent of clockwork cats.

Dear John,

Whether my three cats (all I have) are enough to keep away all the mice in the world, I'm not sure; nor whether it is fair that they should be allowed to. Anyway, your chap shall be given his chance. Thank you very much.

I hope you have hated Christmas. I seem to remember that you were plotting to be back by the New Year. If you are back, dine with me on the 1st; notifying me by postcard. If you can't, don't bother to write.

I don't know when I first began to call you by your first name. What I do know is that, whenever I have used your second name, I have dropped the e in it. With the New Year, I give you the e that belongs to you (apparently).

Yours ever,

H. W. Garrod.

In case my account of Garrod makes him sound soft in the head it's worth pointing out he was a formidable scholar and still at work when I knew him. The revised edition of his Oxford University Press *Works of John Keats* had come out the previous year. As a young man he'd been a classics don, but his edition of the second book of Manilius' *Astronomica* – a first-century AD poem about astrology – had been so savagely reviewed by A. E. Housman that he resigned his classics fellowship and took up English studies. He became Oxford's professor of poetry in 1923 and Charles Eliot Norton Professor at Harvard in 1929. In 1911 he had edited the *Oxford Book of Latin Verse*, and the introduction to that is his masterpiece, breathtaking in scope – it surveys Latin poetry from the first century to the fifth – monumental in learning, eagerly distinguishing the passion and sensuousness he loved in poetry from mere imitations. It's difficult to imagine any professor of English literature in the world being able to write it today.

Training of research students in 1950s Oxford was minimal, but the English faculty ran two useful introductory courses. In the first we learned to decipher seventeenth-century handwriting, often excruciatingly difficult. In the second we learned how to set up a page of type from trays of metal letters, as a seventeenth-century compositor would, and how to ink the page up and print it, using an ancient hand press in the Bodleian Library. This gave us a glimpse of how modern bibliographers, by tracking bits of damaged type, and other microscopic clues, can tell, for example, which compositors set up which sheets of the First Folio of Shakespeare. At the end of our first term we all set up and printed fake seventeenth-century Christmas cards and felt very pleased with ourselves.

But none of this helped in finding a research subject. Science graduates join teams, headed by a professor, so their subject is found for them. But arts graduates are on their own – or on their own with a supervisor. In the 1950s many Oxford supervisors were useless. Kingsley Amis's *Memoirs* recount, hilariously, how he was neglected by Lord David Cecil, who had been appointed his B.Litt. supervisor, and proved chronically unavailable. George Steiner once told me how he had been let down by his supervisor Hugo Dyson. He was writing a thesis on 'The Death of Tragedy', and when he had a supervision with Dyson, which was seldom, Dyson would slam down a fistful of coin on the mantelpiece, explain derisively that this was all the university paid him for the supervision, and suggest he and Steiner go off and 'drink it' in a pub. Eventually Steiner submitted his thesis and at his viva it was 'referred', that is, he had to rewrite it, because of elementary mistakes in presentation any supervisor should have picked up. He left Oxford and got a job on the *Economist*, but one day Humphry House (the brilliant young scholar who later lectured to us on Aristotle) sought him out, said that he knew Steiner had had a raw deal, and offered to take on his supervision free of charge. He did, Steiner got his D.Phil., and Faber and Faber published *The Death of Tragedy* in 1961.

I was lucky. Helen Gardner, who was Queen of English Studies at Oxford, appointed herself my supervisor. She was much feared. Female students, it was said, left her room in tears. Nor did she intimidate only young women. I joined Merton at the same time as Nevill Coghill, who was taking up his appointment as Merton Professor of English literature. It was generally agreed that Helen should have got the chair – a view she strongly endorsed – and some said she had been passed over only because Merton's statutes barred a woman from becoming a fellow. I met Coghill, a tall, twitchy, gentle man with a face full of care, and shortly afterwards he asked me to his room and explained that, later in the term, he was due to give his inaugural lecture as Merton Professor. The prospect, he said, filled him with trepidation, and he wondered whether, if, on the day, he found himself unable to speak, I would step in and read his lecture for him. It seemed a singular proposal to make to a first-year graduate student, but I didn't see how I could refuse. So on the day of the inaugural I sat in the front row in academic dress, clutching a copy of the lecture, and praying Coghill would not break down. He didn't, so all was well. But his terror was a tribute to Helen's power.

To me, though, she was kindness itself. When I first called on her, in her big airy room looking out over St Hilda's College garden, she struck me as elegant, vain, bright and very feminine. She was almost the only member of the English faculty who knew anything about research. The introductory courses for graduates had been her idea (and it was she, as examiner, who had referred George Steiner's thesis). Her landmark edition of Donne's religious poems had come out in 1952, and when we met she was working on her edition of his love poems. What fascinated her was establishing the text of Donne's poems – that is, trying to decide exactly what words he wrote by comparing the differing versions that survived in seventeenth-century manuscripts. I could see this mattered a lot, but at the same time it seemed a bit mechanical.

What interested me more was why Donne wrote the poems and who they were for. I wondered this particularly about his love elegies, written when he was in his early twenties. They are swashbuckling poems, modelled in part on Ovid's erotic *Amores*, in which Donne presents himself as a reckless Lothario, leading wives astray, deflowering maidens, cuckolding fat old burghers, stealing into grand houses and seducing heiresses under their parents' noses. There was quite a vogue for boastful fictions of this kind, and it centred on the Inns of Court where Donne had been a student. I began to wonder whether what love elegies were really about was the anxieties Inns of Court students felt in Elizabethan and Jacobean London. Many of them came from country districts, and in London they were an easy prey for prostitutes, cheats and conmen of every kind. Portraying themselves in their poems as irresistible Don Juans might, I thought, be a kind of compensation. But there was a wider issue too. The vogue for love elegies had replaced the vogue for sonnets, and whereas sonneteers were courteous and adoring, love elegists treated women as natural inferiors. Could this be part of a readjustment in sexual attitudes? Of course, men have always found reasons for disparaging women, but in the 1590s the reasons seem new, and are directed against a new phenomenon – the London woman. London women were educated (the female literacy rate was far higher in the capital than anywhere else in Britain), they were authoritative (Elizabethan widows could, and did, inherit and run their husbands' businesses, and there was a queen on the throne), they were shamelessly extravagant (exploiting the market for luxury goods that London had developed) and they were upwardly mobile, with the daughters of wealthy London tradesmen marrying into old county families whose income from land had diminished. Elizabethan and Jacobean satires buzz with indignation at these disgraceful goings-on, and love elegies, I conjectured, might be similarly motivated.

Of course, to make this thesis go anywhere required work on two fronts. I had to read through virtually the whole of Elizabethan and Jacobean poetry and drama, plus a lot of pamphlets, collecting material about attitudes to women, and I had to track down as many love elegies as I could. Luckily the Bodleian has a huge collection of manuscript poetry from the seventeenth century, much of it in so-called 'commonplace books', where gentlemen copied out poems they fancied, and I set myself to work through this. In the vacations I made inroads into the British Museum's equally rich collection. Sometimes I worked in the great circular reading room where Dickens and Marx had read, but more usually I was in the manuscript room, poring over faded ink in little vellum-bound notebooks, so that it was a mild shock to emerge at lunchtime and find myself among buses and newspaper sellers and people in modern dress. I used to eat my sandwiches in Russell Square, shake out the crumbs for the pigeons, and hurry back, eager to get on with the search. Being lewd and salacious, a lot of love elegies were in Latin – what Gibbon calls 'the decent obscurity of a dead language' – so Mr Brigden's teaching came in useful. I'd not realised so much Renaissance Latin poetry existed. There was even a learned periodical devoted to it called *Neo-Latin News* which I read in the Bodleian. I often wondered what its print run was. I saw Helen Gardner regularly. She would greet me archly – 'So you've come to tell me more about those disgraceful young men!' – then she'd sit by the fire knitting, while I read out the bits and pieces I'd found. Few supervisors, I imagine, knit nowadays, but I found it soothing.

About halfway through my Merton year I got a letter from J. I. M. Stewart, the English don at Christ Church, to say he was going to America for the next academic year and would I like to take over his Christ Church teaching. The pay was better than the Harmsworth, so I said yes. Stewart was a Scot, shortish and rather pigeon-like, with a puffed-out chest and a way of twisting his mouth wryly when he talked. He was best known for his Michael Innes detective novels, and got up, he told me, at five every morning to write them. When we met he gave me a run-down of the students I'd be in charge of, and introduced me to John Burrow, who looked after the Anglo-Saxon and Middle English teaching. John later moved to Bristol where he got a Chair, but at the time he and his wife, who was to become celebrated as the writer Diana Wynne-Jones, had a big, welcoming flat, littered with books, which overlooked the Iffley Road sports ground where, four years earlier, Roger Bannister had run the first under-four-minute mile.

Christ Church was (is) just at the end of Merton Street, a minute's walk away. But in the 1950s it was another world. It was reputed to be Oxford's most aristocratic and exclusive college, and just walking through it was an object lesson in how architecture can be used to make people feel small. The gargantuan main quadrangle (Tom Quad), built with money robbed from monasteries by Cardinal Wolsey, announces the grandeur of 'the House' (as Christ Church calls itself) as clearly as if it was blaring out W. S. Gilbert's 'Bow, bow, ye lower middle classes' over a tannoy system (though that would have been much jollier, of course). In 1950s Christ Church people would ask you quite seriously and directly what school you were from and who your parents were, as if such things really mattered. One of my students told me it was a joke among the cognoscenti that grammar-school boys always got housed on the outer rim of the college in the uninviting Meadow Building, while the grand rooms in Peckwater Quadrangle were reserved for entrants from the major public schools.

I noticed that another of my students had clearly sustained

some damage to his left eye, and he told me how it had happened. Apparently there was a tradition in Christ Church that on a certain night in the year you would, if you were a young blood with a feeling for family history, try to smash as many windows in Peckwater Quadrangle as your father and grandfather had smashed when they were up. My student had been innocently making his way from Canterbury Gate to Tom Quad when this mayhem was at its height, and a fragment of a tonic-water bottle had bounced back from the wall into his eye, blinding him. What impressed me was his lack of resentment. He was from a public school himself, and his ethos seemed to be that young gentlemen would cut loose from time to time and it was just bad luck if you were in the way. The whole episode was an illustration of Evelyn Waugh's famous reference in *Decline and Fall* to 'the sound of English county families baying for broken glass'. But that was in 1928 and I'd not expected to find the tradition alive and well thirty years later.

Christ Church – or, for that matter, Oxford – can damage people in less obvious ways. Among my first-year students was a boy from a lower-middle-class background who took to aping the high life around him. He dressed like a Proustian dandy and appeared each day with a fresh carnation in his buttonhole. He did no work, and was sent down after failing his preliminary exams twice. Apparently he was one of the last expelled students to be ritually carried to the railway station in a coffin, borne by fellow-dandies. Forty years later I got a letter from him, written in an exaggeratedly flamboyant script – the kind of writing that you might expect from the quill of a *grand seigneur* of the *ancien régime*.

He was, he told me, serving a life sentence in a high-security prison, and wondered if I could spare some review copies when I'd finished with them, as reading matter was hard to come by.

I looked up the account of his trial at the Old Bailey, where it emerged that he had acquired a taste for an aristocratic lifestyle while at Christ Church, and for thirty years had pursued a career of crime, mainly involving art thefts, to fund his fantasies. He pretended to be an old Etonian and to have worked at the Foreign Office. Landowners, bankers, widows and small cash-strapped charities had all fallen prey to his guile, and he had received ever-increasing jail terms. It was while he was serving ten years for the violent kidnapping of a rival antique dealer that he evolved a plan to kidnap and extort twenty million pounds from a 'Mr G', described as one of Britain's wealthiest men. Unfortunately the accomplice he chose was an undercover policeman. I did send him some review copies, feeling that I and Christ Church had to take some of the blame for what had happened.

Another student who quickly disappeared was the future film and TV director Michael Lindsay-Hogg, a plump young man who was later to write an autobiography claiming to be the illegitimate son of Orson Welles. I am not sure whether it was the syllabus or my teaching that he took against. All the others stayed the course and put up with being taught by a graduate student rather than J. I. M. Stewart. They were a bright bunch, and the third year, whom I saw through Schools, all did well. Several got first-class degrees. One became a professor at Birkbeck, another, a High Court judge, another started his own film and TV company and a fourth went to California to teach film theory. The infectious snobbishness of Christ Church left them untouched – but they were exceptional. Even the college servants succumbed to it. I got the impression they would have gone to the stake to defend the right of their employers to exploit them. I had a room – a rather dingy bedsitter – in 2 Brewer Street, opposite the college, and my scout, called Edwards, never tired of telling me, with evident relish, of the good old days when, if one of his young gentlemen was throwing a party, you couldn't see the banisters for fur coats. He chuckled over his memories of the treatment meted out to 'a communist gentleman' by the other undergraduates. They used to take his copy of the *Daily Worker* and flush it down the lavatory while holding the communist gentleman's head in the pan. Regrettably, he explained, he had to put a stop to this jape because the paper blocked the plumbing. He was, in other respects, a kind man, and used to carry a lighted candle under his budgerigar's cage when he moved it from room to room, lest the bird should catch cold.

Though Britain was still struggling out of austerity, the meals at Christ Church high table were more luxurious than anything I'd come across before. It was there that I first tasted oysters – and thought wonderingly of my mother's fondness for them. The dons I saw most of were the small band who lived in college, among them the economist Sir Roy Harrod, who pointedly refrained from ever addressing a single remark to me in my three terms' residence. One night I was sitting opposite him at dinner when he had a guest, for whose benefit he was identifying the various notables seated round the table. I heard his guest ask who I was, and Harrod

replied, quite audibly, 'Oh, that's nobody.' The guest gave me
a pitying glance and looked away. From Harrod's viewpoint
it was, of course, a perfectly accurate description, but I felt he
could have phrased it more tactfully.

A consolation was W. H. Auden. He was Oxford's professor of poetry at the time, and came over from America
for a few weeks each year, staying in Christ Church, and
quite often dining in college. He was the first great poet
I'd met (later ones were Larkin, Hughes and Heaney), and
I'm surprised, looking back, I wasn't more awestruck. That
was because he made things easy by being so unaffected. He
used cosy English words like 'peeved', which sounded unexpected in his gravelly American voice. Getting to sit next to
him at dinner or dessert wasn't difficult because, curiously,
no one else seemed to want to. I don't know whether the
other fellows (or 'Students' as they call themselves in Christ
Church) resented him as an intruder, or still bore a grudge
about his staying in America during the Second World War,
or just weren't interested in poetry, but I quite often found
myself in his company, sometimes accompanied by Canon
Demant, the Regius Professor of moral theology. Demant
was a member of the Wolfenden Committee which, the
previous year, had recommended the decriminalisation of
homosexual practices. As a young man he had written for A.
R. Orage's modernist literary magazine the *New Age*, and he
and Auden used to talk about that. I remember Auden saying how, as an undergraduate at Christ Church, he had sent
some poems to T. S. Eliot for publication in the *Criterion*,
and felt flattered that Eliot had bothered to send them back,
and had even enclosed an encouraging letter. One night he

talked about rhythm in poetry, and how his poems – or some of them – came to him as rhythms rather than as words or ideas, and how he had to find words and ideas to fit the rhythms. Auden famously likened his face to a wedding cake left out in the rain. But what I noticed more than his wrinkles was how he turned his head – slowly and carefully, as if it was someone else's head and he might break it. Perhaps this was just when he had a hangover. There was a rule at dessert that the port had to circulate twice before you could smoke. He was always dying to light up and would remark acidly on the fatuousness of such a restriction. I suppose that didn't endear him to the 'Students' either.

Meanwhile, in the intervals of teaching J. I. M. Stewart's undergraduates, I'd had rather a breakthrough in my research. Looking for unpublished seventeenth-century love elegies I'd noticed a group of poems that recurred in various manuscripts, often bearing the initials N.H. I was keen to find who this unknown poet was, and followed several leads, without success. Then one day in the British Museum I found a manuscript where one of the N.H. poems bore a name – Nicholas Hare. I was very excited, and in the next few weeks turned up quite a lot about Nicholas Hare. He was born in 1582, the son of a wealthy lawyer and Member of Parliament, went to Christ's College, Cambridge, and studied law at the Inner Temple before going into partnership with his father. But he seems to have soon tired of the law and decided to travel – a rare and risky thing in the early seventeenth century. In 1610 he was in Venice, bound for Constantinople, and a year later was on his way to Malta via Cyprus, having just returned from Jerusalem. He sounded exactly the sort of unconventional type Donne would have been intrigued by – but I still could not prove he knew Donne. That final piece slotted into place when I tracked down his will in the Public Record Office. One of the witnesses was Isaac Walton, Donne's friend and first biographer (and author of the *Complete Angler*), and Hare left a bequest for the poor of St Dunstan's in the West, stipulating it should be administered by the Dean of St Paul's – that is, John Donne. So I had discovered a new English poet (even if not, to be honest, a particularly marvellous one) and new member of the Donne circle. I sent Hare's poems and my account of his life to the *Review of English Studies*, where they were published in 1960, and now it was just a matter of writing up the rest of the thesis.

That would take time though, so I put in for research posts for the following year and was offered, on the same day, a junior research fellowship at Merton and an Andrew Bradley Junior Research Fellowship at Balliol. I didn't want to offend Merton by refusing theirs, but I went to see the Warden, Geoffrey Mure, who was kind and understanding and advised me to go to Balliol as I'd get to know a new academic community. So I did. At about the same time Gill, very courageously, agreed to marry me, and share my worldly goods, which still amounted, in effect, to the Bakelite radio and the electric coffee pot. So quite early in the morning on Ascension Day, 7 May 1959, I bought a bottle of champagne from Christ Church buttery, and Gill and I and Gillian Thomas and Del drank to one another's futures beside the round pond in the middle of Tom Quad, while the goldfish gleamed and the waterlilies spread their petals and Mercury, with jets of water dancing round him, stood on one leg on his plinth and pointed to the sky. It was a most un-Carey-like episode. Champagne! In the morning! Looking back I'm amazed, and realise I was touched by the Christ Church infection, just like all the others.

Christ Church stopped paying me at the end of term and the Balliol job didn't start till the autumn, so I needed some money to tide me over the summer, and my father, with typical thoughtfulness, employed me as his assistant. This took me, each working day, into a sanctum of English cultural life as strange and secluded as any Oxford college. It was (still is) tucked away behind a modest, Jane-Austenish facade in Mayfair, halfway up Brook Street on the left-hand side, at Number 39, where a grey-painted sign announces its name – Sybil Colefax and John Fowler Limited. It had been founded in the 1930s and became known as the most chic and expensive decorating firm of the twentieth century, specialising in the 'English country-house look', which, so far as I could make out, combined extravagant frou-frou draperies, painted French furniture, and the faded splendour of sun-bleached silks, velvets, damasks and brocades. I could see that my father loved the place. It reminded him, I think, of his youth, when he had collected beautiful things himself. The old house was said to be haunted by a 'grey lady', and though he never claimed to have seen her, he said that when he unlocked in the morning he would find chairs arranged around a spinet or a harpsichord, as if there had been a phantom concert.

Nancy Lancaster, the American socialite who bought the firm from Sybil Colefax in the 1940s, occasionally looked in, but John Fowler ('The Prince of Decorators' as his biography subtitles him) was there all the time, very dapper, very camp, immaculately suited, with dazzling white shirt-cuffs on display, fussing around like an agitated cockatoo among the artists and designers who brought his ideas to life. One wall in his office was his 'palette', covered with favourite samples for which he and Mrs Lancaster had invented a jokey language of colour-names like 'dead salmon' and 'mouse's back'. He wondered, I think, what I was doing around the place, but was far too courteous to ask.

As my father was the firm's accountant I suppose I might have claimed to be the assistant accountant, or, rather, the second assistant accountant. The first assistant accountant was a gaunt Dickensian clerk called Mr Hobbs. Sober-suited, bowler-hatted, punctual and unconversational, Mr Hobbs was a vegetarian, a very rare thing at that time, and one that I vaguely associated with a naturist magazine called *Health and Efficiency*, which carried photos of naked ladies and gentlemen on beaches and at campsites. But I could not imagine Mr Hobbs in such a situation, despite his vegetable diet. Healthy eating did not seem to make him happy. When my father and I went off each day to eat our packed lunches in Grosvenor Square, we left him at his desk, slowly munching his way through small heaps of shelled nuts like a disconsolate squirrel.

I was touched to see how much my father was loved by everyone in Colefax and Fowler – even Mr Hobbs managed a watery smile when speaking of him. But then, he was a loveable man. He used to buy sweets on his way home at a little shop round the corner from Brook Street, not to eat, but to give away, often to children. I suppose he would be arrested if he did that nowadays, but for him it was just a natural expression of kindness. When he first met Gill they instantly took to each other, and I distinctly remember him slipping her a Fox's Glacier Mint. When I went to the sweetshop with him he introduced me to the lady serving behind the counter as 'My son who is at Oxford'. I was embarrassed, of course, and assumed a village-idiot grin to show I was harmless. But I oughtn't have felt awkward, because his pride was so honest and open.

As I had just spent a year in Christ Church I couldn't help thinking how Sir Roy Harrod, and people of his ilk, would have despised my father, as he had despised me. That thought was the seed of my book *The Intellectuals and the Masses*, though my father died long before I wrote it. The chapter that his shade particularly hovered around, in my imagination, was the one about the Bloomsbury Group and their contempt for office workers, generically referred to as 'clerks'. Harrod had been the friend and biographer of Geoffrey Keynes, so in my reckoning he was tarred with the Bloomsbury brush.

I moved into Balliol in the autumn. It was not a beautiful college. Its Victorian architecture was often mocked, and it did not go in for grandeur or opulence. But it seemed perfect to me. On my first day after lunch a square-jawed man with a lively face, pointed eyebrows and dark curly hair walked up and said, 'Hello, I'm Christopher Hill. Can I get you some coffee?' For a moment I was speechless with shock. Christopher Hill was one of my gods. I'd no idea that he was a fellow of Balliol. I only knew him as the leading British Marxist historian, who championed Puritans and Parliament in the English Civil War, and whose work had introduced me to the Levellers, the revolutionary movement in Cromwell's army who had demanded equality before the law. He was also the only historian I'd come across who wrote intelligently about seventeenth-century literature, and placed it, as I wanted to do with Donne, in its political and cultural context.

Christopher's friendliness and informality were typical of Balliol in the 1950s. It was full of brilliant minds, and the class distinctions that mattered in Christ Church counted for nothing with them. All they seemed to care about was whether you could talk intelligently. Apart from that common factor they were a rather motley assortment. There was Russell Meiggs, the historian of Roman Ostia – wise, genial, bumbling, with an explosion of grey hair like a crazy birdnest, and Tommy Balogh, the cheerfully obscene Hungarian economist, and the philosopher John Searle, a couple of years older than me and finishing his D.Phil., and Gordon Williams, a young Irish classicist with a sardonic grin, whose sceptical view of academic life reminded me of Kingsley Amis's Lucky Jim. I used to go to him if I had a problem with Latin translation and he would roar with laughter at the oddities of the Latin language and put me straight. He later became Thatcher Professor of Latin literature at Yale.

I saw quite a lot of the fellow in English literature, John Bryson, though we never discussed English literature, which would, I think, have seemed a bit parochial to him. I felt he was not quite at home in the mid-twentieth century. He wore finely cut tweed suits, like an Edwardian gentleman, and might have stepped out of a Thomas Mann novel, specifically, I suppose, *Death in Venice*, for he was what we now call gay, though the word seems silly and trivial when applied to him. He was a man of means – the family money came, I think, from Belfast linen – and he was expensive to entertain. Soon after my arrival I asked him round for a drink after dinner in my room and we – or, mostly, he – polished off almost the whole of a bottle of whisky which I had hoped would last the term. It had no discernible effect on him whatsoever.

When I first visited him in his flat in Belsyre Court – a rather pricey block of flats on the Woodstock Road – I noticed hanging over the stairs a drawing of a violinist, seated on a wooden chair and seen from behind, which I thought vaguely might be a print of a Degas, though not one I recognised. My eye strayed to other prints hanging nearby which also seemed half-familiar, at least in their styles, and the thought flashed through my mind that these might be – no, surely not! – originals rather than prints. John watched me, smiling, and then took me round his collection. It was jaw-dropping. There were three Degas drawings, a male nude by Cézanne and a female by Modigliani and a lovingly chosen selection of Pre-Raphaelites, including three Rossetti studies of Elizabeth Siddal and Millais's early drawing *Apple Gatherers*.

The strangest picture was of a young woman's head resting on a pillow and viewed from above and behind, so that what you see most is her beautiful light brown hair, neatly parted and divided into three tresses, the centre one tied with a dark green ribbon. It was a sketch by Ford Madox Brown for his first major oil painting, *The Execution of Mary Queen of Scots*, but this seemingly severed head is not Mary's. In the completed painting, now in the Whitworth Art Gallery in Manchester, you can see that John's sketch is for the head of a waiting woman who has fainted, and is lying propped up on the knee of another woman in a green dress.

The gem of the collection was a miniature by Nicholas Hilliard of an unknown young man, painted in around 1588. He has dark, clustering curls, the lowest, dangling tendrils reaching almost to his shoulders, but his little moustache and his eyebrows and the fuzz of incipient beard, like an inverted halo, that goes round his chin and up to his ears, are all blond. His grey eyes and his lips convey something slightly mocking, not a smile, exactly, but a hint of playfulness. Two interlinked gold rings hang from his left ear. Against his tunic of dark blue velvet an intricate white lace collar gleams. The background is dazzling blue, like the brightest Mediterranean sky. John Donne admired Hilliard intensely and I liked to think, whenever I saw John's young man, that Donne might have known him.

On that first occasion he showed me round his collection with modest pride, commenting in little gruff bursts like a friendly dog. He had, he explained, two flats, one above the other, and lived in the lower one because he did not like hearing noises in the rooms above. His pictures lived in the upper flat. When he died in 1976 he left them to the Ashmolean, where they can now be seen, except the Hilliard which is in the Victoria and Albert Museum.

I do not know if John ever wrote anything about English literature, but he did something much more important, for it was he who discovered, in 1959, the Lothian portrait of John Donne which now hangs in the National Portrait Gallery. It particularly interested me because it shows Donne in the mid-1590s, when he was writing the elegies, got up as a melancholy lover in a black floppy hat and a lacy collar, and it bears a blasphemous Latin inscription to his mistress, very much in the love-elegy style. It had hung unrecognised for centuries among the Marquis of Lothian's pictures – ever since Donne bequeathed it to his friend Robert Kerr, the Marquis's ancestor – and had been mistaken for a portrait of the medieval schoolman Duns Scotus. It took John Bryson's knowledge of literature, art and history to seek it out and identify it. Amid all the hoo-hah about raising £1.4 million to acquire it for the nation in 2006, no one mentioned his name.

Politically Balliol was leftist. The previous Master, 'Sandie' Lindsay, had been the first socialist head of an Oxford college, and had famously opposed appeasement and the Munich agreement in 1938. The Master when I was there was Sir David Lindsay Keir, a constitutional historian for whom the fellows had little respect. They ostentatiously read newspapers, shuffling the pages noisily, when he spoke at governing body meetings. It was even said that one fellow used to bring a tape recorder along (enormous contraptions in those days, like suitcases, with big revolving coils) and lean forward ostentatiously to switch it off whenever Keir opened his mouth. I'm not sure why they disliked him. He was, admittedly, a bit off a stuffed shirt, and he had foolishly accepted an honorary appointment, dating from medieval times, which notionally authorised him to fix the price of grain within the city boundary, and bore the title Clerk of the Market. This generated considerable ridicule, but I think the real reason for the fellows' attitude was that they just didn't think him intelligent enough to be Master of Balliol – a post for which the great Victorian Master Benjamin Jowett had notoriously set the standard ('I am Master of this College/What I don't know isn't knowledge', as a contemporary satirist chaffed). Christopher Hill, who succeeded Keir as Master, did not have an easy ride but at least no one doubted his intelligence.

Balliol's leftism was not dogmatic but liberal and tolerant, and there were plenty of fellows who weren't of the left at all. Bryson was one, and another was the Dean, the Reverend Frank McCarthy Willis-Bund. He had a high domed forehead which looked as if it had been freshly polished, and a slit of a mouth like a crack in a board. I think of him as wearing a wing collar and bands, like a Victorian clergyman, though perhaps he only did that in my imagination. Despite this forbidding exterior he was boundlessly good-natured. I saw him quite a bit because I had been appointed Junior Dean, a dogsbody job you were likely to get if you were a junior fellow and lived in college, as I did. I had the most beautiful room I've ever lived in in Oxford. It looked out across St Giles at the east wing of the Ashmolean, with its four soaring Ionic columns topped by gesticulating stone ladies, and it was the only room in the whole college with a balcony – though we reckoned it too rickety to use. Gill was teaching in Cheltenham, and used to come over by bus on Sundays, so we did some entertaining. One Sunday we asked Frank to sherry before lunch because we had decided to get married and wanted him to marry us. The conversation turned to politics, as it often did in Balliol. At that time, I'd guess, every intelligent young person in Britain was somewhere to the left of centre, and Gill and I were entirely conformist in this respect, though I was further left than her, being dogmatically republican as well as socialist, edging on communist. Frank listened to me with incredulous amusement as I outlined my opinions, and when it was time for him to go he plonked down his empty sherry glass and enunciated, 'Labour stinks!' All three of us laughed – each, I suppose, for a different reason. It was a moment that summed up for me the spirit of Balliol – a civilised place where disagreement could resolve itself in laughter, not anger.

We could afford to get married because I had got a job. I'd applied for and been elected to the fellowship in English at Keble College – not quite the same as Balliol, but who was I to be choosy? At the end of the Trinity term I was viva'd on my D.Phil. thesis. My examiners were Leishman and John Sparrow, the Warden of All Souls. I'd met him through Helen Gardner, and he had lent me some rare volumes of Renaissance Latin poetry, a subject on which he was an expert. So it was hardly a hostile judiciary. Neither of them much liked my socio-cultural speculations, and Sparrow enjoyed himself pointing out false quantities in some of the elegiac lines I had quoted. But apart from that it went off smoothly, and Leishman handed me at the end a dozen pages of notes on points that might repay further consideration, closely written in brown ink and totally illegible.

At the time couples had to choose between two alternative wordings in the wedding service. Either the bride could promise to 'love, honour and obey' her husband, or she could choose just to love and honour him. For some reason I found the first alternative rather appealing, but Gill rather firmly preferred the second. Frank, when we consulted him, said flatly that he would not conduct a service with the 'obey' clause in. So that settled it, and on 13 August 1960 he married us in Balliol's Victorian chapel, which is striped in two shades of pink like a boiled sweet (architect, Alfred Waterhouse, who also designed the Natural History Museum – an indiscretion on a much larger scale). John Burrow was my best man. John Bryson gave us an eighteenth-century print of Oxford's Divinity School; Garrod gave us a book called *Came to Oxford* that Gertrude and Muirhead Bone had published in memory of their son Gavin. He had been the English tutor at St John's – Philip Larkin was among his pupils – and was richly talented, a translator of *Beowulf* and a fine watercolourist. He died of cancer in 1942, aged thirty-five. Garrod had known the family well, and I think perhaps he chose his gift not only for its illustrations of St John's, which he knew had been my college, but also as a wise reminder that marriage could bring sorrows as well as joys.

7

Keble

Despite Garrod's warning, if that's what it was, our four years at Keble seem, in retrospect, to have passed in a haze of happiness. We lived in a flat on the top floor of the Warden's Lodgings, watched over by a looming imitation-Gothic gargoyle on the gable end outside. Keble College is Victorian, built of red, white and blue bricks in decorative patterns, and it was widely regarded at the time as a monstrosity. Sir Kenneth Clark called it the ugliest building in the world. But we thought it was fun – like living inside an enormous Fair Isle cardigan.

Gill was teaching at a school in Abingdon – St Helen's and St Katherine's – and earning more than me, and after a year she bought our first car, a white Mini. We also bought a kayak which we christened Pip, after my Westgate-on-Sea donkey – it had to have a name so that it could be legally registered with the Thames Conservancy, which seemed rather grand for such a small boat. It was made of wood and canvas – white, with light blue trim and two plywood seats. We got a roof-rack for the Mini which it could be strapped to, sticking out fore and aft like a spear, and on summer evenings we used to drive out to launching places on the Thames or the Cherwell or stretches of canal threading through the Oxfordshire countryside.

Because Pip was so light we could rest our paddles and slide across shallows to deserted backwaters and silent pools that only a canoe could reach. Shoals of tiny fish darted an inch or so beneath us, and electric blue dragonflies flashed through the shadows. Sometimes we would push our way through overhanging willow branches and come upon sheets of yellow kingcups, wide open to the sun, their leaves so dense and flat you felt you could walk across them. We'd disembark on the long grass, eat our supper, and read. It was my time for catching up on the great books, and I wolfed them down in no particular order – Thomas Mann's *Buddenbrooks* and *Felix Krull*, Dostoyevsky's *Crime and Punishment* and *The Idiot* and *The Brothers Karamazov* (hard going, I thought), Flaubert's *Madame Bovary*, Zola's *Germinal* and *Thérèse Raquin*, Tolstoy's *War and Peace*, Stendhal's *Scarlet and Black* and *The Charterhouse of Parma*. I read them in Penguin Classics paperbacks, and forced myself to make notes on the endpapers of each one to remind myself of the plot and the highlights, before hurrying on to the next.

Reading so much of the world's great literature at one go was probably not a good idea. But it was tremendously exciting, and I felt free, after years of working for exams, to do what I liked. Given that I was so happy, you might expect I'd remember the happy parts of what I read. But nearly all the scenes that come back to me from those novels are violent or ironic or blackly comic. Maybe that's not so surprising, because most of them are about catastrophes of one kind or another and, like all the great works of European realism, they reflect a century of violent upheaval, cruelty and change.

Thomas Mann, whose novels I started with, surprised me by being so funny. It wasn't how I'd been brought up to think of Germans. *Buddenbrooks* is about the decline of a great nineteenth-century merchant family, so it ought to be sad. But it constantly subverts the feelings you'd think it proper to have. The passage I instantly recall whenever the novel is mentioned describes the death of a senior citizen in Mann's native Lübeck.

James Mollendorpf, the oldest of the merchant senators, died in a grotesque and horrible way. The instinct of self-preservation became very weak in this diabetic old man; and in the last years of his life he fell a victim to a passion for cakes and pastries. Dr Grabow, as the Mollendorpf family physician, had protested energetically, and the distressed relatives employed gentle restraint to keep the head of the family from committing suicide with sweet bake-stuffs. But the old Senator, mental wreck as he was, rented a room somewhere, in some convenient street, like Little Groping Alley, or Angelswick, or Behind-the-Wall – a little hole of a room, whither he would secretly betake himself to consume sweets. And there they found his lifeless body, the mouth still full of half-masticated cake, the crumbs upon his coat and upon the wretched table. A mortal stroke had supervened, and put a stop to slow dissolution.

It's remarkable how the thought of that arrests your hand when reaching for a second slice of *Sachertorte*.

Unlike poor Senator Mollendorpf, the hero of *Felix Krull* is an adroit and likeable trickster, completely without principles, who undermines everything a good German should believe in. His talent for dishonesty is a family trait, and a passage I treasure from the novel is about his father, a manufacturer of substandard champagne:

The firm of Engelbert Krull paid unusual attention to the outside of their bottles, those final adornments that are technically known as the coiffure. The compressed corks were secured with silver wire and gilt cords fastened with purplish-red wax; there was moreover an impressive round seal – such as one sees on ecclesiastical bulls and old state documents – suspended from a gold cord; the necks of the bottles were liberally wrapped in gleaming silver foil, and their swelling bellies bore a flaring red label with gold flourishes round the edges. This label had been designed for the firm by my godfather Schimmelpreester and bore a number of coats of arms and stars, my father's monogram, the brand name, *Loreley extra cuvée*, all in gold letters, and a female figure, arrayed only in bangles and necklaces, sitting with legs crossed on top of a rock, her arm raised in the act of combing her flowing hair. Unfortunately it appears that the quality of the wine was not entirely commensurate with the splendour of its coiffure.

Although Mann is being funny, I came to feel, as I worked through my little pile of Penguin Classics, that you could regard Engelbert's bottles as a kind of symbol of what realism, as a literary mode, does. It operates, that's to say, through absolute attention to the external appearance of things, just like Engelbert. I don't mean to disparage realism, which is the mode in which all the greatest novels I've read have been written. But I was just interested in how it worked.

Realism, like reality, is infinite (that is, there are as many versions of it as there are people in the world), and by the same token attention to external appearances differs according to who is doing the attending. I tried to register this as I read. In Dostoyevsky, I found, the images that nail scenes in your mind are raw and simple. When Raskolnikov first sets eyes on the old woman he is going to murder in *Crime and Punishment*, for example, he notices that her long, thin neck, with a flannel rag wound round it, is 'like a hen's leg'. When he smashes her head in with the back of his hatchet, blood gushes out 'as from an overturned tumbler'. The simplicity authenticates the horror. In *Madame Bovary*, by contrast, the vivid physical images express the Swiftian disgust that human beings seem to have aroused in Flaubert – Hippolyte's gangrenous leg, covered in oozing pustules, for instance, or, when Emma has swallowed arsenic, and her corpse is being arrayed in her wedding dress for burial, the stream of dark liquid that suddenly pours from her mouth 'as though she was vomiting'.

In *War and Peace* the whole vast panorama is created by thousands of tiny dabs of imagery like a pointillist painting. The crowd scenes come to life because images pinpoint selected individuals – the huge, pockmarked Russian cavalryman on his coal-black charger, for example, who scowls viciously at Rostov and almost runs him down as the Horse Guards gallop into the attack at Austerlitz. Images differentiate characters from each other – Princess Bolkonsky's short upper lip, which makes her look like a vicious little squirrel when she's angry; Hélène's gleaming bare shoulders, suggestive of shamelessness and indecency; the artilleryman Tushin with his stumpy pipe, dependable and down-to-earth. Through images, too, we get an instant understanding of historical figures – Tsar Alexander peering at a dying soldier through his gold lorgnette; Napoleon being dressed by his valet and daubed all over with cologne.

But seeing just what is there – absolute attention to externals – serves another purpose for Tolstoy. It is the mark of the innocent eye, which banishes pretence and dispels false glories. When Rostov takes a French dragoon prisoner the event is stripped of martial splendour. The dragoon falls off his horse more from fright than from the glancing blow of

Rostov's sword, and hops around desperately trying to dis-entangle his foot from the stirrup, looking up at Rostov in terror. Rostov, meanwhile, looks at the dragoon's pale, mud-stained face – fair-haired, boyish, with a dimple in the chin and clear blue eyes – and feels moral nausea at the thought that he has struck this being with a sword.

The execution of the prisoners (Book 4, Part 1, Section 11), one of the most unbearable scenes in literature, is written throughout from an innocent eye perspective. Tolstoy also finds it useful for comedy or satire. When Natasha, fresh from the country, goes to her first opera (Book 2, Part 5, Section 9) she is bewildered by what she sees. Some painted canvas at the sides of the stage represents trees. A fat girl in a white silk dress is sitting on a bench which has a piece of green cardboard glued to the back of it. A man with stout legs encased in silk tights goes up to her and starts to sing and wave his arms about. To Natasha it all seems grotesquely unnatural, and the actors make her feel ashamed and amused by turns. This is how the innocent eye sees grand opera, gen-erally accounted a crowning triumph of European culture.

So far as I could make out the innocent eye was Stendhal's invention, and Tolstoy seemed to have copied it from him. In *The Charterhouse of Parma* the naïve Fabrizio manages to get involved in the Battle of Waterloo, and attaches him-self to a group of French hussars. He's riding along beside them when he notices something singular happening to the ploughed field they're traversing. Mud from the furrows is flying about in little black lumps, flung three or four feet in the air. Fabrizio takes this in absent-mindedly, but he's busy daydreaming about the glorious Marshal Ney whom he has just caught sight of. Then he hears a sharp cry and, looking back, sees two hussars falling, struck by shot. At that moment the other hussars spur their horses to a gallop and only then does he realise that it's fire from the enemy's guns that's making the earth fly up all around him.

Naïve heroes like Fabrizio and Julien Sorel in *Scarlet and Black*, who don't understand what's going on around them, are naturals for the innocent eye technique and the mixture of affection and mockery it implies. Stendhal also uses external appearance, as Tolstoy was to do with the Tsar and his gold lorgnette, to fix a character in a single shot. Julien Sorel is torn between a longing for military glory and hopes of attaining eminence in the church. On the occasion of a royal visit to Verrières he serves as a member of the guard of honour and also, arrayed in ecclesiastical gear, assists the priest at mass in the ancient abbey church. As he kneels, his spurs poke out beneath the folds of his cassock, capturing his dilemma in a single comic image.

I suppose I could be accused of reducing these great novels to picture shows, and that's probably true. They did seem primarily visual to me. When, later, I saw the 1956 film of *War and Peace* I thought that for all its changes and omissions it belonged to the same kind of artistic reality as the novel, and nowadays when I reread *War and Peace* Natasha is always Audrey Hepburn. Besides, I'd argue that from the perspective of cultural history the nineteenth century was essentially a struggle towards visual representation. Dioramas, daguerreotypes, lithographic newspaper illustrations – step by step they all brought camera and film closer. So it's not surprising the century's great novels should strive in the same direction.

The exception is Dostoyevsky, who is far more spiritual and psychological than visual, which is probably why I was less keen on him. I found his plots rambling and his sentimental religiosity – well, just sentimental religiosity, especially in *The Idiot*. I know this may seem shallow and philistine, but I think it's a reaction Dostoyevsky tempts you to have, to see if you've got the depth he requires of you, and I hadn't. In the famous Grand Inquisitor section of *The Brothers Karamazov* what I admired most was Ivan's sardonic, unanswerable rejection of Christianity. Ivan is a rationalist and he's arguing with his brother Alexei, a religious idealist, about why a supposedly loving God should allow suffering. He tells Alexei a terrible, true story about a Russian general, a rich landowner with aristocratic connections, whose great pride was his pack of thoroughbred hounds. One day a little serf-boy, aged eight, threw a stone in play and hurt the paw of the general's favourite hound. The general assembled all his serfs, including the boy's mother, to witness the punishment. The terrified child was stripped naked, and made to run. Then the hounds were released, hunted him down, and tore him to pieces.

Christians are bound to forgive the general, Ivan points out. They must forgive everyone. But he finds the idea of such a monster being forgiven abhorrent, whoever does the forgiving. 'I do not want a mother to embrace the torturer who had her child torn to pieces. She has no right to forgive him.' He acknowledges that forgiveness is necessary if the world is to attain divine harmony. But for him the suffering of the innocent is too much to pay for divine harmony, and he wants no part in it.

Too high a price has been placed on harmony. We cannot afford
to pay so much for admission. And therefore I hasten to return my
ticket of admission. And indeed, if I am an honest man, I'm bound
to hand it back as soon as possible. This I am doing. It is not God
that I do not accept, Alyosha. I merely, most respectfully, return him
the ticket.

Alexei is shocked. 'This is rebellion!' he whispers. But the
genius of Dostoyevsky, like the genius of Milton when he
wrote the part of Satan in *Paradise Lost*, is to put the reader on the side of God's enemy, by making the case against
Christianity almost irresistible. I wished he'd done it more
often.

Zola is as far away as you can get from Dostoyevsky, and
his lack of interest in spirituality was a great relief. I knew
he was friends with the Impressionists, and I kept remembering paintings I'd seen in the Jeu de Paume – eight years
before – as I read him. I could see that his novels were, in a
way, documentaries, tracing the causes of poverty and violence in Second Empire France. It made them different, and
more real than anything I'd come across in English literature.
I knew too that he was a real-life socialist hero, a defender of
Dreyfus against the rabid anti-Semitism of the French es-
tablishment, and a believer in mankind's moral progress who
foresaw the workers' revolution decades before it happened.
Germinal, published in 1885, ends with its hero, Étienne, imagining, as he walks through the spring countryside, that he
can hear his dead comrades still tapping away at the coal face.

Everywhere seeds were swelling and lengthening, cracking open
the plains in their upward thrust for warmth and light. The sap was
rising in abundance with whispering voices, the germs of life were

opening with a kiss. On and on, ever more insistently, his comrades were tapping, tapping, as though they too were rising from the ground. On this youthful morning, in the fiery rays of the sun, the whole country was alive with the sound. Men were springing up, a black avenging host was slowly germinating in the furrows, thrusting upwards for the harvests of future ages. And very soon their germination would crack the earth asunder.

Germinal tells the story of a miners' strike in northern France in the 1860s and, like all Zola's novels, it is about cruelty – not the flaring, aristocratic cruelty of Dostoyevsky's general, but the ordinary everyday cruelty suffered by working people going about their normal occupations, and the cruelty which, because they are made callous by deprivation, they are capable of themselves. There is a scene during the strike in *Germinal* where a frenzied mob of women, miners' wives and others, lynch the shopkeeper Maigrat, who has made their lives wretched by his extortions, tear off his genitals, and parade through the town with the bloody lump of flesh held aloft on a pole like a banner. This is matched in its horror by the description – exact and terrible – of what happens when a platoon of soldiers, called in by the authorities, open fire on the miners and their families.

For me, though, the novel's most powerful scene wasn't about deliberate cruelty – or even cruelty at all, so far as those who take part in it are concerned. It describes how a new pit pony is trussed up and lowered down the mine shaft to start his working life underground.

Soon Trompette was lying on the iron flooring, an inert mass. Still he did not move, but seemed lost in the nightmare of this black and endless cavern, this vast chamber full of noises. As they were setting about untying him, up came Bataille, who had just been unharnessed. He stretched his neck and sniffed at this new pal who had dropped down from the earth. The miners laughingly made room for him in the circle. Well now – what did he think of this nice new smell? But Bataille did not let their jibes damp his enthusiasm. Perhaps he found in his new friend the good smell of the open air, the long-forgotten smell of the sun-kissed grass, for all of a sudden he burst into a resounding whinny, a song of joy with a sob of wistfulness running through it. This was his act of welcome, made up of delight in this fragrance of the old, far-off things and sadness that here was one more prisoner who would never go back alive.

On the riverbank, among the kingcups and dragonflies, I was, I suppose, especially susceptible to the pathos of Bataille's memories. Not that I can really have read all those novels on summer evenings by the river. But I certainly read them all during my first months at Keble, and it's the riverbank and the evening sun and being newly married that I still remember now when I pick one of them up and glance through it, or sniff its cover to find if the smell of crushed grass lingers.

Meanwhile, back in the real world, I was discovering what a strange place I had landed up in. All colleges are different, but Keble was out on its own. One reason was that it was very poor. Oxford colleges differ greatly in their wealth, and fellows in the richest colleges earn far more in pay and allowances (not to mention access to travel grants, study leave and other perks) than those in the poorest, which at that time included Keble. Once the rent for our flat had been deducted, my salary, as a junior fellow, was scarcely enough to live on. We depended on what Gill earned. The other fellows were similarly disadvantaged by comparison with the rest of the university, and this bred a sense of isolation.

One way this showed itself was in exaggerated formality. At lunch and dinner fellows were required to sit strictly in order of seniority, so that you were likely to find yourself next to the same two people day after day. This was obviously absurd, but it was, I suppose, a bid for some kind of identity in an institution that feared it had none. The person who gave most thought to the college's public image was Vere Davidge, the law tutor, who was also the bursar and the uncrowned king of Keble. As an undergraduate at Pembroke College, Oxford, where he gained a second-class degree in law, Davidge had been a keen oarsman, and he hit on the idea of making Keble a great rowing college. To this end he admitted, year by year, as many of the Eton College first eight as possible. Inevitably, these young athletes could not always meet the usual entrance requirements, but Davidge used his influence and also sought out obscure courses – Diplomas in Forestry, and suchlike – to which the less academically gifted might be admitted. He was quite open about this, referring to Eton jocularly as 'Slough Grammar', so as to suggest an intimate familiarity with the place. A florid, raucous, powerfully built man, he was a keen follower of the Pytchley Hunt and had been High Sheriff of Northamptonshire – all of which weighed with the other fellows and led them to view his activities with a kind of resigned acquiescence. His strategy was remarkably successful, if accumulating Etonian oarsmen can be accounted success. During the 1950s and early '60s the Oxford crew in the university boat race regularly contained Keble men.

Davidge's other ploy to get Keble noticed was his guest nights. Each Thursday after dinner he would preside, by virtue of his seniority, at dessert in the common room. In other colleges it was the rule that port should circulate only twice before hosts and guests retired for coffee. But during Davidge's reign the decanter circulated non-stop into the small hours, frequently replenished by the hapless common-room butler. In terms of publicity this weekly binge was less successful than the Eton rowers. It was known about only locally, and attracted ridicule even among undergraduates. One night, shortly after I left the college, a group of Keble students came upon some building materials – sand, mortar, bricks – left by workmen in the front quadrangle. It was a Thursday. Davidge and his friends were engrossed in their dull and deep potations. The common room had only one exit into the quadrangle, and the students neatly and efficiently built a wall entirely blocking it off. They went to bed happy, knowing that the mortar would have several hours to set before Davidge discovered he was immured. Apparently, when the door was at last flung open, and the inexplicable presence of a wall entered the consciousness of the befuddled revellers, they made frantic attempts to dislodge it, but it stoutly resisted them and the emergency services had to be called.

In the days of Davidge's supremacy such an outrage would have attracted fearful retribution. But by the mid-1960s his influence was on the wane. A new power had arrived in the college, and was to redirect it towards the success it enjoys today. This was the theologian and philosopher Austin Farrer, who had been elected Warden the previous year and moved into the Lodgings in the same week as Gill and I took up residence in the top flat. Farrer had a brilliant academic record – a Balliol scholarship, a double first in Mods and Greats (Latin and Greek literature, philosophy, ancient history) and a string of original and controversial books that are still read and argued about today. He was lean, quick and witty, and seemed to me – though he was well into middle age – like one of Jane Austen's young clergymen – Henry Tilney in *Northanger Abbey*, say. His wife Kay was tiny, sharp and so neurotic you imagined she'd emit a shower of sparks if placed in a dark room. She wrote detective novels (*The Cretan Counterfeit* is the best) and talked in a series of rapid squeaks that were hard to interpret.

Farrer was the nearest thing to a saint I have met, but he was capable of asperity, as saints no doubt need to be. One night, a week or so after we moved into our rooftop flat, the doorbell rang and I trudged down the fifty-two stone steps, arriving at our front door just at the moment that the Warden, whose doorbell had evidently been rung too, arrived at his. Confronting us in the porch was a woebegone freshman from some other college, apparently looking for a friend in Keble, and he asked us where he could find the college porter. Farrer did not seem inclined to reply, so I said, 'In the porter's lodge.' 'Where else?' Farrer snapped, as he closed his front door. It was a retort addressed, I think, to the world at large – a cry of despair at the world's folly – rather than a missile aimed at the hapless boy on the doorstep, but I am afraid he probably took it personally. Gill and I treasured it for its succinctness, and adopted it as a private code, to be used in relation to anyone who asked stupid questions.

Not that Farrer was usually impatient with undergraduates – unless they were idle or foolish – and he was considerate to Gill and me, allowing us, for example, to store Pip in the Lodgings' cavernous cellars. Shortly after the front-door episode we were asked to lunch to meet C. S. Lewis, a close friend of the Farrers. We were both a bit awed at the prospect, having read Lewis's prodigiously learned *The Allegory of Love* and his history of sixteenth-century literature. Besides, he had a ferocious reputation as a tutor and was famed for having challenged an undergraduate who failed to share his passion for Matthew Arnold's 'Sohrab and Rustum' to a sword-fight. However, he was not at all intimidating that day. He had walked down across the University Parks from his home in Headington Quarry, and strode into the room, rubicund and tweedy, with a knapsack slung over his shoulder, like a farmer on holiday. There were just the five of us at lunch, and the mahogany-and-damask splendours of the dining room set me wondering what Victorian luxuries were in store. Turbot? Sirloin? Ortolans? But, the Farrers being ascetic, we were served stuffed onions by their bustling, motherly housekeeper.

The conversation was about literature and at one point Lewis quoted a line from a half-remembered poem – 'It was a little budding rose' – wondering who wrote it. A nonplussed silence fell, and Farrer laughingly suggested it might be by Ella Wheeler Wilcox, an American poet noted for triteness. It happened, though, that I had come across that very line when reading the poems of Emily Brontë just the week before, and it was apparent to me that this presented a character test for all three of us, though the other two were not aware of it yet. My test, of course, was whether to shut up or proclaim my superior knowledge, and I failed it almost instantly with flying colours. 'Actually, it's by Emily Brontë,' I ventured modestly. Both Lewis and Farrer were obviously glad to be enlightened, and showed not the least trace of pique, so in character-test terms they won by an enormous margin – as I glumly reflected while finishing off my onion.

Confronting Davidge at governing body meetings, however, Farrer was a different person – needle-sharp, every particle of his being a living, quivering reproach to what Davidge represented. It was like watching Squire Western from Fielding's *Tom Jones* confronting Savonarola on one of his fire-and-brimstone days. In the pulpit, too, Farrer's personality changed. He would start very quietly, almost in a whisper, and gradually work himself up into a soaring climax, as if the Holy Spirit had entered him, as perhaps it had. I was not a regular chapel-goer but I tried not to miss his sermons because I was interested in the histrionics. Besides, I wanted him to know I backed him in the great anti-Davidge crusade.

Readers will probably have already gathered I was not over-fond of Davidge, and he quite understandably loathed me. However, we avoided open confrontation except on one occasion. It happened quite by chance. I'd been disconcerted when I arrived to find that Keble's main auditorium, the Pusey Lecture Room, in which all the fellows had to deliver their university lectures, was furnished with an assortment of ramshackle chairs and desks which looked as if they had been acquired at an elementary school's closing-down sale. This seemed to me symptomatic of a general neglect of the academic side of college life, and I had pestered Davidge repeatedly to have the place refurnished. He always pooh-poohed the idea, insisting that there was no money to spare for incidental luxuries of this sort, and I retired from our encounters baffled and seething.

There was a tradition at the time that when a college eight came head of the river in the annual bumping races a Bump Supper would be held, and afterwards a bonfire would be lit in the quadrangle on which the winning boat would be ceremonially burned. In my first year at Keble the college eight came head of the river – as usual – and permission was granted for a Bump Supper and a bonfire. Davidge's oarsmen were splendid creatures, wandering around the quadrangles like polar bears in their white flannels and blazers, and on the eve of the Bump Supper one of them came up to me with a perplexed look and asked if I knew where they might procure wood for the bonfire. It seemed too good an opportunity to miss, and I replied instantly, 'Well, there are all those old desks and chairs in Pusey Lecture Room for a start. It's high time they were disposed of' – or words to that effect. Something akin to intelligence glimmered in his eyes, and he scurried off.

I retired early that night, not being given to watching bonfires. But next morning I heard that it had been a huge success, a spectacular blaze, the best for many years, and everyone had had a wonderful time. The locked doors of Pusey Lecture Room had been beaten in at an early stage, and a party of jubilant polar bears, attended by eager assistants, had gone back and forth carrying the old furniture into the quadrangle and committing every atom of it to the flames.

Davidge was naturally furious – though as his oarsmen were responsible there was little he could do, except, of course, refurnish Pusey Lecture Room. In retrospect I'm rather ashamed of my role as agent provocateur. Or rather, I'm ashamed until I put myself back into that time and remember how I felt. For to me Davidge was not a well-meaning senior academic, as of course he was in reality. He was a symbol of the monstrous injustice of Oxford, its crooked admissions policy and its shameless favouring of wealth and privilege, and I was determined – perhaps fuelled by my incendiary reading of Zola – to put the world to rights.

The part of it I could put to rights was admittedly small, but it did include the English literature students at Keble College, and they certainly needed attention. When I interviewed the second and third years at the start of my first term I was alarmed at how little they knew. No one, so far as I could see, had taught them anything – how to read, what to read, how to criticise. With the second year there was time to put this right. But the third year had only nine months before Schools. However, they seemed bright and eager, so I arranged twice-weekly 'rescue' tutorials, taking each Schools paper in turn and clarifying where they must focus. The third-year student who worried me most was also the cleverest – a reticent twenty-year-old with watchful eyes and a mouth that tilted slightly on one side in a sardonic smile. This was Ian Hamilton, later celebrated as poet, literary critic and biographer and as the founding editor of the *Review* and the *New Review*, which published a generation of new writers including Ian McEwan, Julian Barnes, Martin Amis, James Fenton and Clive James. What worried me about Ian was that he clearly ought to get a first and, as clearly, would not, bar a miracle. I told him both these facts, and added that I wanted him not just to get a first but to stay on and write a D.Phil. thesis on contemporary English poetry (which, at that time, no one in Oxford had dreamed of doing). The idea appealed to him and he applied himself seriously to filling the gaps in his knowledge. But he had other things to do – among them editing the poetry magazine *Tomorrow* – and his justifiable contempt for the antiquated Oxford syllabus stood in his way. In the end he got a third-class degree, a crass assessment of his abilities that only Oxford could have made.

Maybe it was for the best in the long run. The British literary scene over the next forty years would have been immeasurably poorer if he had become just another academic. But I felt Keble had let him down, and I resolved that the English students who remained would not be let down in the same way. So I saw to it that they worked – harder, I think, than many of them had supposed anyone could. I was talking to one of them just the other day (Val Cunningham, who became a professor at Oxford and authored, among many other books, the magnificently abrasive *British Writers of the Thirties*) and he said, only half jokingly, that working with me had been like military discipline. I took it as a compliment.

Besides making sure they fulfilled their utmost potential I wanted to open doors for them beyond English literature, so, inspired by my discovery of Penguin Classics, I set them to read during each vacation great European works in translation. My diary for October 1963 records the third year sitting a start-of-term three-hour paper, based on their long vacation reading, with questions on Dante's *Inferno*, selected poems of Baudelaire and Rimbaud, *Scarlet and Black*, Balzac's *Old Goriot*, *The Idiot*, *Madame Bovary* and *Germinal*. During term, in addition to the normal English literature tutorials, we had weekly classes to discuss these and other continental masterpieces. More than one ex-student told me later that it was the most worthwhile part of their time at Oxford.

The range of comparison this reading gave them, and its impact on the way they thought, talked and wrote about literature, was huge, and Keble's English results improved dramatically. My other innovation was to write, after the entrance exam each year, to scores of English teachers in non-public schools whose pupils had failed to get a place at any Oxford college, encouraging them to send applicants to Keble in future, and I made a point of admitting, if I possibly could, candidates from schools or homes that had never sent anyone to Oxbridge. Nowadays this kind of liaison with disadvantaged schools is commonplace. All colleges do it. But back in 1960, so far as I know, no one else did, and when news of it got around it was frowned on in some quarters, partly on the grounds that I was 'poaching' on other colleges' territory, and partly because many people, both in and out of the university, thought there was nothing wrong with Oxford selecting more than half its undergraduates from public schools. Public-school all-rounders were more suitable material for Oxbridge, it was argued, than swots from grammar schools could ever be. Here is P. G. Wodehouse expressing that view in 1962, in a letter to a friend whose son ('a cert for his cricket, hockey, and racquets blues') had been turned down by Pembroke College, Cambridge (though he got into Magdalene):

> I do agree with you about the folly of the Cambridge authorities in not paying attention to 'on the field' excellence. I think they're all wrong making the standards so high. Cambridge ought to be like it was in my young days, a place where you could get in if you could read and write. Bertie Wooster and his pals just walked into their university, presumably purely on charm of manner, and I think that's how it ought to be. Too much of this business of East Salford Secondary Grammar School nowadays.

Davidge, and many others in Oxford, would have concurred.

But there were those in Keble who didn't, and who supported what I was doing. Austin Farrer was one. Another was Malcolm Parkes – later internationally known as an expert on early manuscripts, but then just a young lecturer looking for a job whom I signed on to teach Anglo-Saxon and who helped me reform English at Keble. Actually what he helped me with at our first meeting was our flat's electrical system. He turned up to see me on the off chance one morning when I was trying to sort out the bewildering main fusebox and the wires perilously dangling from it. Rapidly taking charge, he displayed electrical skills far in advance of anything I had expected in an Anglo-Saxonist. It seemed to me that on both counts he was too good to lose, and that was the start of Malcolm's distinguished Keble career which lasted till his retirement some forty years later.

The other fellows I thought of as being on my side were really, of course, simply the ones with a serious interest in their subjects and in Keble's academic future who were prepared, from that point of view, to indulge my intemperate outbursts.

There was Denys Potts the French don, an opera fanatic and authority on Saint-Évremond, and the archaeologist Christopher Hawkes, and Hans von Engel, an urbane, witty physicist who had fought on the German side in the First World War, and the young historian Eric Stone, and the philosopher Basil Mitchell, who had been Farrer's advocate in the wardenship election, and Spencer Barrett, who was working on what was to be a landmark edition of Euripides' *Hippolytus* (published in 1964) and who, as a devout atheist, had refused to become a fellow of Keble – though he was treated as one – until 1952 when the college statutes ceased to require fellows to declare themselves members of the Church of England.

Our favourite fellow was Douglas Price, a rotund, jolly, pipe-smoking historian who, before Gill bought the Mini, used to take us out for night-time drives to prehistoric sites around Oxford. We stood in pitch dark among the Rollright Stones and, encouraged by Douglas, imagined that we could hear them walking. We looked out from Wayland's Smithy at the lights of Swindon twinkling far below, while Douglas told us how, if you left your horse to be shod there, and put a silver sixpence on the entrance stone, the job would be done in the morning and the sixpence gone. He never claimed to have seen the phantom smith himself, but he did see ghosts, or one ghost anyway, in the kitchen at Chastleton House, a Jacobean manor near Oxford, and seemed keen to see more. One night he drove us out to the escarpment of Edgehill where, on 23 October 1642, the first battle of the English Civil War was fought. Though the conflict was inconclusive, the idea of Englishmen fighting and killing Englishmen left a terrible mark. For years afterwards on the anniversary of the battle there were sightings of spectral armies, with the faces of combatants clearly recognisable, and even in modern times motorists report having to swerve to avoid galloping cavaliers on the roads around Edgehill. Douglas showed us where Prince Rupert and the Royalist cavalry had charged, and where Sir Edmund Verney had died defending the royal standard, and he told us how, in the parish churches on the roads radiating away from the battlefield, the registers record the deaths of the wounded who started out for home but did not make it.

He had a cottage in the village of Wigginton, which is near Hook Norton, a small town famous for its brewery and local ale. The area around there has long been notorious for witches and the black arts, and when his cottage was being renovated Douglas found a seventeenth-century doll buried under the hearthstone – a substitute for what, a couple of centuries earlier, might have been a sacrificed child. But Gill and I brought back something much less grim from Douglas's cottage. He knew we wanted a cat and he acquired one from a local farm – a handsome tabby kitten with white front and paws. We named him Wigginton, naturally, and he was our pride and joy. Being ignorant first-time cat-owners we didn't realise that he ought to be 'doctored' (as the euphemism sinisterly terms it) and in any case we came to feel that his little furry testicles were quite as beautiful as everything else about him. He soon left kittenhood behind, and his amorous quests took him far afield. Lodge porters would phone from colleges as distant as Magdalen, asking us to come and collect him. He had his name, address and telephone number neatly inscribed on a disc round his neck, so was readily identifiable. He made friends easily and was always kindly treated. Often we would find him curled up by the lodge fire or lapping a saucer of milk. In Balliol he was elected an honorary member of the junior common room and allocated a special chair.

Admittedly he was not quite perfect. He was rather prone to sexual stereotyping, and if Gill was slow putting his plate of food down for him he would bite her ankles, which he would certainly never have thought of doing to me. But this was just because he recognised her as the female and therefore held her responsible for nourishment, which was natural. When I was working late at night he used to climb up and lie across the back of my neck, his forelegs and head hanging down over my left shoulder, his back legs and tail over my right, and go to sleep, occasionally snoring. I found it a comfort, like wearing a live scarf. The reason for my late-night sessions was that I had taken on a new task. When I was putting the final touches to my D.Phil. thesis Helen Gardner told me that Yale University Press had contacted her as they were looking for someone to translate Milton's Latin treatise *Christian Doctrine* for their great new international scholarly project, the *Yale Complete Prose Works of John Milton*. Would I do it? I said yes. I'm not sure I was right, or that she was right to ask me. But I think she reckoned it would be good for my career, and it probably was. It was made clear from the start that I would not be paid for my labours. The honour of taking part in the Yale project was considered payment enough.

It took me five years – not full-time of course. I had a teaching job. But five years of what would have been my spare time. That may seem slow going, but it was a tough assignment. My translation occupies seven hundred printed pages in the *Complete Prose Works,* and runs to a quarter of a million words. The real gain of doing it was what I learned about the mind that created *Paradise Lost* and *Paradise Regained.* Milton wrote it (or dictated it, for he was blind by this time) in the late 1650s, and it spells out his most considered thinking on what he saw as the nature of reality. He derived every statement in it from the Bible, backing up his claims with thousands of biblical quotations. But despite its biblical basis it glaringly contradicts fundamental Christian beliefs – to such an extent that publication in his lifetime was unthinkable. It has been estimated that, under the Presbyterian Blasphemy Ordinance of 1648, it would have rendered him liable to five death sentences and eight terms of life imprisonment.

In *Christian Doctrine* he rejects belief in the Holy Trinity, and with it the belief that Christ, the Son of God, is of the same essence as God the Father. 'If the Father and the Son were of one essence', he briskly observes, 'it would follow that the Father was the Son's son and the Son the Father's father. Anyone who is not a lunatic can see what kind of a conclusion this is.' With similarly robust common sense he rejects the orthodox belief that God created the universe out of nothing. It is impossible, he asserts, to make anything out of nothing, and since only God can have existed before the creation of the universe, He must have made the universe out of Himself. As the universe is made of matter, it follows that God must be made of matter too (a heresy the Christian church called 'materialism'). 'Spirit', Milton argues, is really just a refined form of matter: everything that exists is matter – an advanced view for his day. Other assertions, distressing to orthodox Christians, found in *Christian Doctrine* are that the soul has no separate existence from the body, and dies with the body, and that polygamy is a perfectly acceptable form of Christian marriage.

These were the kind of inflammatory claims I pored over as Wigginton purred and snuffled across my shoulders. They caused widespread alarm when *Christian Doctrine* was rediscovered and published for the first time in 1825. Many refused to believe our great Christian poet could have written such things. Some modern Milton scholars also find it hard to swallow, and when news got around that I was working on a translation I received several anxious letters urging me to consider whether Milton's Latin might not allow a less scandalous interpretation. I forwarded these plaintive missives to the volume's editor, Professor Maurice Kelley of Princeton University, who greeted them with sardonic amusement. Kelley was a hard-bitten old Miltonist of impregnable erudition and taciturn epistolary manner. I had met him only once, and it occurred to Gill and me that, as I was not being paid for my work, some small portion of the ample funds at the disposal of the editorial board of the *Complete Prose Works* might be diverted in our direction to pay for a couple of economy-class transatlantic flights, which would give us a holiday and a chance of one-to-one collaboration with Kelley. Sure enough, a year or so after I started work a thick envelope arrived at the flat covered in American stamps. We felt certain this was our air tickets, and tore it open excitedly, only to find that it contained a wad of handwritten slips, each relating to a sentence in the translations I had sent Kelly so far that he felt needed reconsideration.

One problem with the translation was that the thousands of biblical quotations Milton based his arguments on did not always appear in the same form. Generally he quoted from a sixteenth-century Latin Bible, popular with Puritans. But he tended to adapt its wording to fit the argument he wanted it to support. If he had supplied a biblical index, listing the various contexts in which each text appeared, it would have made it easy to check where the wording had changed. But of course he didn't. So Gill supplied one, recording every biblical text in Milton's vast work together with the page number and paragraph in which it appeared. It was a colossal labour and done out of sheer loving kindness because she could see I was worried I'd never finish. So the fact that, after five years, the job was completed was her doing as much as mine. We treated ourselves to a dinner out to celebrate – and almost didn't get there because the last page took longer than I expected. But luckily they held the table. Editors of earlier volumes missed their deadlines so publication of *Christian Doctrine* was delayed, but our translation, with Kelley's introduction and notes, eventually appeared in 1973 as Volume VI of Yale's *Complete Prose Works*.

Another time-consuming activity that Helen – with, I'm sure, the best intentions – steered me into was the New English Bible. Oxford University Press published the New Testament in a modern English translation in 1961, and a team of Hebraists was assembled to give the Old Testament the same treatment. A 'literary panel' was also got together and Helen, as a delegate of the Press, suggested I should be on it. Surprisingly, this was approved. I suspect they hoped I'd breathe the youthful spirit of the sixties into their venerable deliberations. If so, it was a bad mistake. Gill and I did go to see *Yellow Submarine* when it came out, and thought it quite fun, and Gill made herself several 'sack' dresses, waistless and miniskirted, in which she looked irresistible. We also had a Jackson Pollock, or the next best thing, which a friend of ours made by squeezing tubes of coloured paints onto a huge rectangle of hardboard. We hung it over the fireplace in our cavernous drawing room, where it helped to use up wall space. But apart from that the great tide of pop culture – Buddhism, hippyism, mind-expanding drugs, and the prophets, saints and martyrs of the drop-out ethos, Antonin Artaud, Hermann Hesse, Timothy Leary, Herbert Marcuse – swept by leaving us untouched. We were just too busy to notice it, and the bits we did notice seemed noisy, vulgar or senseless. Maybe we'd been brought up wrongly. Or maybe pop catered for some need that the post-war generation felt and we didn't. Whatever the reason, I couldn't see that pop mattered in the way that Tolstoy or Dostoyevsky or Stendhal or Zola or Mann, or, of course, Shakespeare or Donne or Milton mattered. They seemed deep and fixed, whereas pop was just a ripple on the surface.

Anyway, the literary panel was an experience not to be missed, even if I was there under false pretences. The other members were all impeccably distinguished – Basil Willey, the King Edward VII Professor of English literature at Cambridge, Sir Roger Mynors, professor of Latin at Oxford (who had been at Eton with George Orwell and Cyril Connolly and said he preferred Connolly), and the poet Anne Ridler, who had worked with T. S. Eliot at Faber and Faber. The chairman was Sir Godfrey Driver, professor of Semitic philology at Oxford. He was head of the whole project and chaired the Hebraists' translation committee as well as our panel, and before each meeting he sent us Xeroxes of the version the experts had come up with. Our job was to apply a sort of cosmetic treatment, turning their literal translation into flowing prose.

It was hopeless. The King James version was always at the back of our minds. The others, I'd guess, knew a lot of it by heart, and even I, as an ex-choirboy, had its language and rhythms thoroughly embedded. Poking modern words into it seemed absurd, and rewriting more extensively was like sacrilege. So we were all a bit subdued and dejected – except Driver. He had a wonderful time, because in quite a lot of places he and his colleagues had found the accepted translations were wrong, and the Bible actually said something different. So he came to the job with fierce exultation, like an archaeologist digging treasure out of the desert sand. He had a strange manic grin – or grimace, I was never sure which – and read out the new translation to us, page by page, in a triumphant, croaky voice, like an excited rook. Then we would make our feeble suggestions, which, as often as not, he would overrule, with a gabble of the original Hebrew to keep us quiet.

Years later I met a professor of Hebrew who told me that the translation Driver presented us with was often not the one approved by the Hebraists' committee, but his own highly controversial interpretation, based on his knowledge of Arabic, which he had picked up during army service in the First World War. This happened on such a scale that in the 1980s a new panel of Hebraists was recruited to prepare a Revised Old Testament (published in 1989) which ironed out the Driverisms. We knew nothing of this at the time, of course. We were just four bewildered sheep driven hither and thither by a maverick shepherd, whose own idea of modern colloquial English seemed to be based largely on the schoolboy slang current at Winchester when he was there in the first decade of the twentieth century. T. S. Eliot said of the New English Bible that it 'astonishes in its combination of the vulgar, the trivial and the pedantic', and I think he got it about right. Whenever I hear it read in church now I wince.

Like my *Christian Doctrine* translation, work on the New English Bible was unpaid – which was fair enough, since I learned a great deal about the Hebrew Bible from Driver, even if some of it was rather dodgy. But I needed to find other sources of revenue, so I took on marking A-level English papers, and Gill and I acted as deans (that is, general carers and dogsbodies) on an International Oxford Summer School in Exeter College. We did this for several years and enjoyed it a lot. The students were mainly young Americans, and they came with an eager appetite for Oxford's rituals and legends. From their angle the place wasn't really a university but a gorgeous animated museum, and they greeted each new find – the weird old dons, the mouldering libraries, the white-coated servants ('Isn't he just like Jeeves!') – with delighted surprise. The whole of Great Britain – tiny for them – was a kind of fabulous theme park. They would go to 'Hardy country' or 'Brontë country' after breakfast and be back by dinner. They went to Scotland and returned clad in an assortment of tartans. They were crazy about ghosts, so one night Gill and I took a group to look for the ghost of Archbishop Laud, who is supposed to haunt the old library in St John's. He didn't put in an appearance, but it was deliciously spooky all the same, and we crept around whispering. When we left we did a head count and two of our group were missing. So we went back and found that one young couple had forgotten all about ghosts and were kissing and cuddling among the ancient tomes.

Our pay from the summer school allowed us to take our first ever Mediterranean holiday – not counting our honeymoon, when we had gone to Florence and Perugia. One of my Christ Church students had a family house on Menorca, and told us about the island, so that's where we went, flying to Barcelona and then getting a boat. We stayed in Ciudadella at the Hotel Alfonso III – a lovely, comic-opera hotel with menus in pidgin English ('Muched Meat' was a staple) and bedroom lights that gave out the feeblest glimmer. This was 1961, and there were no tourists, except in Mahon, which we hardly ever went to. Ciudadella had its own little horseshoe beach, but a few pesetas would hire a fishing boat to take you to remote bays with huge stretches of shimmering white sand where you could spend all day completely alone. We bought a green drawstring bag that held everything we wanted – towels, swimming costumes, plastic bottles of Ambre Solaire, and lunch – a loaf, a can of tuna or sardines, dusty-looking figs that glistened red and purple when you bit into them, and big, soft, downy peaches, best eaten standing up to your neck in the warm sea because they were so juicy.

It seemed the right time to tackle a European masterpiece I hadn't tried yet, Cervantes's *Don Quixote*, so I took along J. M. Cohen's Penguin Classics translation and read it day after day crouching in the patch of shade under our blue-and-white beach umbrella. It was a colossal disappointment. I found it boring and hateful. The whole idea of making a joke about the delusions of someone who's mentally ill seemed disgusting to me – partly, I suppose, because of my experiences with my brother. As for the Sancho Panza stuff – the doggily loyal servant who can be kicked around with impunity – it reeked of injustice and class discrimination. This got even worse in the second half, where Don Quixote becomes a sort of court fool for the amusement of the Duke and Duchess. Chapter 53 of Part 2 seemed just about the nastiest, where Sancho is brutally punished for daring to try to rise out of his social class, but there were many others almost as horrible. I'd guess that *Don Quixote* is one of those works which is celebrated because virtually no one has read it.

We went to Ciudadella the next summer too, and again it was idyllic. But, back in Oxford, the winter of 1962–3 was the coldest since the seventeenth century. Heavy snow in December, with drifts up to twenty feet, blocked roads and railways and brought down power lines. The upper reaches of the Thames froze over. One Saturday, well wrapped up, we went for a walk on the river – it was as solid as a road – and met an excited group of nuns walking in the other direction. The snow lay till March, and revealed unsuspected traces of the past. On a country walk near Leafield we noticed a slight declivity in the snow snaking across what were normally green fields, and worked out from the map that this was the Roman Akeman Street that had joined Cirencester with London.

Our flat, though, was not an ideal place in cold weather. It consisted of five huge rooms – one of them had been a dormitory for six maids – and we could not afford to heat any of them, or even furnish them except sparsely. We'd had to do all the decorating ourselves, and I'd built a partition with shelves and cupboards to divide one of the rooms into a kitchen and dining space. The bathroom was the worst – like a large, square igloo. The bath took so long to fill that the water was cool before you got in, and the little round overflow aperture between the taps was positioned so that the wind came through it like an icy blade. You had to lean sideways to dodge it. In the autumn of 1962 dry rot had been discovered in the Warden's Lodgings. Scaffolding was erected, and the wall of our kitchen disappeared. In its place was a sheet of transparent plastic – our only protection from the Arctic outside. Our gas stove which had been against the removed wall now stood in the centre of the kitchen, on the end of an improvised copper pipe. No one thought of suggesting we might have alternative accommodation somewhere else in the college, or even pay a reduced rent, and as I had been appointed Dean by this time I was obliged to live in college so could not just move elsewhere.

I provide these details not out of retrospective self-pity but to explain why, when a letter arrived in the autumn of 1963 from the President of St John's, offering me the English fellowship there (following the death of my old tutor Leishman) and adding that they would give me a college house entirely free of charge and a salary considerably larger than what I was getting at Keble, the decision to accept was not very difficult.

8

St John Street and Catching Up with the Victorians

The house the college provided for us turned out to be in an elegant Georgian terrace built in the 1820s. Nowadays St John Street is one of Oxford's most exclusive addresses, but in 1964 it was engagingly down-at-heel. Many of the houses were rented by college scouts and their wives, who ran them as student digs. The enticing smell of fried breakfasts wafted on the air as you walked past in the morning. Battered bikes lined the pavement. There were almost no cars. Ours, number 38, was the very first house to be gentrified – the college's generous decision, not ours – and they did a thorough job. The front was covered in scaffolding and sprayed with water for several days, returning the stone to its pristine creaminess so that it shone like a beacon among the other soot-blackened facades. The inside was gutted and redesigned from scratch in 1960s Scandinavian style. There were beechwood-clad walls with fitted cupboards and shelves and recesses for hi-fi equipment. Sliding glass doors looked out onto the garden. The kitchen-diner had custom-made furniture. Cooker, sink unit and cupboards fitted into a discreet recess. The bathroom was a gleaming triumph of ingenuity, tucked under the staircase to the third floor. Old features were kept and lovingly restored – the delicately panelled bedroom doors, the slender wooden banisters. The cellar was a masterpiece. That part of Oxford is riddled with underground streams, but our cellar – floor, ceiling, walls – was coated with a material which, it seemed to us, must be similar to what makes submarines waterproof. It housed the central heating boiler and hot-water tank, both of them surprisingly large – the sort of thing you might find below decks on an ocean liner.

Not until it was all finished were we handed the keys, and we tiptoed round, dumbfounded. We had never seen such a house. It seemed like an illustration from some swanky magazine. We could scarcely believe it was for us. The college evidently didn't regard it as anything special. When I went to the bursary to thank them I was given to understand it was just the way St John's treated its fellows. It was rent-free, of course, and they'd take care of any decorations or alterations for free as well. They'd do the garden if we liked. As it was our first garden, though, we decided to do it ourselves. There was a pile of old bricks left over from the renovation and we used them to make a curving brick path down to the back gate. On one side we had a flower bed, on the other a little lawn and, beyond that, blackcurrant bushes, gooseberries and raspberry canes. I got catalogues from specialist nurseries and pored over them, finding it especially hard to resist new varieties. I remember choosing an almost coal-black delphinium – the result, I suppose, of years of misdirected research. Gill chose old-fashioned roses – a blush-tinted Madame Alfred Carrière, a purple Roseraie de l'Hay, and Blanc Double de Coubert with big, dishevelled papery-white blooms and clustered yellow stamens. We tried camellias, which succeeded, despite our alkaline soil – a pink Donation, and a Contessa Lavinia Maggi, white flecked with cherry red, which was a gift from my father. Against the south-facing wall we planted a fan-trained peach, the variety called Peregrine, which fruited year after year. Jasmine and honeysuckle climbed the back of the house.

But our great horticultural discovery lay just beyond the end of our garden, through a little wooden gate. It was a patch of ground, roughly square, and about half the size of a standard allotment, that had for some reason been left untouched when St John Street was developed – we never found out why. Our two theories were that it had been a graveyard (perhaps a plague pit) or part of the city's defences. The walls on the north and west sides were stone, and the ground fell away sharply beyond them, which suggested a defensive purpose – especially as Oxford had been garrisoned by the Royalists in the Civil War. We asked the college if we could use it as a vegetable garden, and they said yes. So we got more catalogues and sent off for seeds. The results were spectacular. I have never been able to grow such vegetables since – and we were complete amateurs. It must have been the soil. Perhaps it really had been a graveyard. Whatever the reason, our potatoes came plump and gleaming from the earth, our cabbages spread huge leaves to catch reservoirs of rainwater, our buttercrunch lettuces had hearts as tight as fists, our turnips were neat white spheres, daintily haloed in purple, our outdoor bush tomatoes sagged with fruit, our onions bulged, our parsnips drove themselves deep into the ground like miners. We grew mangetout peas as well as standard kinds, and they were all heavy with pods. I built a makeshift greenhouse out of corrugated plastic sheets which produced long, juicy cucumbers (F1 hybrid, variety Femina) and glossy purple aubergines. Just for fun I planted rows of cornflowers and marigolds among the vegetables, and great thistly cardoons, like discarded Corinthian capitals, and there was room for a row of strawberries under the north fortification, if that's what it was.

It seemed as if we had started a new life, and to add to the novelty I was writing my first book. It was in a series called Literature in Perspective, and the general editor was Ken Grose, the senior English master at Bradford Grammar School, where I had gone to do a recruitment talk. The aim, set out by Ken, was 'to make literary criticism lucid to the general reader'. Each volume was on a single author and mine was on Milton. The *Times Educational Supplement* described it as 'a very useful series indeed', though I suspect that was before my volume appeared. Having to write clearly and briefly (150 pages was the limit) was good training, and I tried to make Milton seem less intimidating as well as clarifying why he was truly great. I also tried to make it funny. What the *Yale Complete Prose Works* team thought of it when it came out in 1969 I don't like to think. On the other hand, I'm pretty sure undergraduates found it useful. A few years after its publication the English faculty librarian phoned to say their copy was falling to pieces and could they have a replacement? I took one along and collected the old one. It looked like something from a waste tip, but almost every page was underlined or highlighted and the margins bristled with ticks, exclamation marks and scrawled comments ('Yes!' followed in another hand by 'No!!' Beside one passage someone had helpfully written 'Irony'). I felt it deserved to be hung up somewhere like one of those bedraggled regimental flags you come across in cathedrals. Whatever else, one good thing it did was introduce some of its readers to

Thomas Mann. Alongside Milton's description of Eden I quoted Hans Castorp's vision of an earthly paradise from *The Magic Mountain*.

The Literature in Perspective series prospered, and some years later Gill wrote the volume on Shelley – she was expecting our firstborn, Leo, and was still correcting the proofs in the early stages of labour. But we'll come to that later. At the time we celebrated my finishing the book by taking the Mini across to Cherbourg and driving down through towns almost wholly rebuilt after the war – Saint-Lô and Carentan (subject of a moving poem by the American soldier-poet Louis Simpson) – for a September walking holiday in Normandy. France, we discovered, was short of footpaths compared to England, but we used large-scale maps to plan walks along tiny roads and tracks, past apple orchards and immaculate smallholdings and moated manor houses and ancient abbeys. It was my first experience of the transformative power of French cooking. I had experienced tripe only as a kind of flocculent horror, served up boiled in a boarding house in West Bridgford when my parents were looking for somewhere to live after leaving London in 1941. Here, in Normandy, at a little hotel-restaurant in St Pierre-des-Nids, we were served a mouthwatering creation called, I was astounded to find, *tripes à la mode de Caen*. The *cidre bouché* and the *crème fraiche* seemed pretty marvellous too, and we went back to Normandy for walking holidays several times. This time, on our first morning, the air was crisp and the sky eggshell blue. But while we were getting our map out of the Mini a sunburnt couple, clearly homeward bound from the Riviera, were huddling themselves into their Mercedes nearby and we heard the male remark, 'Beastly cold.' It's a phrase we've cherished ever since as a shorthand for perfect September weather.

Writing about Milton inevitably makes you feel inadequate, and I decided I ought to brush up my Greek and read Plato's *Phaedo*, a key text for Milton, in the original as he did. So I got a Loeb edition and worked through it, page by page, while shaving each morning. The razor plug was in the top bedroom, which, since the renovation, had a big west-facing window, so I could shave, digest Plato and enjoy a distant inspection of my stalwart ranks of vegetables all at once. I was worried about Plato, though. I'd read quite a bit of him in translation, and it seemed to me that his belief in absolute truth, beauty and goodness, and his notion that some kind of ideal perfection exists, which humanity always falls short of, were not only groundless but dangerous and damaging to human life. However, knowing he was considered a great philosopher, I kept these doubts to myself. In the event, they were resolved quite by chance. One Saturday morning I was passing Blackwell's bookshop in the Broad when I spotted the tubby figure of Sir Maurice Bowra approaching at a fast waddle. He was a legendary presence in 1960s Oxford, a distinguished classicist and President of the British Academy, but also a mischievous power-broker, renowned for fixing university appointments and delighting in the 'bad blood', as he called it, that his interference caused. He had been kind and welcoming to Gill and me, and invited us to lunch in Wadham, where he was Warden, so I felt fairly at ease with him. We exchanged pleasantries, and he asked me what I was reading. I explained I was having another go at Plato, and his face lit up. 'Ah! Wonderful stuff, wonderful stuff!' he growled. 'Of course, the philosophy's nonsense' – and with that he stomped up the steps and disappeared into Blackwell's. I felt greatly relieved. It was just what I wanted to know.

Alongside the Milton book I worked on an edition of Milton's poems for a series called Longman's Annotated English Poets. The general editor was Freddie Bateson, the English fellow at Corpus Christi – a man much hated by the senior members of the English faculty because of his determination to update the syllabus and his low estimate of Anglo-Saxon literature. He was very distinguished – editor of the *Cambridge Bibliography of English Literature* and founder of the periodical *Essays in Criticism* – but shamefully he was never invited to examine in the Final Honour School. I once asked at an English faculty board meeting why this was, and there was a shocked silence as if I'd uttered an obscenity. Freddie organised several younger dons – among them Christopher Ricks, Roger Lonsdale, Emrys Jones, Alastair Fowler and me – into a discussion group, and invited speakers from outside Oxford. The only time I heard F. R. Leavis speak was at one of these gatherings. He seemed very much the actor and, once Freddie had introduced him, he sat in silence for quite a while, apparently deep in thought, as if at a loss what to talk about and waiting for a spark from heaven to fall.

The idea behind Longman's Annotated English Poets was to print the entire poetic output of each poet, in chronological order, with explanatory notes, and each poem had to have a headnote summarising all the criticism that had ever been written about it. Alastair Fowler and I split Milton between us. He did *Paradise Lost*, I did all the rest including *Paradise Regained* and *Samson Agonistes*. Checking out everything that had been written about such well-known poems meant a lot of reading, but Oxford was the ideal place to do it because the Bodleian is a copyright library, getting a copy of every book published in Britain. The Bodleian's catalogue is now online, of course, but in those days it was an antique in its own right, virtually the same as it had been throughout the nineteenth century. It was housed in hundreds of huge leather-bound volumes, about two foot high and six inches thick, with leather straps for lifting them at the top, and they were shelved, two deep, on both sides of two free-standing, chest-high bookcases, with sloping tops, that ran the whole length of one of the library's biggest rooms. To a fanciful eye they looked like upturned longships, with the wooden ridge at their apex as the keel. You had to track down the volume you wanted, lug it out, and plonk it down on the sloping top. Younger readers tended to help older ones with the lifting, so the catalogue room had a pleasantly communal feel – a place for whispered scholarly gossip. When you opened your volume you found that the thick parchment pages had flimsy slips of paper pasted all over them, each with the title and shelf-mark of a book written on it in longhand. You copied these details onto a special slip, interleaved with carbon paper, and handed it in, and next day the book would be waiting for you when you asked for it at the reserve desk. Sometimes the volume of the catalogue you wanted was missing and you would find it in a room off at the side where a team of ladies worked, hour by hour and day by day, writing out and pasting in new slips as new books arrived in the library. My favourite time in the catalogue room was on winter evenings after the end of Michaelmas term, when the undergraduates had all gone away, and almost no one was about, and the tall windows looked out on a sprinkle of snow under the street lamps in Radcliffe Square. You could imagine you were part of a Victorian Christmas.

Reading academic Milton criticism en masse over the course of several months gave me a vivid idea of how awful most of it was – ill-written, obscure, trivial, full of misplaced erudition and calculated to repel any sensible ordinary reader. Another book I was working on at the same time was a selection of the criticism that had been written about the poet Andrew Marvell, from the seventeenth through to the twentieth century. This was for a series called Penguin Critical Anthologies, with Christopher Ricks as general editor, and it showed me that the dire state of academic literary criticism was by no means limited to studies of Milton. I offered some opinions on these issues in my Introduction to the Marvell anthology, and got an amused letter from Christopher Hill, asking, 'Are you allowed to be as funny as that about a sacred subject?' I also got a letter from William Empson saying he would like to meet. I admired Empson intensely, particularly his breezy unacademic style combined with an intelligence obviously far in advance of most academics, so I was flattered he had even bothered to look at my Marvell anthology. I asked him to lunch in college, and he came and talked at some length about the Mary Marvell who published Marvell's poems in 1681, and about what her relations with the poet might have been. It was all a bit beyond me, but I was fascinated by Empson's beard, which was unlike any beard I'd seen before – or since. It grew only along the angle of his jaw – a narrow fringe of greyish wisps, a couple of inches long. I learned later, I forget who told me, that this kind of beard is called a 'hangman' because the wisps resemble dangling nooses. I don't know whether that's true, but Empson's beard remains fresh in my memory whereas his views about Marvell's putative sex life have, I'm ashamed to say, faded.

The morasses of academic literary criticism I had to wade through when researching these two books made me resolve never to write such stuff myself, and to deride it whenever I came across it. Needless to say, this personal protest movement had no effect whatsoever on the relentless march of the armies of academe. In 1997 the publishers asked for an updated edition of the Carey–Fowler *Complete Poems of John Milton*, and I had to read – or, anyway, skim – an astonishing total of seventy books and seven hundred articles relating to Milton that had appeared in the quarter-century since the first edition. It was purgatory, but at least sifting through it enabled me to direct students, who had less time for reading than I had, towards the small residue of stuff that was worth a look. A new custom that had mushroomed since I did the first edition, I found, was for authors to preface their terrible tomes with pages of effusive thanks to all those – teachers, academic colleagues, friends, parents, partners, children, childminders, and as like as not the family dog – without whom the volume would never have come into being. I cursed them all fervently in my heart.

A lot more enjoyable was the reading I had to do for another assignment in the late 1960s – writing the chapters on sixteenth- and seventeenth-century prose for the second volume of Christopher Ricks's *Sphere History of Literature in the English Language*. I had felt, when Christopher asked me to do it, that writing about the prose of the period wasn't exactly the most exciting job. But I soon found I was wrong. I realised, as I read, that I was watching the modern world come into being. For between the early 1500s and the mid-seventeenth century two world-changing events took place, the Protestant reformation and the scientific revolution, and reading through the writings of those who were at the centre of these movements I found I was experiencing them not as dry historical facts but as living fears, hatreds and hopes.

Reading the controversy between Thomas More and William Tyndale, for example, I began to see why Protestantism seemed so outrageous to conservative souls like More, and why it turned him from the witty, open-minded humanist who wrote the *Utopia* to a rabid heretic-burner. But I saw, too, why Protestantism seemed so wonderful and liberating to its converts, especially the poor and powerless, and why they were ready to go to the flames for its sake. More was a lawyer and he felt, quite understandably, that he had justice and reason on his side. He believed that if you do good deeds on earth you will be rewarded in heaven. That fair and sensible arrangement was what the Catholic church taught and it was called 'justification by works'. Tyndale and the Protestant reformers proposed something entirely different, something which seemed, to Catholics, monstrous and mad. It was called 'justification by faith' and it meant, in effect, that if you believed you were saved you were saved. Being good, Tyndale teaches, is not doing good but feeling good. You feel God's spirit in your heart. It's like sunshine inside you, 'soul health', organic not outward. You don't have to try to do good any longer. Indeed, trying to do good is pointless because, as Tyndale observes, no one ever has obeyed or ever could obey the ten commandments. Morality, effort, laws are things of the past. If good deeds do not come as naturally as leaves to a tree – as Keats said of poetry – they had better not come at all. The tree image is fundamental for Tyndale. The words 'tree' and 'fruit' fill his pages, along with other garden language: planting, weeding, ripeness; root, blossom, pith. This reflects his Gloucestershire farming background, but there is also a doctrinal reason for it. His basic manoeuvre is to capture the horticultural texts like 'a good tree bringeth forth good fruit' (Matthew 7:17) which had traditionally been in the justification-by-works camp. The fruit, Tyndale points out, does not make the tree good, but the tree the fruit. You have to be good before you can do good. The Catholic church, he insists, by teaching that good deeds make you good, 'turneth the roots of the tree upward'. This intensely personal idea of faith as something internal and special to every believer struck at the economic fabric of Catholic Christendom. Basic to that was the assumption that spiritual assets are transferable, and can be bought and sold – hence the Church's machinery of pardons, indulgences, chantry chapels and prayers for souls in purgatory. Tyndale dismissed it all as nonsense. One tree cannot bear fruit for another. It was this simple logic that would set Europe alight. Armies would march, thousands would be massacred, martyrs on both sides would die horrible deaths, and centuries of priceless artistic endeavour – abbeys, shrines, cathedrals – would be reduced to rubble and broken glass.

The scientific revolution was quieter, though eventually more world-shaking, and it too was clearly visible in the prose works I was reading. Science depends on observation and on the belief that observation will show you what is real. In his *Novum Organum* Francis Bacon (who was looked upon by the mid-seventeenth-century founders of the Royal Society as the father of modern science) makes his observations in a winningly amateurish way, but deduces scientific truths from them. He notices, for example, how the nails in garden walls holding the wires for fruit trees grow loose in winter, and he sees it as an illustration of the fact that iron contracts with cold and expands when heated. This was a new way of looking at things. Neither More nor Tyndale would have bothered with such an observation or thought it of any importance if brought to their notice. Bacon applied his observational method to other subjects besides the physical world – to economics, for example, expressing his findings with gnomic terseness: 'Money is like muck, not good except it be spread.' When it is applied to psychology the method can sound callous: 'Deformed persons, and eunuchs, and old men, and bastards, are envious. For he that cannot possibly mend his own case will do what he can to impair another's.' But callousness is not its purpose. The aim is simply to see things as they are. It can generate patience and tolerance:

There is no man doth a wrong for the wrong's sake, but thereby to purchase himself profit or pleasure or honour or the like. Therefore, why should I be angry with a man for loving himself better than me? And if any man should do wrong merely out of ill nature, why, yet it is but like the thorn or briar, which prick and scratch because they can do no other.

Compared to the fury that religion bred, science seems here sane and liberating. Bacon's *New Atlantis*, the world's first science-fiction novel, depicts an island utopia ruled by wise scientists.

Sir Thomas Browne, who won European fame with *Religio Medici*, written in the 1630s, was a scientist as well as a Christian, and he inherited Bacon's sanity. He muses with satisfaction on the difference between his own reasonableness and the prejudices of his Norfolk neighbours: 'I could digest a salad gathered in a churchyard as well as in a garden.' He is perfectly happy to eat frogs, snails and toadstools. At the sight of snakes or scorpions, 'I find in me no desire to take up a stone to destroy them.' Though a Protestant, he deplores Protestant vandalism: 'I should cut off my arm rather than violate a church window'; 'I could never divide myself from any man upon the difference of an opinion.' Nearly all his scientific knowledge was wrong, nevertheless he is a shining advertisement for science. He was not afraid to think in new ways – about sex, for example:

I could be content that we might procreate like trees, without conjunction, or that there were any way to perpetuate the world without this trivial and vulgar act of coition. It is the foolishest act a wise man commits in all his life, nor is there anything that will more deject his cooled imagination, when he shall consider what an odd and unworthy piece of folly he hath committed.

Nowadays, partly because of the anxieties of an ageing population, we consider sex the highest good, so Browne seems outrageous. But he is simply being rational, and comparing, in a spirit of scientific detachment, the human species and its curious means of reproduction with other forms of life.

This ability to look at human beings in a new and objective way reached its apogee, in the period I was covering, in Thomas Hobbes, whose *Leviathan* came out in 1651. Here is Hobbes on laughter.

Joy, arising from imagination of a man's own power and ability, is that exultation of the mind which is called glorying . . . Sudden glory is the passion which maketh those grimaces called laughter, and is caused either by some sudden act of their own which pleaseth them, or by the apprehension of some deformed thing in another by comparison whereof they suddenly applaud themselves. And it is incident most to them that are conscious of the fewest abilities in themselves, who are forced to keep themselves in their own favour by observing the imperfections of other men.

Years after reading that I was asked by Adam Phillips, who had been a student of mine at St John's, to write an introduction to Freud's *The Joke and Its Relation to the Unconscious* for the new Penguin Modern Classics translations of Freud that he was editing. Freud's examples of jokes seemed to me unfunny, and I found his speculations about why human beings laugh much less persuasive than Hobbes's caustic Baconian realism.

By comparison with these great works of sixteenth- and seventeenth-century non-fiction the literary fiction of the period – the romances of Lyly, Sidney, Greene, Lodge and so forth – struck me as feeble-witted. The exception was Thomas Nashe, best known as the author of *The Unfortunate Traveller*, whose writing boils and bubbles with a figurative richness only Shakespeare can match. But even in Nashe thought and ideas are in short supply. It reads like a howl of laughter modulating into a howl of despair, and I wondered whether he was generally drunk when he wrote.

Soon after my arrival in St John's the English faculty decided, partly because of the grumbles of the Bateson set, to drag itself into modern times. A date was fixed, a couple of years ahead, when Victorian literature would enter the syllabus and a later date when the twentieth century would. Luckily I'd finished the *Christian Doctrine* translation and the Milton edition (published 1968) and the *Sphere History* chapters (published 1970) by this time, so I could get ready for teaching the new periods, and I started with Christopher Ricks's edition of Tennyson, which had just come out. Reading the poems in chronological order – as the Ricks edition prints them – it was easy to see how they deteriorated as he got older, especially after 1850 when he accepted the poet laureateship, married, settled down and became respectable. When I got to the high Victorian bunkum of *The Idylls of the King* I wondered how Christopher could have had the patience to edit such stuff. But the young Tennyson was very different. For one thing, he was distinctly feminine – which contemporary critics noticed and mocked. Both 'Mariana' and 'The Lady of Shalott' are written from the perspective of lovelorn women yearning for a man. The Lady of Shalott relishes Lancelot's male accessories while peering secretly at him in her mirror.

> All in the blue unclouded weather
> Thick-jewelled shone the saddle-leather,
>   The helmet and the helmet-feather

> Burned like one burning flame together,
> As he rode down to Camelot.

Arthur Hallam, the college friend whose early death Tennyson mourned in *In Memoriam A.H.H.*, was still alive when 'The Lady of Shalott' was written, and it is hard not to connect the Lady's adoration of Lancelot with Tennyson's love for his perfect knight, Arthur.

Death was Tennyson's great subject. He was drawn to it from an early age. As a little boy he used to lie on the grass in Somersby churchyard and pray to be dead. As a young man he wrote a poem mourning his mother's death. In fact she was perfectly fit and lived on for many years, and from this angle it might be said that Hallam's death – though personally distressing – was just what Tennyson's poetry had been waiting for. The early poems make death gentle and alluring. The mythical Tithonus, granted immortality but not eternal youth, bemoans not being able to die as he lies in the arms of his love, Aurora, the goddess of the dawn:

> The woods decay, the woods decay and fall,
> The vapours weep their burthen to the ground,
> Man comes and tills the field and lies beneath,
> And after many a summer dies the swan.
> Me only cruel immortality
> Consumes; I wither slowly in thine arms,
> Here at the quiet limit of the world,
> A white-haired shadow roaming like a dream
> The ever-silent spaces of the East,
> Far-folded mists and gleaming halls of morn.

In 'Ulysses' the old warrior, home from the Trojan War, finds peaceful life in Ithaca empty and boring, and urges his comrades to gather their strength for one last adventure which will be a quest for death.

> Some work of noble note may yet be done,
> Not unbecoming men that strove with Gods.
> The lights begin to twinkle from the rocks:
> The long day wanes: the slow moon climbs: the deep
> Moans round with many voices. Come, my friends,
> 'Tis not too late to seek a newer world.
> Push off, and sitting well in order smite
> The sounding furrows, for my purpose holds
> To sail beyond the sunset, and the baths
> Of all the western stars, until I die.

But *In Memoriam* replaces the myth and marvel of these poems with a more realistic way of facing death, which finds no escape from the emptiness death leaves.

> He is not here; but far away
>   The noise of life begins again,
>   And ghastly through the drizzling rain
> On the bald street breaks the blank day.

In Memoriam is not just about Hallam's death but about the death of humanity. Tennyson had read Sir Charles Lyell's *Principles of Geology*, which traced the changes in land-masses and oceans that had taken place over millions of years and foretold that the same processes of change would eventually eliminate the human race and every trace of its existence. Tennyson incorporated this fearful knowledge into *In Memoriam*, imagining geological change as a kind of speeded-up film:

> The hills are shadows, and they flow
>   From form to form, and nothing stands,

> They melt like mist, the solid lands,
>   Like clouds they shape themselves and go.

One great poem interrupted Tennyson's post-1850 decline – 'Maud', published in 1855. Ostensibly a dramatic monologue spoken by a crazed killer, 'Maud' gives voice to the black passions that had been boiling inside Tennyson for decades. He hated and envied his uncle's family, the Tennyson d'Eyncourts, who had inherited the wealth and status that should, he thought, have gone to his own father. He detested what he saw as the vulgar upstarts who were making fortunes in Victorian commerce and industry. Their success was an affront, he felt, to old aristocrats like himself, descended (as he fancied) from the Plantagenet kings. He nursed a grudge against Rosa Baring, the daughter of a banking family, who, years back, had discouraged his advances. All these resentments come roaring to the surface in 'Maud', and the poem ends in an apocalypse of warmongering bloodlust as the hero, having murdered Maud's (or Rosa's) brother, goes off to fight in the Crimea. But amid the fury is passionate love – linked to death as in Tennyson it always is:

> She is coming, my own, my sweet,
>   Were it never so airy a tread,
> My heart would hear her and beat,
>   Were it earth in an earthy bed;
> My dust would hear her and beat,
>   Had I lain for a century dead;
> Would start and tremble under her feet,
>   And blossom in purple and red.

Browning seemed the obvious big poet to tackle next. We had read 'The Pied Piper of Hamelin' at school, but otherwise he was a blank, and it seemed hard to believe, once I started reading him, that he belonged to the same century as Tennyson. By comparison he is a modern, almost a modernist poet. His dramatic monologues anticipate stream-of-consciousness techniques. His knotty syntax is based partly on Donne, whom, like T. S. Eliot, he much admired. To decipher it you need to use your intelligence, whereas with Tennyson you can safely switch off your intelligence before you start. Browning was fascinated by the contradictions inside people ('The honest thief, the tender murderer,/The superstitious atheist'), especially artists and those entangled in the complexities of religion. The monk who speaks the 'Soliloquy of the Spanish Cloister' is both pious and poisonous. He hates Brother Lawrence, who is trying to grow melons as a treat for his brethren, and Browning makes us laugh with him, becoming complicit in his hatred.

> Oh, those melons? If he's able
>   We're to have a feast! So nice!
> One goes to the Abbot's table,
>   All of us get each a slice.
> How go on your flowers? None double?
>   Not one fruit-sort can you spy?
> Strange! – And I, too, at such trouble,
>   Keep them close-nipped on the sly!

The wily old sinner who pours himself onto the page in 'The Bishop Orders His Tomb at St Praxed's Church' is more repellent, but still recognisably human in his longing for beauty. On his deathbed he tells his sons where to find a lump of lapis lazuli, hidden away long ago, that will be the glory of his monument:

> Big as a Jew's head cut off at the nape,
> Blue as a vein o'er the Madonna's breast . . .

The suddenly shocking similes reveal – it seems inadvertently – the brutality and lust coiled within the bishop's aestheticism.

The poem the Victorians regarded as Browning's masterwork was *The Ring and the Book*, and in it his focus changes from the complexities within single individuals to the complexity of human nature, as shown in differing accounts of the same event. Based on a real-life murder that Browning had read about in an 'old yellow book' picked up in a flea market in Florence, it tells the story of an impoverished nobleman, Count Guido, who, in 1698, was found guilty of murdering his wife Pompilia and her parents because he suspected her of having an affair with a young canon, Giuseppe Caponsacchi. The poem's twelve books are allocated to different speakers. Guido, Pompilia and Caponsacchi all have their say; so do their lawyers, the gossips on the streets of Rome, and Pope Innocent XII, whom Guido unsuccessfully appealed to. Each book is a marvel of rhetorical ingenuity, and you finish it convinced of the case it makes out, until you read the next book and feel your certainties unravelling. Browning is able to empathise even with Guido. In the condemned cell he thinks about the new, purpose-built, red-painted scaffold outside, on which he will be executed.

> . . . the twelve-foot space of scaffold, railed
> Considerately round to elbow-height,
> For fear an officer should tumble thence
> And sprain his ankle and be lame a month
> Through starting when the axe fell and head too!

Being capable of irony at such a moment earns our admiration, whatever Guido is guilty of.

My favourite character though was (is) Guido's lawyer Dominus Hyacinthus de Archangelis. Because he is superfluous, just an extravagant frill on the poem's edge, with no real part in the story, Browning can use him as an outlet for sheer creative exuberance. Vain, pedantic, keen on the pleasures of the table, eager to display his erudition and dotingly attentive to his little son Giacinto, Hyacinthus cares nothing for the moral questions that worry his creator. He is simply in it for the money – 'Tra-la-la, for, lambkins, we must live!' is his exit line.

Reading Browning after Tennyson I began to see how vital escapism is to Victorian poetry. The dramatic monologue is an escape into another personality. Browning's move to Italy was an escape, so was his fascination with Italy's gorgeous and sinful past. The Victorian age – booming, expansive – made Britain the greatest power on earth. Yet its poets wanted nothing so much as to be out of it. Browning's strangest and greatest poem, 'Childe Roland to the Dark Tower Came', is another escape and what it escapes from is meaning. It is spoken by a knight who describes a quest across a blighted landscape full of horrors. At the end the object of his quest, the dark tower, is suddenly before him. Around stand rows of phantoms. It is like a chivalric legend reworked by Hieronymus Bosch. None of the suggested meanings makes sense, and Browning himself said he had no idea what it meant. It came to him 'as a kind of dream'. The loss of conscious intention frees him to reach beyond morality to something deeper. At one point the knight comes upon a wretched, blinded horse standing alone in the wasteland, and he reacts with loathing.

> I never saw a brute I hated so;
> He must be wicked to deserve such pain.

The contorted reasoning takes us to a primitive level where suffering is ugly, and prompts not sympathy but loathing.

Another of Browning's most haunting poems, 'Waring', is about a friend who escapes by emigrating. Browning thinks of him as flitting anonymously from land to land – India, Russia, Spain – and perhaps being glimpsed, just for a few seconds, accompanied by a mysterious boy, in a small sailing boat off Trieste –

> The boat,
> I know not how, turned sharply round,
> Laying her whole side on the sea
> As a leaping fish does; from the lee
> Into the weather, cut somehow
> Her sparkling path beneath our bow
> And so went off, as with a bound,
> Into the rosy and golden half
> O' the sky, to overtake the sun . . .

So Waring escapes. All that's certain is he's somewhere:

> Oh, never star
> Was lost here but it rose afar!
> Look East, where whole new thousands are!
> In Vishnu land what Avatar?

I had to look up 'avatar', but finding its meaning didn't add much. What I loved was the blaze of noise it makes at the poem's end, triumphant as the blare of a trumpet.

The most poignant dreams of escape I found came in Matthew Arnold. I'd read, and loved, 'Sohrab and Rustum' at school, but reading his poems right through only made me admire him more. 'Dover Beach' is about the Victorians' loss of religious faith. But it also describes how it feels to be alive in any age, including ours.

> . . . we are here as on a darkling plain,
> Swept with confused alarms of struggle and flight,
> Where ignorant armies clash by night.

The escape the poem offers, now that Christianity has failed, is faithful love ('O love, let us be true to one another . . .'). In 'The Forsaken Merman' though, another favourite of mine, love fails. The faithless human mother leaves her children and her Merman mate, and they creep up onto the land and see her praying in church. It has the cruel tang of a fairy tale.

Arnold's best-known escape poem, 'The Scholar-Gipsy', is based on a legend that there was once a poor scholar at Oxford who forsook his studies and joined a band of gipsies to learn their secret knowledge. For many years people reported catching glimpses of him in woods and fields and country villages. The poem imagines him as immortal, still wandering, still alone, and advises him to shun the 'strange disease of modern life'. A gloriously complicated simile at the close suddenly escapes from the poem altogether into another story. The scholar-gipsy is likened to a Carthaginian ('Tyrian') trader in classical times, who catches sight of a boatload of Greek merchants heading his way. Wanting to escape them, he sails through the Straits of Gibraltar to the west coast of Spain. Here, according to legend, there lived a race who avoided contact with the rest of mankind. To trade with them you had to leave your goods on the beach and return to your ship. Then, when you had gone, they would come down from the hills, take what they wanted, and leave gold in payment, which you could return and collect when they had gone. Arnold advises his scholar-gipsy to follow the Tyrian's example.

> . . . fly our greetings, fly our speech and smiles!
>   – As some grave Tyrian trader, from the sea,
>   Descried at sunrise an emerging prow
>   Lifting the cool-haired creepers stealthily,
>   The fringes of a southward-facing brow
>   Among the Aegean isles;
>   And saw the merry Grecian coaster come,
>   Freighted with amber grapes, and Chian wine,
>   Green, bursting figs, and tunnies steeped in brine –
>   And knew the intruders on his ancient home,
>
> The young light-hearted masters of the waves –
>   And snatched his rudder, and shook out more sail;
>   And day and night held on indignantly
>   O'er the blue Midland waters with the gale,
>   Betwixt the Syrtes and soft Sicily,
>   To where the Atlantic raves
>   Outside the western straits; and unbent sails
>   There, where down cloudy cliffs, through sheets of foam,
>   Shy traffickers, the dark Iberians come;
>   And on the beach undid his corded bales.

The word I liked best was 'indignantly', which reminded me of Yeats's 'The Second Coming', where the monster slouching towards Bethlehem is surrounded by 'shadows of the indignant desert birds'. In both places 'indignant', often a rather petty word, becomes serious.

'The Scholar-Gipsy' had a special closeness for us, because Gill and I had got into the way of doing country walks round Oxford, so the places the poem mentions – Cumnor, Bablock Hythe, Godstow, Fyfield – were familiar. The 'lone alehouse in the Berkshire moors', where 'smock-frocked boors' catch sight of the wanderer, has always reminded me of South Leigh. We had gone there to see the medieval wall paintings in the church, and dropped into the pub for a drink. There was quite a din as we pushed the door open, and the bar was full of rustic types, all male, mostly old, and each, it seemed, accompanied by a dog – though it was hard to be sure through the fog of tobacco smoke. The instant we entered everyone stopped talking. It was as if a film had suddenly jammed. Tankards were arrested in mid-air. One or two of the dogs growled. I ordered a beer and Gill asked for lemonade. This caused some difficulty, but the aged lady behind the bar eventually unearthed a cobwebbed bottle and poured Gill a drink. Every eye was fixed on us, and not a word was spoken while we drank. Then we left. The moment we closed the door, the hubbub broke out again inside. It was like stepping into history, and out again minutes later. I feel a pang now when I hear that the place has become an upmarket gastropub with a helipad for celebrity customers.

Whereas Arnold is undervalued as a poet, he is praised as a thinker, and *Culture and Anarchy* is optimistically quoted by academics hoping to reverse the government's cuts in arts funding for universities. This seems wrong-headed. As a thinker Arnold is at best useless and at worst malign. Every thought that comes to him is drenched in the assumptions of his social class. He disparages Keats's love letters to Fanny Brawne, among the most heart-searing in the language, as 'the love letters of a surgeon's apprentice'. They are 'under-bred and ignoble', and shouldn't have been published. He longs for a central authority – constituted of people like himself – that will decide what should and should not be thought and admired. He detests those, such as noncon-formists, who think for themselves. He equates 'dislike of authority' with 'disbelief in right reason'. His famous advice that to acquire 'culture' we should get to know 'the best which has been thought and said in the world' carries with it the assumption that the best which has been thought and said has already been identified by him and his peers, and is not open to individual judgement, which he considers 'anarchic'.

I started trying to fill the gaps in my knowledge of Vic-torian fiction after weeks of immersion in poetry, with the result that I found myself reading novels as if they were patches of poetry interspersed with relatively uninteresting prose – which I still tend to do. My catch-up reading began with Emily Brontë's *Wuthering Heights*. I'd always meant to get round to it but never had, and I found it unexpected-ly tiresome. The idea of Cathy and Heathcliff as wild chil-dren on the moors has great poetic power, of course. But it's essentially timeless, and fitting it up with a plot and a full supporting cast is cumbersome and extraneous. Besides, the minor characters are feeble, and the narrative is tangled and disrupted as if it's trying to hide the unlikelihood of the events. The story is exasperating because the one thing all the passion and violence obviously ought to lead to is forbidden by the conventions of Brontë's day. So instead we have two characters going mad with frustration. Cathy at one point is said to dash her head against a sofa and grind her teeth, almost reducing them to splinters. Besides being ridiculous, this is no substitute for seeing her and Heathcliff in bed together. I realise that these objections may appear coarse and masculine, and apologise if they do. However, an aspect of the novel that appears coarse to me is the simmering female desire, running through the narrative, for males to be brutal and violent, like hugely sexy Heathcliff, and not weaklings like Edgar and Linton.

The principle behind the poetry in Charlotte Brontë, on the other hand, seemed to me to be self-control, which no one in *Wuthering Heights* could be accused of. Self-control means despising passion and taking pride in austerity. When Lucy Snowe in *Villette* wakes in the cold dawn she revels in the discomfort. 'How deeply I drank of the ice-cold water in my carafe!' The same thirst for bleakness draws young Jane Eyre, when she is reading Bewick's *History of British Birds*, to the 'solitary rocks and promontories' where sea-fowl gather. Fierce frugality of this calibre breeds a sharp critical intelligence – another thing *Wuthering Heights* lacks. Blanche Ingram and the other young ladies in Rochester's luxurious drawing room are scrutinised by Jane with relentless contempt. Lucy Snowe is equally critical of Rubens's painting of Cleopatra. An 'enormous piece of claptrap', depicting a woman who must, she estimates, weigh fourteen stone 'lounging away the noon on a sofa'. Actually Charlotte Brontë invented the painting that Lucy hates. Rubens's *Cleopatra* is a more subdued affair, showing Cleopatra about to commit suicide with an asp.

Puritan distrust of passion and luxury seemed to me the bedrock of George Eliot's art too. Beneath the bright surface of upper-middle-class marriage in *Daniel Deronda* – yachts, casinos, carriages in the park – she exposes an inner world crawling with hate and terror, racked by visions of fangs, serpents and throttling fingers, which eventually erupts in murder. In *Felix Holt, the Radical* Mrs Transome, a doomstruck eagle of a woman, looks out, we're told, across a frozen landscape at 'far-off unheeding stars'. She lives 'in the midst of desecrated sanctities, and of honours that looked tarnished in the light of monotonous and weary suns'. In the structure of the novel her forlorn grandeur is set against the vitality of the little black boy Harry, whose mother was a slave. In one surreal scene Harry, dressed in red and purple, flits 'like a great tropical bird' among the classical statues at Transome Court, while two squirrels scamper around with him and peer down from among the stuccoed angels on the ceiling. Written in the wake of Darwin's 1859 *The Origin of Species*, the novel seems to contrast, through images like these, animal naturalness and the worn-out facades of western culture.

But the most powerful poetic images in Eliot's novels cluster around the figures of Dorothea and Casaubon in *Middlemarch*. On their honeymoon in Rome Dorothea is confused by the vastness of St Peter's, and the red drapery, hung round the interior for Christmas, seems 'like a disease of the retina'. Poor Casaubon's 'frigid rhetoric', when he tries to address Dorothea as a wooer, is 'as sincere as the bark of a dog or the cawing of an amorous rook'. His antiquarian research is a 'small taper of learned theory exploring the tossed ruins of the world'. The contempt is relentless and devastating. But when Casaubon has a heart attack and finds himself facing death, Eliot makes us recognise this dusty freak as a fellow creature, with our wants and fears. The rehabilitation has the educative value of all great writing. Eliot is by a long stretch the most intelligent of English novelists, and she is unusual in using poetry in the service of thinking. Take this:

> If we had a keen vision and feeling of all ordinary human life, it would be like hearing the grass grow and the squirrel's heart beat, and we should die of that roar which lies on the other side of silence. As it is, the quickest of us walk about well-wadded with stupidity.

The tenderness of the heartbeat and the shock of the roar would be marvellous simply as a poetic moment. But it is also part of an argument.

The complete set of Dickens's novels that I read, and still possess, used to be my father's. He was keen on Dickens, and I think got his set free by taking out a subscription to the *Daily Express* in the 1930s. I daresay it doesn't reach the highest modern textual standards, but it's neatly bound in blue and gold, and the back pages of each volume are now so thickly covered with my annotations that I couldn't use any others. Reading Dickens straight after George Eliot made the differences between them very clear. Eliot is great because she is serious and rational. Dickens is great because he is not. He is an anarchic comic genius, and critics who treated him as a moralist seemed to me way off course. Further, he has a weird set of fixations – some sinister, some grotesque, some wildly funny, some all three at once – that have nothing to do with rationality. I started making lists of these as I read – wooden legs, walking coffins, waxworks, stuffed creatures, land-ships, murderers, bottled babies, rickety tenements, public executions, junk-littered wastelands, living furniture, dwarfs – the more the lists grew the more excited I got. I began to see that I might be able to make a sort of map of Dickens's imagination, showing the things that fired it and the things that didn't, and how they connected up. To try out my ideas I made the lists into a set of undergraduate lectures, and they proved more popular than any lectures I'd ever given. I even risked giving them at 9.00 a.m. – an un-heard-of time for Oxford arts undergraduates to stir out of doors – and got an audience.

Somehow Charles Monteith, who was a director of Faber and Faber, got to hear of my ideas about Dickens and asked me to lunch in All Souls. I was awed. He was very grand – tall, with a deep patrician voice and a slight stammer that somehow suggested generations of aristocratic breeding. He also had a limp – a hunting accident, I assumed. Later I found that all this was wrong. He was the son of a Belfast draper, and won a scholarship to Magdalen College, Oxford, where he was taught by C. S. Lewis and got a first in English. When war broke out he was commissioned in the Inniskilling Fusiliers, fought in Burma, and was wounded by a mortar bomb – hence the limp. After the war he came back to Oxford, got a first in law and won a prize fellow-ship to All Souls, entitling him to a room in All Souls for life, which was useful for entertaining Faber authors and for having a look at young hopefuls like me. He had meant to be a barrister, but Geoffrey Faber, who was also a fellow of All Souls, offered him a job in publishing, and in his first few weeks at Faber he rescued William Golding's *Lord of the Flies* from the reject pile. It went on to sell twenty million

copies, and over the next couple of decades Charles recruited an astonishing list of authors for Faber, Samuel Beckett,
Philip Larkin, Ted Hughes and Tom Stoppard among them.

When he joined the firm in 1954 Faber were still in their
original Russell Square offices and he had a little room on
the top floor which had been a maid's bedroom. Across the
passage in another maid's bedroom was T. S. Eliot, then a
director. Eliot died in 1965 but over the years I learned a lot
about him from Charles's affectionate stories. Several related to Eliot's attempts to conform to English ways. He was
under the impression that gentlemen were expected to raise
their hats when passing the sentries at St James's Palace,
which caused some embarrassment to his friends. He was
also fond of traditional English dishes of a kind the English mostly avoid – jugged hare, for example. Once when
Charles was lunching with him at the Garrick Club a distinguished American academic, who was a fellow guest, asked
rather insistently for the name and address of Eliot's tailor.
Eliot, with some reluctance, yielded up the required details.
When the menu arrived jugged hare was listed, and Eliot
instantly chose it. 'Ah! Jugged hare! One of the great English
achievements. I shall certainly have that. Will you two join
me?' Charles, having tried it once, had roast beef, but the
American enthusiastically opted for jugged hare. It arrived,
exuding a powerful gamey smell and surrounded by a pool of
thin, bloody gravy. Eliot tucked in, but his American guest
eyed his helping with dismay and left most of it. In the taxi
on the way back to Faber Eliot was meditative, but broke
the silence to remark, 'Strange fellow, that, don't you think,
Charles? He wanted the name of my tailor,' adding with a

brief smile, 'I don't think he cared for that jugged hare.'

Of course, no anecdotes of this sort were on offer at my first meeting with Charles. I had never been in All Souls before – it is the most exclusive of Oxford's colleges, having only fellows, no undergraduates – and we lunched in the most beautiful room I had ever been in. A perfect oval in shape, higher than its width, with tall, round-topped windows and a curved, coffered ceiling, it was known in All Souls as the Buttery, and had been designed by Nicholas Hawksmoor in the 1730s. The ancient retainers who served us at table were also a surprise – dignified and doddery, like characters from Mervyn Peake's *Gormenghast*. In the course of lunch Charles's friendly, unobtrusive questioning elicited more or less all there was to know about me, and over coffee he said that Faber would be happy to offer me a contract for a book on Dickens. It was published in 1973 as *The Violent Effigy* – rather a silly title, I now realise, but I wanted something that would suggest both Dickens's appetite for violence and his obsession with things, from ships' figureheads to the cast-offs in old clothes shops, which, though not human, took on human shape. I had been torn between *The Violent Effigy* and *The Violent Waxwork* as title – for waxworks were a kind of effigy Dickens had a special interest in – and one Saturday morning I ran into Charles outside Oxford's Covered Market where, I guess, he was buying provisions for a dinner in All Souls that evening. Islanded among the bustling shoppers and delivery vans we held our brief literary conference. I asked him whether 'Effigy' or 'Waxwork' was better. He answered instantly 'Effigy'. So that settled it. On publication day he sent me a congratulatory telegram. It was a thing he did with all his authors when they brought out a book, but it made me feel special.

It didn't get many reviews but the ones it did get were pretty good. Paul Bailey was generous in the *Observer,* and Sylvère Monod, the great French translator of Dickens, called it 'exhilarating' – though unfortunately in an obscure scholarly French periodical. It got a rave review in, of all places, the *Australian*, which kind Charles, always on the lookout for the least scrap of encouragement, was quick to spot ('Dear John, What an absolutely splendid review in the *Australian* . . .'). A young reviewer called Martin Amis roughed it up in the *New Statesman*, but a letter arrived from him, typed on *Times Literary Supplement* paper, confessing that he'd been feeling 'rather guilty' about it. As I would appreciate, he said, it was necessary sometimes to take 'an imperious line' in a review to avoid 'just being wetly descriptive', but he had failed to do justice to my 'perceptive and above all marvellously entertaining' book. As a consolation he gave me advance notice that 'a highly-favourable front page review of *The Violent Effigy*' would appear in the next issue of the *TLS* – as it gratifyingly did. Actually I'd much admired the style of his *New Statesman* piece, so I was relieved he wasn't entirely hostile.

I'd started reviewing myself in the mid-1960s – poetry to start with, for Alan Ross in the *London Magazine* and Karl Miller in the *New Statesman*. In one of the earliest batches I got from Karl there was a pamphlet, *Eleven Poems*, by an unknown poet, Seamus Heaney, and I read it with mounting astonishment. If this was the kind of stuff that regularly came the way of poetry reviewers, I thought, then it was a job to hang on to. I found the whole collection masterly, and said so. Two years later Charles and I judged the Geoffrey Faber Memorial Prize and gave it to Seamus for his collection *Death of a Naturalist*. When we met at the prize-giving he thanked me for the review and I confessed it was about the first I'd ever written. He laughed and said it was about the first he'd received. In the years that followed I reviewed each of his collections as they came out, and marvelled again and again not only at the greatness of his gifts but also at the deep personal modesty and naturalness that ran through everything he wrote and said like the grain through wood.

When Karl moved from the *New Statesman* to become editor of the *Listener* in 1967 I wrote radio reviews for him until 1969 when he decided to switch me to television. I knew nothing about television. We didn't even have a set. But it was not for me to reason why, so we hired a set from Radio Rentals and I became one of the *Listener*'s four regular TV reviewers – another was the Cambridge critic Raymond Williams – covering a week's TV each month. I made dreadful mistakes at first, because I didn't recognise even the most famous TV personalities when they appeared on screen – people like bow-tied Robin Day, then a ubiquitous pundit. However, no one seemed to notice, possibly because no one read the column. I didn't trust the post so I used to deliver my copy by hand to the *Listener* office, which was in the Langham Hotel, a BBC annexe opposite Broadcasting House. When it was built in the 1860s the Langham had been the most modern hotel in London, boasting thirty-six bedrooms and a hundred water closets. Famous guests who had passed its portals to use these amenities included Mark

Twain, Napoleon III and Oscar Wilde. But it had been requisitioned by the army during the war and by the 1960s it was in a sad state – shabby corridors, dark lift shafts behind metal grilles, with clashing doors that made everything shake. I seldom got to see Karl. The drill was that I handed my copy to his assistant, Mary-Kay Wilmers, who sat in an outer office, and she read it through while I watched, hoping she would laugh at the jokes, which she never did. Then I was dismissed and she took it into the inner sanctum. It was all a bit tense. But Karl was a superb editor – scrupulous, unsparing. However humiliated I felt when he cut anything, I always came to see he was right in the end. Gill realised I was in terror of him and once, as a joke, she came out to where I was gardening and said that Karl's secretary was on the phone – just to see me go white. I thought it unwifely at the time, but my ideas about wifely conduct were probably a bit out of date. It was in Karl's office that I first met Clive James – well, not actually met, but caught a glimpse of. He dashed in, handed over some copy, and left. I have a vague sense he was wearing running shoes, but that surely can't be right. I was impressed by the speed of metropolitan life.

I was lucky because my years as a television critic coincided almost exactly with the years of *Monty Python's Flying Circus*, which was always by far the most intelligent thing to come out of the screen. I was surprised that the high-ups at the BBC tolerated it, because it was essentially anti-television television. It concentrated on ridiculing the conventions and inherent weaknesses of the medium – the mannerisms of continuity announcers, the constant needless visual aids (film of a bus when talking about buses) and the reduction of serious subjects to idiocy ('The All-England Summarise Proust Competition', 'It's the Arts!'). It was a training course in how to criticise television, and I watched it gratefully. The other programme I liked was the late-night snooker. Our set was black and white – almost no one had colour in those days – so the state of play was hard to follow. But I was gripped by the dramatic details – the waistcoats, the silence punctuated by tiny flurries of applause, the nervous sips of water taken by the player waiting his turn. When Karl switched me from television to book reviewing in 1974 the snooker was what I missed most. However, we felt there was no point keeping our set, so we phoned Radio Rentals to tell them. The two men who came round were built like heavyweight boxers, evidently expecting to have to wrest their property from the bosom of a distraught family unable to keep up the payments. They seemed disappointed we gave it up without a struggle.

The lure of reviewing – TV or books – was that it kept me in touch with what was going on. The theatre did the same. Oxford's Playhouse was round the corner from St John Street, and we went there a lot. Neither of us had ever lived so close to a theatre before, and we used to joke that we could get home and do the washing-up in the interval – though I don't think we ever did, partly because we got to know Elizabeth Sweeting, the Playhouse manager, and she used to invite us up to her office for interval drinks. We once met Kenneth Tynan there, shimmering in a white suit and with his beautiful second wife Kathleen Halton in attendance. He looked haggard and ill, already suffering from the emphysema that would eventually kill him, and seemed like a bit of decoration left over from a party.

The Playhouse's resident company was Frank Hauser's

Meadow Players, which included Judi Dench, Felicity Kendal, Prunella Scales, Leo McKern and Ian McKellen, and their extraordinary repertoire ranged from Camus and Genet to Jonson, Shakespeare and Aristophanes. We saw Sartre's *Huis Clos*, with Jill Bennett and Constance Cummings, then Sartre's *Kean*, with Alan Badel as the swaggering anti-hero, then, in fascinating contrast, Badel as himself playing Othello. Hauser invited Minos Volanakis in to direct Elisabeth Bergner and Hugh Paddick in Giraudoux's *The Mad Woman of Chaillot*, and Nevill Coghill directed Richard Burton and Elizabeth Taylor in Marlowe's *Doctor Faustus*, a production memorable for the magnificent clouds of dry ice that almost obliterated the action. In 1964 we saw Judi Dench for the first time as Irina in *Three Sisters* and the next year as Dol Common in *The Alchemist*. Leo McKern was a magnificent Volpone, with Leonard Rossiter as a simpering, abject Corvino, and Philip Voss and Lewis Fiander collaborated in an uproarious production of *The Silent Woman*. Morose's protective headgear with its huge fur ear-flaps remains an indelible memory. Barbara Jefford played Cleopatra to John Turner's Antony, and in an OUDS *Coriolanus* Charles Sturridge, looking boyish as Coriolanus should, exited with a spectacular backward somersault.

Hauser was a keen Shavian and put on a spectrum of Shaw in the course of the 1960s – *Arms and the Man*, *The Doctor's Dilemma*, *Major Barbara*, *Misalliance* (with Barbara Jefford as Lina), *Saint Joan* (Nyree Dawn Porter) and a *Heartbreak House* with a third-act explosion so realistic that the audience squealed in alarm. In addition to all this, Prospect Theatre Company, which Elizabeth Sweeting had helped to found, brought plays to Oxford on tour – Ian McKellen as Shake-speare's Richard II and Marlowe's Edward II and, later, with the Actors' Company, as Giovanni in *'Tis Pity She's a Whore*, coming on at the end brandishing Felicity Kendal's heart on the point of his dagger. Prospect made a point of rescuing plays that were hardly ever performed, so it would have been a sin not to see them while we could, or so we reasoned as we happily set off for Otway's *Venice Preserved* and Wycher-ley's *The Country Wife* and Etherege's *The Man of Mode* and Vanbrugh's *The Relapse* and *The Provoked Wife* (with Trevor Martin and Eileen Atkins as Sir John and Lady Brute) and Maggie Smith in Farquhar's *The Recruiting Officer* (though I think this was a visiting National Theatre production, not Prospect) and lots more.

Although we had theatreland on our doorstep, the bit of Oxford we lived in was more like a village than a city. The vast concrete slab of the university offices had not yet reared itself over Little Clarendon Street. There were just a few small shops – Mr Wiggins's dairy where we got our milk, a tailor who did alterations, and the Duke of Cambridge pub where, it was said, you could get pheasants drawn and plucked. A turning a few doors from us led to a lane with tiny houses called Beaumont Buildings, where Elizabeth Sweeting lived, and at the far end were a few arches, said to be the last remains of Beaumont Palace where Richard I had been born in 1157. On Sunday mornings in summer the Salvation Army brass band would gather in Beaumont Buildings and play hymns – all in uniform, with the women in their smart black bonnets trimmed with red. It struck us that my parents might like to come and live in the house for a week or two in the summer, while we were off walking in Normandy, and perhaps explore Oxford a little without too much exertion. They did, and when we got back it was clear they had enjoyed it a lot. My father talked with interest about Oxford sights and my mother giggled at the modern gadgetry the college had fitted 38 St John Street up with.

It was a comfort, looking back, to think of their happiness, because it was their last holiday together. My father died of a stroke the next year. He'd had a stroke a couple of years earlier but made a good recovery. This one killed him at once. We had driven down to see them, as we did most weekends, just a couple of days before, and he seemed fine. We took him shopping in the Mini in the afternoon and he got us to stop at a greengrocer's where he bought a bag of peaches as a surprise for my mother. It was just an ordinary brown-paper bag with four or five peaches in it, but it was his last present to her, and I often think of it as a symbol of what he was – unshowy, kind and faithful.

I don't think my mother wanted to survive him, and she died two years later in 1968. Marjorie was with her, I was not. She didn't want to see me at the end, partly, I think, to spare me upset. In her code, serious matters like birth and death were for women to deal with, and men should be shielded from them. Soon afterwards Bill went into a psychiatric hospital, first at Basingstoke, then at Banstead in Surrey. As Marjorie had married in 1970 and moved back to Nottinghamshire, and Rosemary was with her husband in Venezuela, we were his only relatives within easy visiting distance. We drove over to see him at weekends, and until his death in 1973 I would collect him and bring him to Oxford for Christmas and Easter. He was frail and withdrawn, and these were not happy times.

For several years, to cheer ourselves up, we took a week's break in January to visit art galleries – in Paris, Brussels or Amsterdam. Currency restrictions at the time banned tourists from taking more than £50 abroad each year, so we lived frugally. In Paris we found a student restaurant (called Il Serail) which served delicious *piperade*, and was run by a stern woman with a ravaged face who might have stepped out of a Toulouse-Lautrec. In Amsterdam we stuffed ourselves with *broodjes* as insulation against the Arctic winds that shrieked across the Damrak. We spent all and every day in the galleries, and learned more than we had ever known before about western art. In Paris, besides the Louvre and the Musée Rodin, we were lucky to find special exhibitions of Ingres and Giacometti. From Amsterdam we took day trips to the Mauritshuis, to Delft and to the Franz Hals museum in Haarlem. I discovered that the Dutch school meant most to me, because it took ordinary life seriously. It was not just the Rembrandts and Vermeers. I was drawn as irresistibly to less celebrated things – Saenredam's bare white church interiors, scraped clean of Catholic decoration, or the still life painters who registered the passing world in an overturned glass, a drop of water, walnut shells, or a lemon, stripped and glistening, with its peel hanging from it in a springy loop.

Actually we did take one day off from gallery duty in Paris to visit the Jardin des Plantes, as an act of homage to Rilke's panther. It was eerie. As it was midwinter, the whole place was deserted. The big cats were in their indoor winter quarters – a circular building with cages facing inwards all round its rim.

We were the only visitors, and when we walked into the huge echoing enclosure several of the lions padded over and looked thoughtfully at us through the bars. The effect was strangely intimate. We felt it was quite on the cards that one of them might push open a door and step out and join us, and we were glad to get back to art.

9

Graves, Larkin and Catching Up with the Twentieth Century

Going back to St John's as a fellow meant a switch in perspective. The remote authority figures of my undergraduate days now reappeared as human beings. The don in whose room shivering entrance candidates had waited, gazing forlornly at a rocking horse, turned out to be a delightful ancient historian with a lisp called Nicholas Sherwin White. The don whose question about Horace and Virgil had so taken me aback at my interview was transformed into Donald Russell, a gentle, wise, learned classicist. There were also younger fellows, appointed since I was a student – Keith Thomas, author of *Religion and the Decline of Magic,* who was said to be intimidating, but seemed witty and genial to Gill and me, and Jim Reed, later the Taylor Professor of German, who did his best to amplify my inadequate ideas about Thomas Mann. Then there was the distinguished architectural historian Howard Colvin, a shy, whimsical figure who waged a long campaign to remove all flower beds from the college garden on the grounds that in the eighteenth century there would have been only trees and bushes. Each year he and his wife gave a party when the colourful display of irises in their north Oxford garden bloomed. My opposite number, teaching medieval literature, was Tom Shippey, a science fiction fanatic who later moved to a professorship in St Louis and became the world authority on the mythical universe of Tolkien.

Teaching at St John's was so enjoyable I felt it was wrong to be paid for it. I was able to choose which entrance candidates to accept, and I had time to teach them singly, if I wanted to, rather than in pairs. I often let tutorials go on well past the usual hour if the discussion was throwing up interesting ideas. Years later I heard that one of my ex-students, when he was appointed to a lectureship at a provincial university, innocently proposed they should give the same amount of time to teaching as I had at St John's. He was laughed at, on the grounds that their staff-to-student ratio made it impossible. All the same I think he had a point, and the current abandonment of regular tutor–student contact in many English universities seems to me a disgrace.

The President of St John's in 1965 was John Mabbott, host of the chilly dessert party in my first term. We got on reasonably well, with one slight hiccup. I thought it would be a good idea if the college made the poet Robert Graves, who had been a student at St John's, an honorary fellow. But when I mentioned this to Mabbott he showed signs of agitation. Did I not realise, he asked, that Graves's extra-marital relationship with the American poet Laura Riding, back in the 1920s, had severely upset the villagers of Islip, where the Graves family had settled – and where Mabbott and his wife now resided? I was surprised. Graves's affair with Riding was, of course, common knowledge, and an important chapter in literary history. When reading about it I'd discovered that I had a kind of – admittedly remote – historical connection with it. For on the far side of Hammersmith Bridge stood a block of flats which my mother and I used to pass on our way to Palmers Stores, and it was from a window on the third floor of this building that Riding had, during some amorous disagreement, suicidally precipitated herself. Graves had prudently run down to the first floor before launching himself into the air to join her. Happily, neither of them was fatally hurt. However, it did not seem the best moment for regaling Mabbott with the serio-comic details of this episode, so I contented myself with questioning whether the sensibilities of the good folk of Islip could really outweigh the college's desire to honour a distinguished alumnus. Mabbott was unpersuadable, and since I declined to withdraw my proposal – as he requested – he did some effective lobbying among the senior fellows. So when Graves's possible honorary fellowship came up before the governing body, it did not get the required two-thirds majority.

However, this story had a happy ending. In 1969 Mabbott retired and Richard Southern succeeded him as President of St John's. Lean, witty and an intellectual to his fingertips, Southern had been Chichele Professor of modern history, coming to prominence in 1953 with a landmark study, *The Making of the Middle Ages*. Something of the medieval abbot hung about him, and it was jokingly said that when the St John's examination results were worse than expected he would call the college together for prayer and fasting. Certainly the end-of-term Collections, when each undergraduate appeared before him for a progress report, became more bracing than they had been under Mabbott. At all events, when Southern heard of the proposal to make Graves an honorary fellow he was instantly in favour, and it went through the governing body unopposed.

Graves was delighted, as I'd guessed he would be. Though he liked to be thought a maverick he was deeply traditional, immensely proud of his old school, Charterhouse, and his old regiment, the Royal Welch Fusiliers, and to show how seriously he took the honour St John's had bestowed he travelled from his home in Majorca to attend the first College Gaudy after his election. I sat opposite him at dinner and he was in high spirits, at one point throwing a small bunch of grapes as a kind of thank-offering which just missed landing in my neighbour's soup. As all the college guest rooms were booked it was arranged that Gill and I should put him up in St John Street, and his wife Beryl had dropped him off during that afternoon. Graves at seventy-eight was still a commanding sight – the ramrod back, the shaggy halo of grizzled curls, the haughty face with its broken nose, like a slightly battered Greek god. Every inch a British officer, this was still the Graves who, as I knew from his masterpiece *Goodbye to All That*, had gone out to the trenches fresh from school in 1914 declaring, 'France is the only place for a gentleman now.'

But the older Graves was a seer and a magician as well as an officer, and from his lips there issued, in clipped, upper-class tones, a bizarre jumble of superstition and fictive history. He showed Gill and me the rings he was wearing and explained their mysteries. One – large, amber-coloured and oval – had an Arabic inscription which a Sufi friend had told him only members of his family could translate, and which, when translated, was found to refer to Graves, though he had picked it up by chance. Another ring had a greyish, smaller, transparent stone carved with a bird. While looking for a cornelian for a necklace for his god-daughter on a stall in London he had turned one over and found it was carved with the same bird, by the same hand. He produced from his pocket a third stone – blueish, veined and dome-shaped, an inch or so across – which he had discovered was a meteorite. He knew this was true because a scientist friend had told him so after looking at it under a microscope, and the stone was now 'working' for the Sufi friend, who had fallen ill. He talked of his friendship with Robert Frost, and of Frost's riddle poem which asks what walls don't like – to which the answer is frost – and he presented us with a rid-dle of his own: what word can have its metrical quantity lessened by the addition of a letter? The answer is 'beatified' which with an added 'u' becomes 'beautified'. He thought Stephen Spender ought to get the Oxford professorship of poetry – 'they should let him have it', he said, pityingly – and that W. H. Auden was a 'traitor' for staying in Ameri-ca during the war, and he never wanted to meet him again. Then there were the Etruscans. They had discovered nuclear radiation, which was proved by the hardness of their clay. A young relative of his by marriage had developed hard clay for use in nuclear reactors, but the Etruscans had done it first. Their mazes at Chiusi and on Lemnos were for the disposal of nuclear waste, and probably of contaminated workers too, and Hephaestus, the god with a forge, limped because he had been maimed in a nuclear accident.

So it went on, leapfrogging from subject to subject, and we listened, incredulous but spellbound. When I mentioned our vegetable garden he insisted on seeing it and, seizing a spade, turned over my compost, comparing it (favourably) with his own compost on Majorca where, he said, his broad beans were already quite tall (it was May). He regretted not being able to grow broccoli, but his potatoes were his especial pride and he grew his own oranges and lemons and also his own olives which, he explained, he harvested by waiting until they fell and picking them up from the ground. It was hard to get them pressed because there was only one working press left on the island.

On the Saturday morning he was giving a poetry reading at the Oxford Union and I walked down Cornmarket with him. There were early shoppers about and the majestic sight of Graves in full flow turned heads. But he seemed quite oblivious, holding forth in resonant soliloquy about Siegfried Sassoon, whom he had saved from court martial after he made a public anti-war statement, and about Wilfred Owen, from whom he had received a postcard on the day the war ended, but had thrown it away ('I didn't know he'd been killed'). He had an eager audience at the Union, and improvised on various themes in between reading poems. There had been an announcement in *The Times* that John Betjeman had written his first poem since becoming poet laureate, describing a beautiful woman he saw in church, and Graves joked about this 'indiscretion in the vestry'. Viticulturalists, he said, would like to know where the world's oldest Malvoisie vine was and it was in Majorca near his Deia home. It had been there since 1229 and had supplied wine for James of Aragon when he was fighting the Saracens. A butt of Malvoisie used to be the poet laureate's annual allowance, but he now got £200 in lieu – 'which would not buy even half a dozen bottles of this very rare twenty per cent above proof wine'. *Playboy* had reported that he was poet laureate, and he had written 'absolving myself from the charge'. The laureate, he recalled approvingly, used to have to compose and declaim in Latin, but did not now even need a degree in classics.

When it was over he was given a standing ovation, and a crowd of excitedly chattering undergraduates followed us back to St John Street and stormed into the house. Graves seated himself on a rocking chair in the drawing room, and as many of his young worshippers as could cram themselves onto the floor-space sat at his feet, while he talked non-stop, until Beryl and his two sons Juan and Tomas came to pick him up and take him home.

The reason I knew about Graves and Riding and the important ideas about poetry they worked out together (acknowledged by Empson as one source of *Seven Types of Ambiguity*) was that I had, for some months, been filling the gaps in my knowledge of twentieth-century literature ready for the second stage in the Oxford English syllabus update. I had started with D. H. Lawrence because I knew almost nothing about him, and because I'd agreed to write an essay on his ideas for a book Stephen Spender was editing, to be called *D. H. Lawrence, Novelist, Poet, Prophet* (which was eventually published in 1973). So when we went away in the summer I packed a batch of Lawrence to keep me busy.

We'd discovered a cheap travel firm called Murison Small which organised holidays for small groups of young people – usually about a dozen – in Greece, Turkey and the Mediterranean islands – Sicily, Crete, the Cyclades, the Ionian Islands. You flew out in fairly rickety planes – Dakotas – and tended to land on remote airfields not in normal use. On our first Murison Small trip to Greece, I remember, we landed on a grassy strip somewhere along the Gulf of Corinth, with no buildings in sight, and no signs of life at all, until eventually a jeep appeared on the horizon with some Greek officials in it. Murison Small food and accommodation were generally fairly basic, but there were delightfully cheerful girls, dubbed Muribirds, to look after you, and dusty Land Rovers to take you to archaeological sites which, this being the pre-mass tourism era, were often deserted. On one holiday Gill and I went off by ourselves for a day to Olympia, and wandered among the ruins completely alone apart from the cicadas. Anyway, on my Lawrence-reading holiday we flew to Athens, got a boat to Rhodes and a ferry to Kos, where we stayed a fortnight. Then, back in Rhodes, we boarded a caique and sailed to Simi, where we took a bus up through the mountains to the monastery. So my thoughts about Lawrence have ever after been suffused with hot Greek sun and whitewashed churches and the huge plane tree in Kos main square, where the father of medicine, Hippocrates, allegedly did his cures, and the beach we cycled to each day, which had no one but us on it as far as the eye could see, and the shallow bowls of unimaginably delicious Greek yoghurt put to cool each evening on a table outside the creamery.

Looking for Lawrence's ideas, I quickly found, leads you to a contradiction. His writing swarms with ideas, but he also rejected ideas as a falsification of life. Ideas, he maintains, are like dead leaves thrown off from the living tree. They form an 'insentient husk' between man and the universe. 'All the best part of knowledge is inconceivable', and consists of something quite other than ideas. 'All scientists are liars.'

These objections to ideas are, of course, ideas themselves. Lawrence can't get out of the trap, because there's nothing else to think with except ideas. But he tries to make us see that, if he could, he'd communicate in some other way, freed from the limitations of thought. The word he adopted for the kinds of human activity he approved of was 'blood'. 'My great religion is a belief in the blood, the flesh, as being wiser than the intellect.' It follows that education, as we normally understand it, is worse than useless. 'Let all schools be closed at once. The great mass of humanity should never learn to read and write.' Instead, boys should attend craft workshops and learn 'primitive modes of fighting and gymnastics'. Girls should study cooking and needlework.

Once I got over the initial shock, there seemed to me something intoxicating in even the silliest of his ideas, because they were so contemptuous of sense and reason. The very outrageousness kept me reading, agog to see what monstrosity he'd come up with next. Encountering an old convict in Messina whose face displeases him, he comments:

It is a great mistake to abolish the death penalty. If I were dictator, I should order the old one to be hanged at once. I should have judges with sensitive, living hearts, not abstract intellects. And because the instinctive heart recognised a man as evil, I would have that man destroyed. Quickly.

Thinking with your blood, instead of your brain, will not only, as we can see from this, simplify the legal system, it will also considerably alter relations between men and women. The opinions and personality of one's partner will become utterly insignificant. Couples will renounce 'the weary habit of talking and having feelings'. Ideally the man will become simply 'a voiceless column of blood', and humans will learn to make 'weird, wordless cries, like animals'. Gill and I didn't try that. But being on a beach in the blazing sun makes you more aware of your body than usual, and it also makes it easier to read Lawrence without dismissing it all as nonsense. I began to feel quite like a voiceless column of blood as I basted myself with Ambre Solaire. Besides Lawrence is such a master of words that you almost understand what he means when he writes about the blood's power. Cipriano in *The Plumed Serpent* makes 'the air round him seem darker' just by standing still; Lydia Lensky in *The Rainbow* stands in her black coat 'like a silence'.

Sight, like thought, is ultimately an irrelevance in Lawrence, a distraction from the 'vast, phallic, sacred darkness' in which blood contact occurs. He thought that making love in the daylight was 'an evil thing'. The cinema was 'an impertinent curiosity'. If only we could be struck blind, he said in a letter, 'we should find reality in the darkness'. Maurice, in the short story 'The Blind Man', illustrates this. His wife, jumpy from being educated and reading books, hates going into the stables. But Maurice tends the hot horses with sensual power and confidence, though he can't see. The drugged sacrificial victim in 'The Woman Who Rode Away' also comes to apprehend at a profounder level than the visual. She *hears* the womb of her pet bitch conceive, and the earth revolving 'like an immense arrowstring booming'.

Negating sight seems strange in a writer so rapturously alive to the visible. But his apparently visual descriptions often escape the eye's confines. The bright orange crocuses in 'Flowering Tuscany' are heard and felt as much as seen, 'you feel the sound of their radiance'. Touch becomes sacramental. Mellors, in *Lady Chatterley's Lover*, rubs his face over Connie's body, giving and receiving 'the warm live beauty of contact, so much deeper than the beauty of vision'.

Not that Lawrence approves of lovers touching each other in the normal way. He was puritanically repelled by 'cuddling and petting', and feared and detested love. It sucked the valour and wildness out of men, he warned, and glued them to their putrid routines. It was 'a vice, like drink', and could lead only to 'slimy, creepy personal intimacy'. Married couples should not be united in love, but fiercely separate in their 'dynamic blood polarity', like two eagles in mid-air, 'grappling, whirling'. The novels and stories teem with characters who resemble birds, animals and plants – men with animal eyes and girls whose mouths or wombs open 'like a flower'.

Animals were preferable to humans for Lawrence precisely because they don't get personally involved with one another. Love is beneath them. Lou, in the novella *St Mawr*, loves her horse 'because he isn't intimate'. But there was a difficulty about animals for Lawrence. They were good, because they were sensitive and mindless, but they were also ruthless indiscriminate killers. Lou, in *St Mawr*, gets round this unpleasant fact by explaining to her mother that what she has in mind is a higher, composite kind of animal.

I don't consider the cave man is a real animal at all. He's a brute, a degenerate. A pure animal man would be as lovely as a deer or a leopard, burning like a flame fed straight from underneath. And he'd be part of the unseen, like a mouse is, even. And he'd never cease to wonder, he'd breathe silence and unseen wonder, as the partridges do running in the stubble. He'd be all the animals in turn.

Besides mindlessness, the other thing Lawrence considered essential in sexual relations was male dominance. 'The old dominant male', 'the phallic wind rushing through the dark', must arise and sweep away foolish modern notions of equality between the sexes. Feminist writers have had fun with this aspect of Lawrence's credo, and it's one reason why he has slipped out of fashion. His political views are also abhorrent to most people. He believed that mankind is divided into natural aristocrats and natural slaves. Some men just are 'more vividly alive' than others, he believed. That makes them aristocrats, and they should be reverenced as divine beings. Others 'have only faculties', and should be enslaved. Lawrence himself was an aristocrat, of course. 'Life is more vivid in me than in the Mexican who drives the wagon for me', so it's right that Lawrence should be waited on and the Mexican should remain one of the common herd.

The natural aristocrats in his fiction come across as arrogant and selfish, but that's their point. They are meant to offend hidebound, normal readers. Yvette, for example, in *The Virgin and the Gipsy*, shows her aristocratic nature by stealing from the church's War Memorial Window Fund to buy herself stockings. Her father, the vicar, is morally outraged by her conduct, and that shows he is a 'natural slave'. Christianity with its 'craven' doctrines about loving one's neighbour, its 'beggar's whine' about the God of pity, is detestable to Lawrence. It thwarts humanity's natural impulses. It is not natural to turn the other cheek, and when Ursula Brangwen tries it she doesn't feel clean again until she has gone back and almost shaken the other girl's head off.

Socialism (encouraged by 'Jews like Marx') and all other democratic movements are hateful to Lawrence too. His natural aristocrats believe passionately that the 'rabble', backed by police and moralists, is devoted to humiliating them. Ursula feels 'the grudging power of the mob lying in wait for her, the exception'. Ordinary people, without 'daring, beauty or passion', who obey the laws and work for their living (a 'vulgar, sordid and humiliating' thing to do), do not deserve to live. 'It would be much better if they were just wiped out,' says Birkin in *Women in Love*. In a letter of 1908 Lawrence wrote:

> If I had my way, I would build a lethal chamber as big as the Crystal Palace, with a military band playing softly, and a Cinematograph working brightly; then I'd go out in the back streets and main streets and bring them in, all the sick, the halt and the maimed; I would lead them gently, and they would smile me a weary thanks, and the band would softly bubble out the 'Hallelujah Chorus'.

Reading this, we can see why Bertrand Russell said that Lawrence's mystical philosophy of blood 'led straight to Auschwitz'.

So what was I doing encouraging undergraduates to read such stuff, and reading it myself? I pondered this as we cycled back from the beach each evening. But I couldn't deny that I was gripped by Lawrence, and when we got back from holiday I went on wolfing him down until I'd finished all twenty-three volumes in the Penguin edition. Why? First, because he is a marvellous writer. If you are new to Lawrence, start with the travel books and you will see this at once. They show you the world with the grime scrubbed off. He writes rapturously about the sun and flowers, his two great loves. When I picked my fifty most enjoyable books of the twentieth century for *Pure Pleasure* (2000) the Lawrence I chose was *Twilight in Italy*. It's about escaping from England in 1912 and tramping across the Tyrol, through the snow, to a village on Lake Garda where he takes lodgings. He lies in bed each morning watching the sunrise, from the first gash above the mountains to the molten flood filling his room. At sunset he watches the far mountain snows grow incandescent, 'like heaven breaking into blossom'. Outside he finds English springtime flowers – primroses in nests of pale bloom, crocuses like lilac flames in the grass. For him the sun meant life – the English winter would have killed him – and flowers symbolised not the frailty of beauty but its strength. He liked to think of their seasonal return outlasting the works of man. 'The pyramids', he wrote, 'will not last a moment compared to the daisy.' It's a sentence I've stored in my mind as a talisman for comfort when I read of more green fields disappearing under concrete and sewage pipes.

But beautiful writing, you may say, is not enough. That is true. Where Russell's comment about Auschwitz misleads, though, is that it misrepresents the kind of person Lawrence was. To imagine him as a Nazi is impossible. He hated regimentation, he hated cruelty. Read the description of a bullfight in the first chapter of *The Plumed Serpent* (you can get it on Project Gutenberg) and see how it throbs with pity, disgust and loathing. Everything else I've ever read about bullfighting fizzles into insignificance by comparison (including, of course, the fat-headed defences of it, like Kenneth Tynan's in *The Sound of Two Hands Clapping* – one of the first books I reviewed in Ian Hamilton's *New Review*).

Besides, to believe Lawrence's writing is dangerous is to assume that readers just suck it in uncritically, and it would be a strange reader who did that. Literature functions by making us imagine what it would be like to be someone else, inhabiting another body, thinking other thoughts. Lawrence is able to bring that about because he writes with such passionate conviction. The force of his ego drenches you like a monsoon. But because he is so sincere and uncompromising he also compels you to see the deliberate irrationality and immorality of his creed – and it is a kind of irrationality and immorality to which we, as readers, are particularly susceptible. His natural aristocrats feel special and individual and separate from the mass, and everyone who is educated and reads books has felt like that. So we are made to see ourselves through them – and learn about ourselves. At least, that's how I think it should work. What I'm sure of is that reading Lawrence was for me a revelation – irreplaceable, unforgettable. I believe that, however the intellect may pick him apart and find fault, he was a master-spirit who revealed deep truths about our instinctual life and our bond with the natural world, and did so in a body of writing that is luminous and intense to a degree unmatched, so far as I know, in the whole of western literature.

The other twentieth-century writer who seemed to me of Lawrence's stature was George Orwell – so unlike Lawrence that you might think they belonged to different species. I had read Orwell's novels and thought them remarkable, even the early ones which are generally rather disparaged. *Burmese*

Days, built from his personal experience of the Raj, seemed far better than Forster's *A Passage to India* with its hogwash about the mystical East. *Keep the Aspidistra Flying*, with its details about what everything costs, gave a sharper picture of what it was like to be young and poor in thirties London than anything else I'd read. But it was the four-volume Penguin *Essays, Journalism and Letters* which came out in 1970 that really overwhelmed me. They are the essential Orwell – Orwell the man, Orwell the political animal.

His aim, he says, is 'to make political writing into an art'. That comes as a surprise, because we don't normally think of him as an artist. He almost never praises beauty, and when he does he locates it in rather scruffy, overlooked things – a glass paperweight in a junk shop, the eye of the common toad, a sixpenny rose bush from Woolworths. The style he developed is the verbal equivalent of these objects. It's plain and simple – or seems to be until you try to imitate it. English, he said, is 'the language of lyric poetry, and also of headlines' – like a song or like a fist, depending on how you use it. His rules for writing were: use concrete words rather than abstract; use short ones rather than long; never use the passive where you can use the active; never use a figure of speech you've often seen in print; say everything in the shortest way possible. But you could obey all these rules and still be dull. What you have to add to be like Orwell is challenge and surprise. He had the timing of a stand-up comic. 'Looking through the photographs in the New Year Honours List, I am struck (as usual) by the quite exceptional ugliness and vulgarity of the faces displayed there.' Or (reviewing his friend Cyril Connolly's *The Unquiet Grave*) 'Even without knowing his identity one could infer that the writer of this book is about forty, is inclined to stoutness, has lived much in Continental Europe, and has never done any real work.'

Realism is another key factor. Looking through American fashion magazines he notices there are no references to grey hair, ageing or death. Everything is set in a fake world of eternal glamour. He does exactly the opposite, stripping off polish and giving life back its ordinariness. He valued 'solid objects and scraps of useless information'. He notices small things that gather a cloud of meaning around them – a cabman in 1914 bursting into tears because the army has requisitioned his horse; freshwater fish – perch – for sale on a London fishmonger's slab in 1942. He enjoys small ads and the pleas for partners in the *Matrimonial Post*. He notices how wartime shortages have upped the price of scrubbing brushes, second-hand typewriters and alarm clocks. His seasonal pleasures include wallflowers, 'especially the old-fashioned brown ones', stewed rhubarb in May, and 'the endless pop-pop-pop of cherry stones as one treads the London pavements' in July.

This kind of realism is what makes Orwell a cultural critic. By 'culture' he doesn't mean high art and civic institutions but the life most people lead. England in 1940 is the land of 'totes, dog-races, football pools, the pictures, Woolworth's, Gracie Fields, Wall's ice cream, potato crisps, celanese stockings, dart-boards, pin-tables, cigarettes, cups of tea and Saturday evenings in the four ale bar'. He kept a list of popular fallacies – that a swan can break your leg by a blow of its wing, that powdered glass is poisonous, that the colour red infuriates bulls. His essays 'Boys' Weeklies' and

'The Art of Donald McGill' are founding texts in what we now call cultural studies because they take a serious look at what most people would consider trash – comics and dirty seaside postcards.

I hero-worshipped Orwell not just for what he had written but for what he had done. The life he led seemed to me deeply and entirely admirable – and there was no other writer, with the possible exception of Chekhov, that I thought that was true of. As a child at St Cyprian's prep school in Eastbourne (scathingly described in 'Such, Such Were the Joys') he was made to feel unclean, unlovable and unlikely to succeed. It left him with a permanent hatred of the rich. Eton, where he was a scholarship boy, reinforced this. But he also internalised aspects of the public-school ethos that distinguish him from the common run of lefties. He was a lifelong socialist, but he acknowledged that socialists are often 'irresponsible carping people who have never been and never expect to be in a position of power'. British socialism is a sham, he observes, because no one wants to make really fundamental changes to society, and certainly not to cut back their own standard of living: 'The truth is that in a prosperous country left-wing politics are largely make-believe'. Socialist intellectuals are given to sniggering at British institutions – the police, the army – but those institutions actually ensure their safety and freedom. Pacifism, which many on the left espoused as war approached, is in Orwell's reckoning a luxury others pay for. 'Those who abjure violence can only do so because others are committing violence on their behalf.' By comparison with the 'boiled rabbits of the left' whose hearts have never 'leapt at the sight of a union jack', the young men – 'public school to the core' – who were ready to die in the cause of freedom seemed to him heroic. This is typical Orwell – truthful even when it offends his would-be allies.

From Eton he went straight into the Indian Imperial Police in Burma, where he saw imperialism from the inside, which means he did not see it simply, as the standard lefty did. It was possible, he realised, to be a decent person and an imperialist – as he felt Kipling had been. He was aware that the empire was a system of exploitation, and was guilty of atrocities, but he understood the pressures that drove men to commit them. As 'Shooting an Elephant' records, he knew what it was like to be hooted at by hostile crowds and surrounded by 'sneering yellow faces', and he was courageous enough to admit how it made him feel. 'With one part of my mind I thought of the British Raj as an unbreakable tyranny, with another part I thought that the greatest joy in the world would be to drive a bayonet into a Buddhist priest's guts.' To set against this there is his essay 'A Hanging' – the first thing to read if you are new to Orwell. There are people – Sebastian Faulks is one – who say that reading this essay as a teenager changed their lives, and that seems to me entirely credible. It describes how Orwell and an armed escort are marching a condemned prisoner – a young Burmese – across the prison yard to the gallows when a stray dog comes bounding over to them, wagging its tail, eager for a game, and playfully jumps up at the prisoner and licks his face. The others are aghast and shoo the dog away because it has – though only a dog – recognised the man they are going to kill as a living human being just like the rest of them. It's a moment Tolstoy would have been proud of, and though it's not known whether Orwell experienced it or just made it up, it hardly matters. What matters is that his imagination has seized on it and seen its depth.

Burma educated Orwell. It also contributed to his spiritual growth because it led to his great renunciation. He realised he had been a tool of tyranny – 'I was conscious of an immense weight of guilt that I had got to expiate.' So he resigned his commission and chose poverty. In the early years he suffered severely. He remembers how he would light a candle to warm his hands when they were too numb to write. No one would publish his work, and in Paris, in the autumn of 1929, he was reduced to getting a job as a dishwasher in a hotel. He deliberately shared the privations of the underclass. This is what he records in 'How the Poor Die' and *Down and Out in Paris and London*. He found out what it was like to be a beggar, standing out of doors in all weathers. It taught him, he said, never again to use the expression 'street corner loafer'. He slept out in Trafalgar Square with the homeless, and found that the police made them sit on the benches, not lie down, so they couldn't sleep. He got himself arrested and spent a night in a cell. He went hop-picking in Kent, and his 'Hop-Picking Diary' records the mix of social outcasts and working-class holidaymakers he worked alongside. The resolve to get first-hand experience stayed with him. In *The Road to Wigan Pier* he records going down a mine and crawling on all fours to the coal face – it took an hour, and he was exhausted when he got there, though for a miner it was just the start of a day's work.

He needed to find out what it was like to be a soldier,

too. He had always regretted missing the Great War because he'd been too young to enlist, and when he went to Spain and joined the POUM anarchist militia it was to regain his self-respect as well as to combat fascism. He was shot in the throat and nearly killed, but for the first time he felt comradeship with men from completely different backgrounds. It was a revelation of how society might work under genuine socialism. The biggest impact of the war, though, was to open his eyes to the ruthlessness of Soviet communism. The communists had no intention of allowing the anarchists an independent role. They were hunted down and killed or imprisoned. Orwell and his wife Eileen only just escaped. He learned, too, how the communist media rewrote events. Battles in which he had fought were completely misreported. The very concept of objective truth seemed doomed. Kingsley Martin, the *New Statesman* editor, refused to publish his article 'Spilling the Spanish Beans'. It was a betrayal he never forgave. The bitter lesson of the war in Spain fed his fear of totalitarianism, which grew into *Animal Farm* and *Nineteen Eighty-Four*. I had been brought up in the war to think of the Russians as our brave allies – which they were – but reading this part of the Orwell story cured me once and for all of my ignorant, sentimental fancies about Soviet communism.

It was after the Spanish Civil War that he finally made up his mind what socialism meant for him. It did not mean the abolition of private property (which he had once advocated), but it did mean state ownership of all means of production – land, mines, ships, machinery – and an approximate equalisation of incomes, so that the highest paid in the country could not earn more than ten times what the lowest earned. Hereditary privileges would be abolished, so would private education. The public schools and universities would be filled with state-aided pupils chosen simply on grounds of ability.

These aims correlated so exactly with my own beliefs that I felt like cheering, and I admired even more Orwell's frugality and contempt for luxury. The cottage he moved into with Eileen in 1938 had no electricity, bathroom or hot water, and the privy was at the bottom of the garden. He kept goats, bred pullets for their eggs and grew his own vegetables. The smallholding on the Isle of Jura he rented towards the end of his life was still more primitive, and his self-help became more ambitious. Cows, a pig, chickens and geese joined the goats, and he shot rabbits and cured their skins. He welcomed wartime food rationing. It meant, he observed, that there were fewer 'grossly fat' people about, and rations provided a healthier diet than pre-war plenty had (post-war statistics proved him right – the nation's health improved during the war and the infant mortality rate fell). Besides, a wartime diet was more realistic because it reduced dependence on imported foods, returning Britons to the 'natural diet of these islands' – oatmeal, herrings, milk, potatoes, green vegetables and apples. You might say that it was easier for Orwell to welcome food rationing because food did not interest him much. He once ate a dish of boiled eels that Eileen had cooked for the cat – the cat had Orwell's shepherd's pie instead. He enjoyed predicting dourly in the queue at the BBC canteen that, with food shortages worsening, the chalked menu-board would have 'Rat Soup' on it in a year's time, and in two years it would be replaced by 'Mock Rat Soup'. However, the fact that he did not care about luxury foodstuffs, as opposed to reluctantly having to give them up, seemed to me to make him more admirable not less.

I suppose this was because I was a wartime child, brought up to think austerity good. But it was also because I was moulded by English literature, in which luxury, especially at the expense of others, is always bad. Orwell welcomed clothes rationing as well, and hoped it would continue 'until moths have devoured the last dinner jacket', even if it meant everyone wearing dyed battle dress in the interim. That was fine with me too. No one, or anyway no male, who grew up in the war cares about clothes as much as those born after it.

I admired Orwell as a critic as well. He is enormously widely read, especially in out-of-the-way authors and 'good-bad books'. He has a sharp aesthetic sense and a rapid intelligence that can outpace most literary scholars. His brief essay on Milton says more, and more acutely, than many Milton specialists have managed in their lifetimes. His essay on Dickens asks political questions that no one had thought of asking before, and notices quite simple things that everyone (including me) had missed – that Dickens writes endlessly about food but never about agriculture, for example, and that he has no idea about work – his London is a city of consumers. Another refreshing aspect of Orwell as a critic is that he says what he thinks and doesn't care about upsetting people – that *Uncle Tom's Cabin* will outlast everything Virginia Woolf has written, that *The Brothers Karamazov* is 'heavy going', that he has never been able to read George Eliot, that Sartre is 'a bag of wind'.

He seemed to me to be right (i.e. to agree with me) about the two giants of modernism, T. S. Eliot and James Joyce. Both of them, he thinks, got worse as they got older. He finds he knows quite a lot of Eliot's early poetry by heart – not because he learned it but because it was instantly memorable. But with *Four Quartets* and other later things this doesn't happen, and it's clear 'some kind of current has been switched off'. What went wrong, he suggests, is that Eliot didn't stick to and develop his early anti-democratic feelings which, even if not politically likeable, could have made him a defiant champion of aristocracy. Instead he retreated into Anglo-Catholicism and 'gloomy mumblings' about prayer and repentance.

In Joyce, Orwell detects a gradual death of feeling and its replacement by literary cleverness. The stories in *Dubliners*, written around 1910, are by a man 'who is intensely sorry for the people about him and indignant over their warped, miserable lives'. But in *Ulysses*, published in 1922, Stephen Dedalus is 'intolerable' and Leopold Bloom 'does not evoke much pity even when his situation is pitiful'. As for *Finnegans Wake*, it is 'an elephantine crossword puzzle', emotionally sterile.

He was a moralist even before he was a critic. 'Decency', a key term in his writing, is moral in its force. It entails being concerned about other people, especially the deprived and victimised. It's also a democratic term. He writes about 'the native decency of the common man', implying that there's a basic human goodness that binds people together. The inherent decency of the English comes out, for Orwell, in their tendency to side with the underdog and their hatred of bullying, terrorism and violent crime. It has a sexual side too. Though the English masses refuse to knuckle down to middle-class puritanism, 'almost no one in England', he believes, 'approves of prostitution'. His essay 'Raffles and Miss Blandish' contrasts the innocent old-style English thriller with the 'poisonous rubbish', rooted in sexual sadism, that he finds in American crime fiction. He is opposed to the notion that moral standards should be relaxed for artistic people. 'One has the right to expect ordinary decency even of a poet,' he writes of Ezra Pound. On the other hand he argues that a writer or artist's moral character is irrelevant to the quality of his work. People need to understand that 'what is morally degraded may be aesthetically right'. Failure to understand this has led to the 'outcry' against D. H. Lawrence. The test case for Orwell is Salvador Dalí, since he admires his draughtsmanship but thinks him entirely despicable as a person – and we need to see, Orwell insists, that these are not contradictory positions. 'One ought to be able to hold in one's head simultaneously the two facts that Dalí is a good draughtsman and a disgusting human being.' Not that, Orwell adds, this should be construed as an argument for permitting anything or everything to be published. 'It should be possible to say, "This is a good book or a good picture, and it ought to be burned by the public hangman."'

The only other twentieth-century writer who, it seemed to me, could challenge comparison with Lawrence and Orwell was Joseph Conrad. He was completely different from them, because he believed in nothing at all. Orwell believed in socialism, Lawrence in his dark gods. But for Conrad all belief was illusory. In a letter to his friend Cunninghame Graham he likens the universe to a knitting machine, which has come into existence by pure chance – the collision of atoms. It has created, and will destroy, everything, including mankind. The sun will cool and the human race will perish 'in cold, darkness and silence', and it will be an insignificant detail in the vast insignificance of the cosmos. 'The most withering thought is that the infamous thing has made itself: made itself without thought, without conscience, without foresight, without eyes, without heart. It is tragic accident – and it has happened.' To believe in anything positive or hopeful is, for Conrad, ridiculous, like believing that you can convert the knitting machine into a machine that does beautiful embroidery by applying 'the right kind of oil'. Everything is meaningless – the chance product of a meaningless universe that creates and destroys us. 'It knits us in and it knits us out. It has knitted time, space, pain, death, corruption, despair and all the illusions – and nothing matters.' In the face of this implacable, alien cosmos, Conrad decided, the only reasonable attitude is 'cold unconcern' – though he admitted to Cunninghame Graham that observing the 'remorseless process' and the human beings caught up in it can also be 'sometimes amusing'.

The mixture of amusement and cold unconcern is the key to Conrad's irony. Nihilism as bleak and total as his ought to be depressing. But his despair expresses itself in an irony that is strangely liberating, because it gives you a sense of being superior to the hopelessness and futility that he describes. The intricate rigour of his style and his ironic distancing work together to produce scenes that can become (or so I have found) a permanent part of your thinking. Here is an example, from *Heart of Darkness*.

Once, I remember, we came upon a man-of-war anchored off the coast. There wasn't even a shed there, and she was shelling the bush. It appears the French had one of their wars going on thereabouts. Her ensign dropped limp like a rag; the muzzles of the long six-inch guns stuck out all over the low hull; the greasy, slimy swell swung her up lazily and let her down, swaying her thin masts. In the empty immensity of earth, sky and water, there she was, incomprehensible, firing into a continent. Pop, would go one of the six-inch guns; a small flame would dart and vanish. A little white smoke would disappear, a tiny projectile would give a feeble screech – and nothing happened. Nothing could happen. There was a touch of insanity in the proceeding, a sense of lugubrious drollery in the sight; and it was not dissipated by somebody on board assuring me earnestly there was a camp of natives – he called them enemies! – hidden out of sight somewhere.

When he wrote that passage Conrad was thinking about nineteenth-century colonialism and imperialism. But I have found that the image of the ship firing into a continent has a way of inserting itself between me and twenty-first-century news items – about Iraq, Afghanistan and so forth – where the western powers try to destroy ideas that they consider wrong with weaponry. Perhaps if more people read Conrad fewer people would get killed – though from the viewpoint of his unflinching pessimism saving life and destroying it are both equally pointless in the end.

The futility of human ideals applies, in Conrad, not only to ideals like civilisation, which the west is keen to impose on other peoples, but also to mercy and kindness. In *The Secret Agent* Stevie, a feeble-witted but kind boy, has an altercation with a cabman about the condition of the cabman's horse. Actually Stevie says almost nothing, but the way he looks at the lame, starving animal is so full of pity and accusation that the cabman breaks out into a defensive monologue about how hard his life is and how he has to feed his wife and four children as well as himself and the horse.

'Poor! Poor!' stammered out Stevie, pushing his hands deeper into his pockets with convulsive sympathy. He could say nothing; for the tenderness to all pain and all misery, the desire to make the horse happy and the cabman happy, had reached the point of a bizarre longing to take them to bed with him. And that, he knew, was impossible. For Stevie was not mad. It was, as it were, a symbolic longing; and at the same time it was very distinct, because springing from experience, the mother of wisdom. Thus when as a child he cowered in a dark corner scared, wretched, sore and miserable with the black, black misery of the soul, his sister Winnie used to come along and carry him off to bed with her, as into a heaven of consoling peace. Stevie, though apt to forget mere facts, such as his name and address for instance, had a faithful memory of sensations. To be taken into a bed of compassion was the supreme remedy, with the only one disadvantage of being difficult of application on a large scale. And looking at the cabman, Stevie perceived this clearly, because he was reasonable.

It is one of Conrad's greatest passages, both terrible and funny, and its power comes from making us see that our longing to put an end to pain and suffering is, strictly speaking, infantile and futile.

But if everything is futile, then recognising that everything is futile is futile too, and Conrad plays out the logic of that in the figure of Martin Decoud in *Nostromo*. Decoud is an intellectual, witty and cynical like Conrad, and, like Conrad, he considers himself superior to all ideals, convictions and beliefs. However, though Decoud is like Conrad, Conrad does not approve of Decoud. Decoud is, it seemed to me, Conrad seeing through himself – seeing the emptiness that lies at the heart of his high disdain for what other people believe. Decoud suffers, Conrad writes, from 'a mere barren indifferentism posing as intellectual superiority' – and that is very much how a hostile critic might describe Conrad. At the end of the novel Decoud finds himself adrift in an open boat on the huge, misty Golfo Placido, and after several days he starts to doubt his own individuality. It seems to him that he is merging into the world of cloud and water, and in the end he shoots himself. It is as if he dies of emptiness.

The heroes in Conrad that I found most moving (and, to be truthful, extravagantly, tearfully, operatically moving, on a par with the ending of *La Traviata*, which I can never watch or listen to dry-eyed) were those who, unlike Decoud, find something to believe in just before they die – Jim, in *Lord Jim*, who finds courage, and Axel Heyst, in *Victory*, who finds love. What Conrad found was art. He records that he once spent eight hours on just three sentences. His English can seem too worked over, as if it has been translated from another language. Of course, that is partly because English was his third language after Polish and French. But it is also because he gave it the unremitting dedication that art demands.

Of the twentieth-century poets I'd read the one who seemed closest to Conrad, because he too believed in nothing except his art, was Philip Larkin. He was close to Orwell also, I thought, in his impatience with pretentiousness and

showing off, and I suspected he was keen on D. H. Lawrence. This was because in Larkin's poem 'The Explosion'
the description of miners coming home from work, and of
how one of them is carrying a bird's nest with eggs in it,
reminded me of a Lawrence short story called 'Adolf' where
a miner finds a baby rabbit on his way home from work and
brings it back for his children. It wasn't until the 1990s, when
I read Andrew Motion's biography of Larkin and Anthony
Thwaite's edition of his letters, that I discovered this was
probably a good guess because Larkin, as an undergraduate,
had been crazy about Lawrence. So, anyway, Larkin seemed
a sort of confluence of my three top twentieth-century writers, and I also bracketed him in my mind with Andrew Marvell, not so much because of the Hull connection as because
no other English poets had gained immortality with such a
small output of poems. (They also both wrote poems about
grass-cutting – Marvell's mower poems and Larkin's 'Cut
Grass', a little masterpiece which soars from death to exultation in just fifty-six syllables – but I wasn't sure whether the
grass connection might be mere coincidence.)

All this made me wonder what it would be like to meet
Larkin, and I found out through Charles Monteith who,
early in 1974, asked me to dinner in All Souls, adding that
Larkin would be there. We met before dinner in Charles's
room and Larkin was notable for his silence. He seemed not
so much withdrawn as guarded and watchful. I learned later
that he had stammered so badly as a boy that he couldn't
trust himself to ask for a railway ticket, but had to write his
destination on a piece of paper and push it across the counter. On that first evening he seemed exactly like that – as if

speech was something he couldn't risk, or as if he was there in some non-speaking capacity, permitted to observe but not take part. He loosened up a bit after a few drinks, but when, at dinner, I mentioned Andrew Marvell, he feigned complete ignorance, as if I'd asked for his views on medieval tapestry. (Ten years later, when reviewing his collected essays, *Required Writing*, I came across his essay on Marvell, and this encouraged me and a BBC producer called Roger Thompson, who ran a programme called *Bookmark*, to ask Larkin if he'd take part in a documentary film about Marvell. He declined, protesting in his letter to Thompson that his essay in *Required Writing* was 'no more than a patchwork of other people's sources, mainly Professor Carey's own'. He added that he felt 'quite kindly disposed to this project, but that is not to say that I think I could contribute usefully or even enjoy trying to do so'.)

Given Larkin's reticence, when I heard that the secretary of St John's middle common room, Rob Watt, had invited him to come and give a poetry reading I did not have high hopes. But, astonishingly, he agreed. Rob later wrote the occasion up for *Critical Quarterly*, quoting from Larkin's nervous letters about the coming event – how he would 'hate to find anything resembling a public gathering there', and feared he might be 'scragged by embryo Leavises'. About thirty of us were invited, and Larkin began by saying that he'd never given a public reading before, and only one private reading which had been after midnight and he had been drunk. He also said he wanted no one to make a recording or take notes. Luckily I was seated behind a large sofa, so was able to take notes unobserved – and still have them. In between readings he chatted about the poems, telling us that 'Essential Beauty' and 'Afternoons' were his favourites, that 'Sympathy in White Major' was a parody of Gautier and spoken by 'a poet who thinks well of himself', that 'Church Going' was written after a cycling tour he had gone on while he was working in Belfast, and that he had sent it to a 'major weekly' but they had lost it and later asked for another copy, that 'At Grass' was based on a documentary film about race-horses that he had never forgotten, and that 'The Building' was written after a visit to Kingston General Hospital in Hull. 'Cut Grass', he said, was his nearest thing to a 'lyric poem', or you might say to a 'Georgian poem' if you were being 'uncomplimentary'. He said he had never had a TV set and never seen a TV advert, but he listened to the radio and it seemed that whenever he switched it on 'Wedding Wind' was being read on *Woman's Hour*.

Mostly his readings were quiet and rather underplayed, but he read 'Mr Bleaney' with passion and the last three words, 'I don't know', were almost an angry shout. He explained that he'd written that poem one night when he'd been aggravated by his landlady's radio, and added that a graduate student who had written to him about the poem had taken 'the jab-bering set he egged her on to buy' to be the landlady's dentures. During question time an undergraduate, one of mine, questioned him about the melancholy view of life expressed in his poems, and he replied sharply, 'I didn't invent old age and death.' Another student asked why he had become a librarian, and he replied that he had got a good second-class degree and it seemed 'an acceptable sort of job'. Actually he had got a first, but this was typical of his awkward modesty.

I'd forgotten this exchange but a student of mine, Robert Dingley, who was present, and later went to a professorship in Australia, reminded me of it quite recently.

There was one slightly embarrassing incident. Larkin had suggested that his 'old friend' John Wain might be invited, and he was. He sat silent throughout but towards the end got unsteadily to his feet and uttered in a muffled bellow, 'D'you know, Philip, the difference between them', waving towards the assembled company, 'and us? It's that we're writers and they're critics, which means they can't and we can.' He added that he never read reviews and couldn't afford to waste time on such stuff. It happened that I had recently reviewed, not very favourably, Wain's book on Samuel Johnson, and this fact was known to most people in the room including, I fancy, Larkin. He did not react at all, however. Nor, of course, did I and Wain subsided grumpily. Later, when I read the Larkin–Kingsley Amis letters with their cruel jocularities about poor Wain, I realised Larkin must have been storing up, behind his impassive exterior, the comic details of this episode to retail to Amis. It was quite a salutary lesson for me, though, because I hadn't been reviewing for very long and it taught me that sentences that delight you with their wit and acuity when you write them can be horribly hurtful to the wretched creature at whom they are aimed.

In the spring of 1974, the year Larkin gave his reading in St John's, our lives had changed. On 10 February Gill gave birth to our son Leo in the John Radcliffe Hospital. At the time, fathers were discouraged from being present at births, so all the stuff I'd learned at the pre-natal classes about giving moral support and how to help with controlled breathing went to waste. I was allowed to sit with Gill till the last stage of labour, though. They had put a sensor on her bump connected to a machine that showed the foetal heart-beat, and either because the sensor kept slipping or because Leo kept shifting about the needle swung back and forth alarmingly against its little numbered scale. So I felt pretty wrung out by the time I was ushered into the corridor to wait while Leo was born. I tried to read an Agatha Christie, but it didn't seem to make any sense. At last a smiling nurse came out and asked if I'd like to see my son. So I was taken to a dimly lit room where there were several new babies, neatly swaddled in a row of Perspex cots, and I was allowed to hold him. He was warm and sleepy and had a light fuzz of reddish hair, and was the most beautiful thing I had ever seen. I drove home – it was about three in the morning – dizzy with happiness.

Fashions in medicine change, and three years later when Leo's brother Thomas was born I was allowed to be present, masked, capped and gowned to look like a doctor. The midwife and nurses pretended I was being useful, which was kind of them, and there was some drama as forceps had to be used. These were wielded by a trainee doctor (with the hospital registrar standing beside him to supervise) and I hoped it was not the first time he had used the alarmingly large tongs with which he approached Gill. However, all went well, and Thomas came slithering into the world. He had lovely long legs like a newborn colt – our family doctor had joked with Gill when he examined her that he thought she was going to give birth to a horse – and there were tears and rejoicing and everyone hugged everyone else as Thomas was cleaned up and given to Gill to hold. The registrar shook my hand and said, 'Congratulations,' which took me by surprise because I felt that what had happened was far beyond anything I could be responsible for. It was as though someone had said, 'Congratulations on creating the world.'

10

Reviewing

In the 1970s everything changed. It was not just Leo and Thomas arriving. That was the main thing of course. But other new directions opened up. We'd been thinking that instead of living in a college house we ought to buy one of our own. The trouble was we didn't have much money. Then we saw in the *Oxford Times* that two derelict farm cottages in a place called Lyneham were to be sold by auction. We knew Lyneham because Stephen Wall, my successor at Keble, and his wife Yvonne lived there. It's in the Cotswolds – only forty minutes' drive from Oxford, but it seems deep in the country. You head for the Wychwoods, a group of villages in what was once primeval forest, and when you get to the top of the hill beyond Ascott-under-Wychwood the valley of the Evenlode lies before you – just fields and woods for miles and, down by the river, a tiny cluster of cottages and a couple of farms, and that is Lyneham.

We went to look at the derelict cottages, and they certainly were derelict. Damp was coming up through the flagstone floors and a lot of the woodwork was rotten. The only piped water was a cold tap over a downstairs sink. There was no mains drainage – an earth closet under a corrugated-iron lean-to served both cottages. An outhouse was partitioned across the middle to provide two laundries, each with a copper and a chimney above it. Beyond the laundries was a pigsty – common in old Cotswold cottages. A pig would be fattened during the autumn, then slaughtered and the meat cured to feed the family in winter. A beam in one of the cottages had a peg to hang hams from. There was a sixth of an acre of land, every square yard yielding a rich profusion of elder, nettles, docks, cow parsley and brambles.

On the other hand the cottages, outhouse and pigsty were all built of beautiful, weathered Cotswold limestone, dotted with stars of brilliant white and sulphur-yellow lichen, and with fluted scraps of seashell and other fossil fragments embedded in it. The corner-stones – or coigns, as I decided to call them, after the coigns of vantage in *Macbeth* – were reassuringly massive, and the roofs had swallows' nests bunched under the eaves, exactly as Banquo's temple-haunting martlet would have wanted. The cottages had been reroofed in Welsh slate, but the outhouse and pigsty had lovely, mossed, uneven Stonesfield slates, made by being left out in the frost to split.

The auction was in the Crown and Cushion pub in Chipping Norton. Quite a crowd had assembled, which was alarming. We'd hoped we'd be the only people interested. I'd come to look on the cottages as ours already, and felt resentful that others wanted to take them away from us. It seemed to me that the auctioneer waited absurdly long each time I made a bid to allow our inconsiderately persistent rivals to put in a higher one. However, eventually the others lost interest and his little hammer clunked down and we had bought the cottages for £11,000. We thought it a huge sum, and calculated (correctly) that we'd have to find as much again for rebuilding work. Still, we felt elated, even after driving back to Lyneham and wandering round our expensive ruins.

A local builder, Mr Dore, did the renovation. He was an undertaker as well as a builder, so building work halted when his men were required as coffin-bearers, which gave the whole business a solemn and timeless air. Work stopped for life as well as death, though. When they were taking down a chimney from one of the cottages Mr Dore's men found that swallows were nesting there, so all operations ceased until the nestlings had flown. We took that as a good omen – and there was another when I found an adult swallow fluttering against a window pane in an upstairs room, and let it out to dart away into the sunlight. We weren't sure how old the cottages were, and the title deeds were frustratingly unspecific, mainly concerned with our right of access to a nearby water pump. But we reckoned they might be late eighteenth-century, around the time of Wordsworth and Coleridge's *Lyrical Ballads*, perhaps. They had been built with care – the lintels over the windows were stone, not wood, as would have been usual in farm labourers' cottages – and we altered them as little as possible, beyond piercing the enormously thick dividing wall between them at ground- and first-floor level so that they became one house. The pigsty was converted into a garage.

Lyneham is old. The name means 'a place where flax is grown', and in the Domesday Book it is listed as home to thirty villagers, seven smallholders and six slaves. At that time Lyneham's tenant-in-chief was Bishop Odo of Bayeux, half-brother of William the Conqueror, but I don't suppose he ever came to have a look at it. A mile up the hill is an Iron Age hill fort and a long barrow where an Anglo-Saxon sword and an iron currency bar were dug up in the nineteenth century. So when I set about clearing the ground around the cottages I felt that many generations had sweated there before me. 'Man comes and tills the field and lies beneath', I grunted as I hauled out yet another entanglement of nettle roots. I can't believe Cotswold weeds have changed much over the centuries. Those six slaves probably ripped themselves on brambles just like me. I dug under pitilessly cloudless skies. It was the summer of 1976, the hottest since records began, and I lost half a stone in weight.

We planted fruit trees – apple, pear, plum and morello cherry – thinking it would be lovely on a spring morning to look out from the bedroom window over a snowdrift of blossom. Chatting about this with a colleague, a zoology professor, I gathered that it would be absolutely vital to have bees for pollination. He was, it turned out, a beekeeper, and he sold me my first hive. That was almost forty years ago and I've kept bees ever since. They are endlessly fascinating creatures and have been around much longer than humans. The earliest bee fossil, caught in a drop of amber, is eighty million years old. A cave painting near Valencia depicts Spanish hunters taking honey from wild bees maybe eight thousand years ago. The ancient Egyptians were the first to keep bees in hives. Tomb paintings show them using smoke to control them, just like modern beekeepers, and making honey cakes.

Almost everything about bees is amazing. Worker bees fly up to three miles from the hive and visit ten thousand flowers in a day. Their wings beat two hundred times a second, and they perform elaborate dances on the face of the comb to tell other workers where and how far away food sources are. In summer there are fifty thousand of them in the hive, and each dies of exhaustion after about five weeks. In its whole lifetime a worker collects about a quarter of an ounce of honey, less than half a teaspoonful, but the yield from one hive in a good year can be over eighty pounds. From our three hives we usually get between two and three hundred pounds, and we market our honey through a friendly butcher in Chipping Norton who sells local jams and pickles as well.

But the real satisfactions of beekeeping are more subtle than just producing or eating honey, and only beekeepers know about them – the humming noise from thousands of bees fanning with their wings to drive surplus moisture from the honey when you put your ear against a hive on a summer night, for instance, or the sight of bees on the landing board waddling up into the darkness of the hives, the orange pollen-packs on their back legs shining like brake lights. Best of all, perhaps, is the living smell of honey and wax which comes up at you whenever you open a hive – and this smell, which is just a pleasure for you, is for the bees an intricate information network, carried by pheromones, giving up-to-date news about the state of the brood, and the health, age and laying capacity of the queen.

Our two little boys helped with the bees as soon as they were old enough, looking like miniature spacemen in their child-size white bee suits, with hoods and face-veils. Their favourite thing in Lyneham, though, wasn't the bees but the smallholding next to our cottages which was owned by a brother and sister, Arthur and Dora Smith. They were true country people, who'd been brought up in the village, lived all their lives there and seldom ventured far from it – though

Dora told us that on one legendary occasion, I'd guess soon after the war, she'd ridden to Nottingham on the back of Arthur's motorbike. Arthur was a farm labourer, kind, courteous and wise. For all I know his and Dora's smallholding may have been one of those listed in the Domesday Book. It certainly looked old enough with its tumbledown sties and pens and its dense nettle thickets, but it was a scene of purposeful activity. They kept two sows, and from time to time a boar would come to service them. He would arrive in a trailer, drawn behind a battered farm truck, and Arthur and the boar's owner would let the trailer's flap down and guide him towards the expectant sow, holding corrugated- -iron sheets in front of their legs – for boars are dangerous, and can slice you open with one sideways swipe of their tusks. Leo and Thomas would perch on the gate, agog with excitement. When it was time for the boar to leave, a trail of oatmeal would be laid from the sty to the trailer and he would come lumbering along, snuffling up the meal as he went, while his two minders kept pace with their shields at the ready. Soon a new litter of piglets would be born, and we would watch them racing round and round a huge heap of pig dung which was the smallholding's most prominent feature. Arthur generously allowed me to wheel barrowloads of it away to our vegetable plot, and it made wonderful manure. The smallholding also had sheep, but they were pets, not for market. They had been abandoned or orphaned lambs from the flock on the farm where Arthur worked, and Arthur and Dora's elderly mother had bottle-fed them by the kitchen fire, so they lived on the smallholding as honoured guests. Dora once brought one on a lead into our kitchen, to show the boys – a kind gesture, but inadvisable, since sheep are likely to excrete quite copiously when nervous. They are also astonishingly strong and hard to budge if they don't want to move. Chickens, pullets and geese were the smallholding's other inhabitants, and we occasionally got a goose egg from Dora – very good for making ginger cake with. Geese are dangerous too, though. Once Dora turned up with her face torn by a goose that had taken exception to something she did or said.

Our other neighbours, in a house that, we later found out, had been an inn in the seventeenth century, were an elderly couple, Reg and Rose Duester. He had been born in the village, but she was from Devon and, until she gave up work, had been the cook at Bruern Abbey, a Cistercian foundation dating from 1147, and later the home of the Astor family, which was a couple of miles away across the fields. Reg was a champion vegetable gardener and won prizes in shows. Gill used to observe, rather hurtfully, that his shallots were the size of my onions. Rose was wonderful with children, though she had never had any of her own. I don't know what her secret was – unmistakable kindness, I suppose – but Leo and Thomas took to her instantly and would have followed her anywhere, trustfully clasping her hand. At the weekend they always went to the Duesters' big kitchen for tea. Reg would be ensconced in his armchair, watching television (which we didn't have). He was keen on horse-racing, but out at Lyneham there was a lot of onscreen interference, so our boys got the impression that television meant black and white horses running through a rainstorm. When we went to collect them they were always quiet as mice, completely entranced.

Around the time we bought the cottages Gill and I both changed our jobs. Gill moved from school-teaching – at Oxford High School – to being the fellow and tutor in English literature at Manchester (now Harris Manchester) College. At the time Manchester College was still only affiliated to Oxford University, and Gill was one of the group of pioneering tutors who helped it gain full collegiate status in 1996. It had been founded in 1786 as a dissenting academy, providing university education for nonconformists who were debarred from Oxford and Cambridge. It championed reformist causes such as the abolition of slavery, and in its early days the scientist Joseph Priestley and the Unitarian minister William Gaskell, husband of Elizabeth, were associated with it. After resiting from Manchester to York and London it came to Oxford in 1893, where it occupies a mixture of seventeenth-century and Victorian buildings on Holywell, opposite New College.

Gill and I already knew about Manchester College because when we were undergraduates it let out its rooms to students from other colleges, and I had digs there in my third year, along with twenty or so other students from different colleges and backgrounds, all studying different subjects. I especially remember a genial American basketball player called Ted Gold who was so tall he could change light bulbs without standing on a chair – a useful accomplishment, though I'm not sure what, if anything, Ted was studying. We all lunched and dined together, presided over by the Revd H. L. Short, the Dean, who was deeply learned in biblical subjects and languages and liked to provoke discussion. I imagine the seventeenth-century inns and halls of residence where undergraduates lived before they were allowed into the colleges were little communities rather like ours. Everyone had to be in by eleven o'clock, as in other Oxford colleges, but we all regularly climbed over the wall after the gates had been locked, and no one seemed to mind. By the time Gill took up her appointment this pleasantly rag-tag stage in Manchester College's history was, of course, over. It was admitting its own students and preparing them for – at first – University of London degrees.

My job change was less adventurous than Gill's, taking me just from one Oxford college to another. Helen Gardner retired from the Merton professorship of English literature in 1973, the post was advertised, and I decided to have a go. One reason was that I'd been teaching undergraduates for nearly fifteen years and feared I was getting a bit stale and repetitive. I was only forty, and doing the same thing for another twenty-five years wasn't alluring. But another reason was that Oxford undergraduate life was going through a phase I didn't much like. Back in 1968 Parisian students had linked up with striking workers, occupying buildings and fighting street battles with the police in the Latin Quarter. *Les événements* and the witty graffiti they inspired ('*Soyez realistes, demandez l'impossible*', '*Même si Dieu existait, il faudrait le supprimer*') became legendary, and rather belatedly, in March 1974, a group of Oxford undergraduates rose in imitation, occupying a central room in the Clarendon Building – then the university's administrative centre. What they were protesting about was never clear, but the university authorities decided that to forcibly eject them would attract adverse publicity, so they were allowed to stay put for a couple of weeks. This decision was, it transpired, wise, for when they eventually departed they left behind bottles of tomato ketchup which, had anyone laid a finger on them, they would have daubed over themselves so as to appear covered in blood when carried out to the waiting TV cameras.

It happened that at the time I was a pro-Proctor, that is, an assistant to one of the Proctors or university disciplinary officers. It was felt that someone must keep an eye on the protestors in case they hurt themselves or damaged the building, and the pro-Proctors were chosen for this task, organising themselves into a round-the-clock rota. So I found myself getting up on several nights at three in the morning to dress in proctorial rig (white tie, bands, gown, MA hood, subfusc) and sit outside the main room in the Clarendon Building, accompanied by a huge contingent of police, drawn from all over Oxfordshire, who were happily sitting on radiators, munching sandwiches and playing cards. On one occasion, sick of hanging around doing nothing, I went into the room and engaged the sleepy occupiers in debate. All they seemed to be worried about was whether they would be punished for their foolish prank. Several down-and-outs and winos from the Oxford streets had joined the protest, for the sake of warmth, and their proximity was clearly proving irksome to the young toffs with whom they had entered into political alliance. I found it depressing that intelligent, highly educated young people could do something so disruptive and pointless, instead of getting on with their work, and more depressing still that they all seemed to be from arts faculties, and included one of my St John's undergraduates. Scientists, it seemed, were more serious, industrious and grown-up.

At all events, I opted to apply for the Merton professor-ship. There were no interviews – evidently the electors de-cided to rely on the written evidence – and I was able to fit my application onto a single sheet, listing just the *Christian Doctrine* translation, the discovery of Nicholas Hare, the Milton edition, the Milton book and the Dickens book. Having sent it in I forgot about it, feeling pretty sure I'd hear no more. When a letter arrived from the University Regis-trar saying that I had been elected, Gill and I were elated, of course, but I was also a bit apprehensive, since accepting the Chair would mean a considerable drop in income. I'd cease to be a tutorial fellow of St John's so I'd lose our free tenancy of 38 St John Street, for which we'd now have to pay a market rent. Still, it seemed dishonourable not to accept, having applied, and accepting would not mean losing touch with undergraduates altogether. Though a lot of my work would be with postgraduates I'd still give lectures and semi-nars which were open to all comers.

So I moved back to Merton – the college my university professorship was attached to – and, as it happened, back to the Old Warden's Lodgings, though this time to a spacious bow-windowed room on the first floor which gradually, over the years, filled with thousands of books. Among the let-ters of congratulation I received were two I especially prized. One was from John Buxton, the English fellow at New Col-lege, who was a truly remarkable man. Captured early in the war during the Norwegian campaign, he was sent to a prison camp in Bavaria, where, being a keen ornithologist, he organised fellow-POWs to observe a pair of redstarts round the clock. The redstart is a small insect-eating migratory bird, a bit like a robin but more orange, and after the war John wrote the standard book on the species. His joy in watching them while he was in the camp came from their freedom and their complete unlikeness to humans: 'They lived wholly and enviably to themselves, unconcerned in our fatuous politics.' He also wrote an entirely original book called *Elizabethan Taste* about the painters and sculptors, often immigrants, at work in Shakespeare's England. The other letter was from Philip Larkin, who wrote that he was delighted to read of my appointment, adding, 'Does it mean that your centre of gravity – or levity – shifts to Merton? If so, I do hope to see you once again before your translation.' I was pleased about 'levity' because it suggested something I'd written must have made Philip laugh, which was more than I'd ever managed in conversation.

Oxford professors were expected to give an inaugural lecture, and I called mine 'The Critic as Vandal', arguing that academic literary criticism, as currently practised, was largely engaged in turning works of literary art into barely readable prose, and inevitably destroying, in the process, the very specific meanings that the words of the original artworks conveyed. After about a quarter of an hour one member of the audience walked out – this was Mary Lascelles, the English fellow at Somerville College, author of a book on Jane Austen. She was of royal blood and, it was rumoured, fifty-seventh in line to the British throne (or some such figure). But she'd always been rather frosty to me, so I was not sorry to see her go. Besides, I harboured a slight grudge against her because when Gill had applied to Somerville as an entrance candidate Miss Lascelles had turned her down, remarking, at the end of the interview, that she hoped Gill had had a pleasant day in Oxford (with the clear implication that she wouldn't be seeing Oxford again). Gill, who is much kinder than me, felt sure this was inadvertent tactlessness, but I wasn't so certain. I think Miss Lascelles took offence because one of my three examples of critical vandalism was taken from C. S. Lewis, whom I suppose she had known. The other two were from Empson and Christopher Ricks. All three were chosen because they were obviously out-standingly brilliant critics, so if vandalism could be detected even in their work it was an indication it was widespread elsewhere. Perhaps I did not make this clear enough. Claire Tomalin published the lecture in the *New Statesman*, so it reached the eyes of Christopher and Empson, and they were both, I think, a bit miffed.

I'd been writing regular reviews for Claire in the *New Statesman* for three or four years when, early in 1977, Harold Evans, who was editor of the *Sunday Times*, asked me to lunch in the Garrick and invited me to become one of the paper's regular reviewers. We agreed that I should write a review each fortnight, and I was introduced to John Whit-ley, the books editor, and Godfrey Smith, who ran the arts pages. They were a contrasting couple, Godfrey cheerful and Falstaffian, John quiet and watchful – a benevolent Prince Hal. I liked them both, and through them I met the great Jack Lambert, who had been books and arts editor before moving on to an associate editorship. He was a true old newspaperman, and had worked on the *Fruitgrower, Florist and Market Gardener*, prior to joining the navy – in which he had a distinguished wartime career. Cyril Connolly and

George Steiner were among the writers he had brought to the paper during his time as books editor, and he welcomed me with warmth and, I think, some scepticism. 'The trouble with you, dear boy,' he once said, 'is that you've been to uniVARsity.' I could see what he meant – but still, so had Connolly and Steiner.

At the time the paper was housed in a rather tatty office block on Gray's Inn Road, and books and arts were on the second floor, in an open-plan office where John and Godfrey had desks, and where among the secretaries clattering away at typewriters sat a young and beautiful Nigella Lawson. Walking up from Chancery Lane tube station to deliver my copy of a Tuesday I would often see lorries loaded with huge rolls of paper, like Brobdingnagian cotton-reels, heading for the printing presses, which I found a curiously stirring sight. When Claire came to the *Sunday Times* from the *New Statesman* to replace John (who moved a bit higher in the hierarchy) we would occasionally go for book-chat over a cup of coffee in an exceptionally greasy greasy spoon across the way. Nearby was Dickens's house in Doughty Street, and sometimes I'd drop in there before going back to Oxford. On a winter's day you could be quite alone, standing in the bedroom where his sister-in-law, young Mary Hogarth, died in his arms. Claire left the paper in protest when Rupert Murdoch defied the print unions and moved the whole enterprise to Wapping, and she was replaced by Penny Perrick, who once – when I was judging the *Irish Times* Literature Prize (won by E. Annie Proulx's *The Shipping News*) – had me to stay in her lovely cottage at Roundstone, the only place I've ever seen with peat-burning fires. It looked out over Galway Bay, where great brown-sailed fishing boats butted through the waves.

After Penny came the witty and ebullient John Walsh – more like I imagine Oscar Wilde to have been than anyone else I have met, though with quite different sexual preferences – and after John, briefly, came Harry Ritchie, a joy to work for and a supporter of Queen of the South, a team I did not believe really existed until I met Harry. He was replaced by Geordie Greig, who suggested, in 2000, that I should write every week for a year, selecting my fifty most enjoyable books of the twentieth century. It was fun to do. Gill and I were in Durham, attending a conference, at the time Geordie suggested it, and we sketched out a list of possibles after dinner one night. At the end of the year Faber published the collection in paperback as *Pure Pleasure*. I felt sure Geordie would end up as editor of the *Sunday Times* – maybe he still will – but in fact he left to edit the *Tatler* and Caroline Gascoigne who had virtually been joint books editor with him took over. She was encouraging and motherly and I felt pretty glum when she phoned to say she was going into publishing. But there must be something about the books editor job that attracts only top-notch people, because Susannah Herbert, who came after Caroline, and Andrew Holgate, who has the job now, and his adjutant Robert Collins, have been every bit as good as any of their predecessors, and Peter Kemp, who was fiction editor from Harry's time on, has one of the most acute literary intelligences of anyone I have ever come across. I know this sounds like sucking-up but it is true.

Totting up the years, and taking into consideration reviews written for other papers before joining the *Sunday*

Times, I calculate that I shall soon write – or perhaps have already written – my thousandth book review. Selecting just a few from a thousand books is a bit difficult. Still, it struck me it might be worth doing as some of them could be ones readers had missed and would enjoy. So I jotted down the titles that, for one reason or another, immediately came to mind, and stopped when I got to twenty. I found – though it wasn't something I'd aimed for – that most of the twenty weren't strictly literary, but belonged to the broad category of social history, including biographies and autobiographies, so I suppose that must reflect my taste. Anyway, here they are.

Probably the most enjoyable literary biography I ever reviewed was James Knowlson's *Damned to Fame: The Life of Samuel Beckett*. True, it verges on hagiography, but it also convinces you that Beckett was unusually hagiographable. I ended up feeling he would have made a marvellous Pope, except that he was a Protestant and didn't believe in God. Otherwise he had all the qualities a great pontiff needs – cast-iron integrity, boundless generosity, saintly self-denial. He hated the body and its pleasures as intensely as the most austere desert father, and his art pursued a spiritual ideal that demanded the renunciation of virtually all recognisable human qualities. His wit would have been a wow on papal walkabouts. Once when a bystander asked him if he minded that she had named her dog after him, he riposted, 'Don't worry about me. What about the dog?'

I was amazed to learn what an un-Beckettian background he came from. Father was a prosperous quantity surveyor and they lived among doilies and finger-bowls in a smart new Tudorbethan villa, with tennis court, in the Dublin commuter belt. At public school young Sam excelled at boxing, golf and cricket. He is the only winner of the Nobel Prize for Literature to appear in *Wisden*, scoring 18 and 12 for Dublin University against Northants in 1926. The philistine atmosphere at home doesn't seem to have bothered him in the least. He enjoyed Sexton Blake and Gilbert and Sullivan, whose operas he knew by heart, and drove a natty sportster, his father's gift. Apart from the death of a pet hedgehog, nothing occurred in his formative years to justify the universal pessimism he later specialised in.

Another biography that has stuck in my mind is *Mauve* by Simon Garfield. It's about a chemist called William Perkin, who, as an eighteen-year-old student in 1856, was trying to synthesise quinine from an alkali called aniline, found in coal tar, and discovered, quite by mistake, a new colour – mauve. He cannily took out a patent, and his second bit of luck was that Napoleon III's Empress Eugénie decided that the new colour matched her eyes. Fashionable Paris turned mauve overnight. Not to be outdone, Queen Victoria wore mauve for her daughter's wedding in 1858, and after that every woman wanted it. Mauve mania swept London, and Perkin's fortune was made.

But that was only the beginning. Once Perkin had shown the way, hundreds more aniline dyes – reds, blues, greens, violets – burst upon the world. They were far cheaper and more brilliant than the old animal and vegetable dyes. Women who had never aspired to colour before could now revel in it. Satirists sneered, and the fastidious French historian Hippolyte Taine, walking in Hyde Park, complained that the glare was insufferable. But what really alarmed these conservative males, as Garfield notes, was the advent of women as independent consumers. Perkin changed the way women smelt as well. Producing coumarin from coal tar, he simulated the perfumes of roses, jasmine, violets and musk.

He seemed to me even more admirable as a man than as an inventor. Exceptionally modest and self-effacing, he shunned publicity, and seems never to have made a clever or witty remark. He retired aged thirty-six, built a pleasant house with large gardens, devoted himself to good works in the local community, and taught his sons to be useful citizens. All became scientists, and one invented non-flammable underclothes, saving many young lives. An evangelical Christian, Perkin died quietly, having first sung a verse of the hymn 'When I survey the wondrous cross'. His last words were 'Proud? Who could be proud?'

Among autobiographies a favourite was – is – Frank Muir's *A Kentish Lad*. I met him just once, at a BBC party, but I'd admired him for years on the radio, where he collaborated with Denis Norden in witty, educated comedy of a kind that is now considered too intellectually demanding to be broadcast. He comes across in the book as modest, funny, heroic and uncomplaining. Born in 1920 in his gran's pub on the edge of Ramsgate he grew up in an England still, as he says, almost Dickensian. Huge shire horses hauled the brewer's dray, the milkman ladled out milk into your jug from a churn. Mum kept a sweetshop, and Muir's tribute to the sweets of yesteryear (tiger nuts, liquorice bootlaces, banana toffee) rivals George Orwell's in *Coming Up for Air* or Clive James's in *Unreliable Memoirs*. I also liked his economical attitude to personal hygiene, contrasting with modern youth's foppish addiction to unguents and aftershaves. All through the Second World War, he wore the same vest, occasionally using it as a back-up towel or for caulking draughty windows at night. Once at a Royal Variety performance he and his wife Polly met the Queen Mother, who asked Polly, 'Does he think up funny things in his bath?' 'It's all I can do to get him *into* a bath,' Polly replied. I was delighted to hear that Frank liked my review and when, a year later, he died his son Jamie told me they put a copy of it in his coffin. I felt very honoured.

Most people are less likeable than Frank but almost no one is less likeable than John Osborne. All the same, his autobiographies – *A Better Class of Person* and *Almost a Gentleman*, taken together with John Heilpern's *John Osborne: A Patriot for Us* (which does not just repeat stuff from the autobiographies), add up to a riotously funny amalgam of spleen and rancour on a par with Evelyn Waugh's diaries and letters. The bane of Osborne's life was his mother, Nellie Beatrice, to the analysis of whose meanness and vulgarity he devotes his full rhetorical and forensic powers. It seems to me that Nellie Beatrice was largely responsible for the revolution in British theatre ushered in by *Look Back in Anger*. Of course, Osborne did the actual writing, but the rage that drove him accumulated gradually during his childhood and adolescence thanks to Nellie Beatrice's goading and belittlement. She ridiculed him for his acne, his bedwetting, his puny physique and any other shortcomings real or imagined, and he was helpless before her cockney-barmaid bluntness. My favourite Nellie Beatrice story dates from

Osborne's days as a struggling actor when he played Hamlet at the Victoria Theatre, Hayling Island. Nellie Beatrice, invited to attend, replied, 'I've seen it before. He dies in the end.' Osborne's attractive traits were few, but one was his gift for self-ridicule. He liked to boast that he was the only actor to be booed by an entire audience, consisting of five pensioners and a dog at a Thursday matinee in Brighton. Even the dog howled.

The autobiographies of people who share your own views are, of course, the best, but I don't think that's the only reason I admired Peter Vansittart's *In the Fifties*. I liked its sardonic wit and the beautifully judged style that scores its hits with a fencing master's grace. He describes taking a group of German students round London and noticing their approval of the bomb sites – a tribute to the Luftwaffe's efficiency. Their only criticism is that St Paul's was left standing. In Britain towards the end of the 1950s, he notes, advanced thinkers had already begun to dismantle the post-war system of secondary education that had been designed to further meritocracy and facilitate social mobility. Anthony Crosland, a public school-educated Labour savant, vowed to eliminate 'every fucking grammar school' in the country, and the philosopher A. J. Ayer agreed, while sending his own son to Eton. Vansittart found himself teaching at an experimental school for the children of 'rich, nervy' Hampsteadites, dedicated to freedom and self-expression. In the interest of rooting out 'bourgeois' tendencies it was laid down that no pupil should be obliged to read or count. Grammar, spelling and decimal points were treated as matters for democratic discussion, not despotic facts.

I came across a different kind of educational idiocy in Oliver Sacks's *Uncle Tungsten, Memories of a Chemical Boyhood*. When Sacks was eleven his mother used to give him dead babies to dissect, to prepare him for the medical career she had decided he should pursue. As a gynaecologist she obtained the corpses professionally – some had been stillborn, others were malformed foetuses that she and the midwife had quietly drowned at birth. Sacks escaped these horrors thanks to two uncles, Dan and Abe, who introduced him to the impersonal beauties of chemistry and physics, and the result is the most alluring account of a child's education I have ever read. Sacks's immersion in science was rapturous, akin to what less gifted boys might find in sexual awakening. When he first set eyes on the model of the periodic table in the Science Museum in South Kensington, with its compartments holding samples of the elements, he thought it the most beautiful thing he'd ever seen. He could hardly sleep for excitement. What's more he makes you feel excited too, even if you know almost nothing about science.

Another unforgettable autobiography, quite unlike *Uncle Tungsten* except that it's about a revelation, is Andrew Brown's *Fishing in Utopia: Sweden and the Future that Disappeared*. Essentially it is a lament for a lost Eden. Sweden in the 1970s, when Brown first went there, was as near as any country has ever come to a socialist paradise. Swedes were bonded together by shared values. Society, it was agreed, would benefit more from co-operation than selfishness. Affluence was bad for people. Failure to want social equality was a handicap to be pitied and, if possible, cured. Drunkenness was an obvious evil, so alcohol could be bought only at government stores ringed with horrific health warnings. There was full employment and no housing shortage. Optimism reigned. It was assumed that as time went on the world would become more peaceful, more egalitarian and more like Sweden. That was what progress meant.

Brown married a Swedish girl, got a job in a factory making wood pallets, read a lot of philosophy and developed a serious interest in – or, to be more accurate, an irrational obsession with – fishing, becoming expert at making his own flies and guessing which of the inexhaustible species of insects on the wing in Sweden during the summer the fish he was pursuing would prefer. It sounds boring but isn't. He conveys with glittering clarity the freedom he felt when he was alone in the wild, surrounded by silence and the smell of trees. When he went back in the 1990s everything had changed for the worse. Only in the remote countryside had life remained timeless. In the closing pages he drives up into the Swedish Arctic. At a lonely farm he finds an old couple who don't just believe in trolls but have seen them. They are, he is told, benevolent spirits, quite likely to take milk from a cow at night, but happy to do humans a favour in return. He joins in a traditional midsummer festival. A maypole is decorated with birch branches and flowers and hauled aloft. Girls and men dance round it through the white midsummer night. The music comes from an instrument, special to the locality, with eleven steel strings and three banks of keys, which sounds like 'an accordion on the verge of tears'. Quite a good description of this haunting book's tone.

Equally offbeat and beautiful is Thad Carhart's *The Piano Shop on the Left Bank*. Walking his children to and from school in the rather run-down Parisian *quartier* where he has made his home, American freelance writer Carhart finds his attention drawn to a sleepy little shop down a cobbled side-street. Stencilled on its window is *Desforges Pianos: outillages, fournitures*, and peering through the glass he can glimpse the arcane materials of piano repair – tuning pins, wires, swatches of felt. He goes in several times to enquire about purchasing a second-hand piano, but is met with impenetrable Gallic reserve. Unfortunately they have no pianos in stock, it is explained, and in any case you need a recommendation from a previous client before you can even be considered as a customer.

However, he persists, and gradually wins the confidence of the younger Desforges partner, Luc, who takes him one day through the mysterious door at the back of the shop and into the glass-roofed atelier that lies beyond. It is enormous, flooded with sunlight, and stacked with pianos – uprights, spinets, grands – in every state of disrepair. A recess houses the oldest inhabitants, delicate little nineteenth-century square pianos teetering on slender legs, their fall boards announcing their provenance – Paris, Amsterdam, Vienna – in curly golden scripts. On workbenches the intimate insides of pianos are exposed to view.

Over the succeeding months Carhart becomes a regular visitor. Luc phones him when a particular treasure is due to arrive – a Steinway in tiger-striped Brazilian rosewood, a shimmering golden Gaveau more than a century old. On Friday evenings a group of addicts gathers in the atelier for piano-talk over a glass of wine – a professor of linguistics from the Sorbonne, a vagabond Dutch piano tuner with a drink problem who spends his nights in carriages parked in various Paris terminals.

A book with a similar charm, at any rate in its secretiveness, is John Harris's *No Voice from the Hall: Early Memories of a Country House Snooper*. After the Second World War Harris, aged fifteen, and his uncle Sid toured the south of England on their bicycles seeking out large country houses that had been requisitioned during the war and were either wrecked or too expensive for their owners to keep up, or both. Echoing, forlorn and deserted, they stood waiting to be broken into, and many had lakes or ornamental canals stuffed with roach, perch and tench that had fattened undisturbed for years, which was convenient, as Sid liked fishing.

In all Harris visited some two hundred houses and his book tells of the surreal visions of decay he came across. Once past the bramble-patch hedge and the Keep Out notices there was no telling what would unfold. Sometimes there were dilapidated classical temples propped on crutches, or spectral greenhouses, smashed and gaping, with trees pushing up through their roofs. On balustraded terraces overgrown topiary figures wagged in the wind like carnival floats. The interiors were dreamscapes of ruin. Tapestries hung in rags. Veneers curled up from table tops like broken springs. Rubbish heaps of leather-bound volumes had avalanched from library walls. In one a colony of wasps had built a nest from the pages. Ancestral portraits stared through films of mildew. The upper floors were open aviaries. Birds rose from the bedrooms with a tornado of flapping.

Some otherwise undamaged houses had been taken over for agricultural use. Pushing open the front door of a pala-

tial pile in Lincolnshire Harris was engulfed by a stamped-
ing flock of sheep that had been living in the marble hall.
Beyond, heaps of grain loomed beside Palladian chimney-
pieces. At Kenwood, in the roof space, he found the Iveagh
bequest pictures, millions of pounds' worth of old masters
– Vermeer's *Guitar Player*, Turner's *Lee Shore*, a Rembrandt
self-portrait – stacked like dominoes without even a sheet of
paper between them.

A different slant on the Second World War is provided by
Daniel Smith's *The Spade as Mighty as the Sword: The Story
of World War Two's Dig for Victory Campaign*. I liked this because it reminded me of my father's transformation into a
vegetable gardener in Radcliffe-on-Trent. Smith estimates
that by 1943 the nation's gardens and allotments were producing over a million tons of vegetables annually, and vegetable growers often kept livestock – hens, rabbits, pigs and bees
– which yielded astonishing quantities of food. In the course
of the war the pupils of a school near Gloucester grossed, on
their smallholding, eight tons of bacon, fifty thousand eggs,
five hundredweight of rabbit meat and five hundredweight
of honey. In tune with the times, the Food Minister Lord
Woolton invented the Woolton Pie, which contained car-
rots, parsnips, turnips and oatmeal under a potato topping,
and was served with brown gravy, and the Women's Institute
organised a network of 5,800 centres, equipped with canning
machines, bottles and Kilner jars, geared to collecting and
preserving perishable fruit and vegetables. Smith's closing
pages remind us of his book's modern relevance. The glob-
al population is expanding by a billion every ten or fifteen
years. Half the world is already gripped by hunger, and it

would be absurd to expect other nations to go on feeding us. The Dig for Victory story is as much a preparation for the future as a hymn to the past.

A morose but strangely touching commentary on a small section of post-war Britain is Edward Platt's *Leadville*. Its subject is Western Avenue, which – for those lucky enough not to know it – is the après-motorway bottleneck, flanked by suburban villas, many of them boarded up, that you get to just after the Hoover Building on the A40 into London. It is also the site of one of the most embarrassing planning fiascos of recent years – a road-widening scheme that was abandoned after half the neighbourhood had been flattened. Platt, a freelance journalist, wondered why anyone should choose to live there, and investigated its history. He found that Western Avenue was part of the post-First World War suburban boom. Lloyd George had promised 'Homes for Heroes' with gardens, hedges and other middle-class amenities, and Western Avenue provided them. Stretching across the fields of West Middlesex it was, the *Acton Gazette* reported, 'probably the finest bit of road in the world ever dedicated to lonely moonlight walks for lovers'.

Platt starts to knock on doors, and finds elderly couples who still cherish a vision of Western Avenue as a tree-lined suburban street. To working-class kids, reared in nearby Wormwood Scrubs, it had seemed a nirvana. They nicknamed it Toffville. The neat front gardens bespoke civic pride. The back gardens were alive with birds and squirrels. You could sit outside on summer evenings and think you were in the country.

These memories are entrusted to Platt in dark parlours, double-glazed against the tumult outside. The din and stench of the highway are now the only reality. Trees and shrubs in the gardens wilt. When it rains, everything goes brown. Fumes rot curtains and fabrics. The noise is so loud you can't hear the TV. The homeless, given temporary accommodation in condemned properties, are another problem. They don't look after their houses. The gardens are waste tips. The rat population of Western Avenue has boomed. One couple found they had devoured almost the whole contents of their garden shed, including two sun loungers. Then there are the gipsies. They deliberately park in front of driveways and threaten you if you ask them to move. They are 'nature's thieves'. One couple have been burgled eight times.

With unchecked population growth, which no politician dares to suggest limiting, it seems likely that in a century or so almost all of England will be like this – congested, polluted, anarchic. Though its geographical focus is small, *Leadville* is a book with big resonances.

Occasionally an autobiography sticks in my mind because someone I've known features in it, and Derek Malcolm's *Family Secrets* is one. It starts fifteen years before Malcolm's birth when his father, Douglas, a bone-headed artillery officer on leave from the Western Front, finds that his wife Dorothy is having an affair with a Russian immigrant called Baumberg, and shoots him dead. Though it is a clear case of murder the jury at Douglas's trial returns a not guilty verdict with patriotic speed, amid cheers from a huge crowd. Given Baumberg's fate you might have thought Dorothy would find it tricky attracting new wooers, but in fact men swarmed around her, particularly from the worlds of art and entertainment – George Robey, Arturo Toscanini, Augustus

John and Nigel Playfair all competed for her favours and so, I was interested to find, did Geoffrey Mure, who had been Warden of Merton when I was a Senior Scholar, and advised me when I had to choose between research fellowships at Merton and Balliol. Dorothy did not hesitate to exploit her friendship with Mure when the time arrived for Malcolm (who later became the *Guardian*'s film critic) to apply for entrance to Oxford. She wrote asking for help, and got a letter back (beginning 'O Seraph') in which the Warden explained that there were many better qualified candidates, but promised to use his influence to secure her son a place – which he did.

In later life Malcolm took up with a Soho dance hostess who was married, he discovered, to an associate of the Kray brothers. One night he awoke to find the wronged husband towering over him with a cosh. On the Baumberg pattern, this should have meant the end of Malcolm. But after beating him about the head a little his nocturnal visitor demanded a cup of coffee and then left. So perhaps, I felt, the gradual moral improvement of mankind is not such an illusion after all.

A moral improvement that warms the heart but is hard to account for is described in Stephen Moss's *A Bird in the Bush: A Social History of Birdwatching*. The Victorians shot and stuffed birds with ghoulish zest, and women ornamented themselves sickeningly with their feathers and corpses. 'Miss Brady looked extremely well', twittered an 1885 society paper, 'with a whole nest of sparkling, scintillating birds in her hair.' The campaigners who started the change were a group of middle-class women in Didsbury who founded their Society for the Protection of Birds (later the RSPB) in 1889. Within ten years it had 150 branches and twenty thousand members, mostly women, and it seems to me that of all the good things that resulted from the empowerment of women, this is one of the most gladdening. Men followed their example, and the change of heart was surprisingly rapid once it started. In the hard winter of 1890–1 national newspapers urged their readers to put out bird food, and the great nature writer W. H. Hudson reported that hundreds of working men flocked to bridges and embankments in their lunch breaks to give the birds scraps from their meals.

Something you could loosely call social anthropology links Moss's book with one that explores a much earlier phase of human development, David Lewis-Williams's *The Mind in the Cave* – an investigation into the origins of prehistoric cave paintings. A key factor in the book's argument is that for thousands of years Neanderthals and new people – immigrants, belonging to our own species *Homo sapiens* – lived side by side in western Europe's stone age sites. The crucial difference between them – or so Lewis-Williams believes – was that Neanderthals, because of the neurological structure of their brains, could not form mental images (what we mean by 'imagining') whereas the new people could. This meant the new people could imagine a 'spirit world' whereas Neanderthals were congenital atheists. It meant too that for the new people one thing could conceptually represent another. So the new people could invent language and paint pictures and carve statuettes – which to Neanderthals would be no more recognisable as pictures and statuettes than they would to an animal.

The new people's social system would also have baffled Neanderthals, because it reflected symbolic values of rank and hierarchy instead of the simple distinctions of age, sex and physical strength that Neanderthals respected. If they could ever have witnessed – as maybe they did – the funeral of one of the new people's dignitaries, in which a human indistinguishable as far as Neanderthals could tell from other humans was buried with a wealth of bracelets, animal teeth, ivory pendants and other treasures, they would have found the whole operation bewildering.

There is rather poignant evidence that Neanderthals admired the new people and tried to imitate them, using ochre body paint as they did. But they were of course grotesquely inferior and Lewis-Williams thinks that what spurred the new people to create cave art was the urge to register their superiority to their conceptually challenged cousins. To call the result 'art' is, he thinks, misleading. For essentially it was a proof of religious superiority, a token of their entry into the spirit world Neanderthals were for ever debarred from, and the artists were shamans – ritual functionaries found in all hunter-gatherer communities – who claim access to supernatural powers.

One reason I was captivated by this book was that its subject matter overlapped with that of William Golding's greatest (in my opinion) novel, *The Inheritors*. So I kept my eye open for reviewable books in the same area and found a compelling one in *Feast: Why Humans Share Food* by Martin Jones, professor of archaeological science at Cambridge. Jones's book has ten sections, each beginning with the reconstruction of an actual meal from the past – the earliest being a feast of roasted horsemeat eaten by a group of Neanderthals in a cave in southern Spain about forty-six thousand years ago. After each reconstruction Jones takes us through the detective work that made it possible – the collection of sediment, debris and bone fragments, the investigation of ash and pollen, the analysis of fossilised human faeces (revealing, in the case of the guests at a dinner party in Roman Colchester about AD 45, that their fare included goat, hare, oysters, scallops, raspberries, dates, figs, grapes and, surprisingly, sticklebacks, though Jones thinks these may have been table decoration).

A typical early human meal with people sitting round a fire talking would, Jones points out, be inconceivable for any other species. To most other animals direct eye contact and opening the mouth to expose the teeth are signs of hostility, fire is terrifying, and placing food midway between several individuals would trigger violence. So how did our abnormal eating habits evolve? Jones thinks the answer must lie in the growth of the human brain's neocortex. For it to grow, some other part of the body had to contract, and that part, seemingly, was the gut. What allowed the gut to shrink, researchers now suggest, was the invention of cooking, which breaks down the fibres in food and so effectively pre-digests it. Neanderthals cooked their food and had big brains. However, they were not modern humans. Something else was needed, namely eye contact and talk. It is hard to tell, from the remains of a prehistoric meal, whether these accompanied it. But a clue, Jones suggests, is jewellery. Beads and other jewellery invite the gaze, so where they are found we can assume eye contact and the opening up of minds that goes with it.

Another book about the origins of human behaviour that I found engrossing was Robert R. Provine's *Laughter: A Scientific Investigation*. Faced with the question of why humans laugh, Provine, a professor of psychology at Maryland, decided not to rely on received opinion or theory but to observe people actually laughing. He and his team of researchers eavesdropped on conversations in shopping malls and city streets, building up a database of thousands of laugh-incidents. His findings were revolutionary. Whereas previous writers had associated laughter with jokes, he discovered that most laughter is not prompted by jokes or other formal attempts at humour, but is a response to quite innocent comments like 'Nice seeing you' or 'We can handle this'. Laughter, he deduced, is a mode of pre-linguistic social bonding and writers who have related it to our higher critical faculties (Plato thought we laughed at evil, Aristotle at ugliness) were on the wrong track.

Also new was Provine's discovery that speakers, on average, laugh more than audiences. Previous studies had assumed the opposite. The only exception, he found, was when the speaker was male and the audience female, in which case it was the females who laughed. This pattern emerges early. Already by the age of six girls are the leading laughers, boys the best laugh-getters. Provine sees this as an expression of power relations between the sexes, and cites instances of laughter-as-subservience from other cultures. The ritualised panting common among chimps and other primates is, Provine believes, an ancestor of human laughter, relating it to older and deeper levels of brain activity than speech or rationality. This is why laughter bypasses our intellect and our conscious control, and why group laughter is irrationally and inexplicably contagious.

I think the most mind-stretching book about the human condition that I reviewed was Michael Frayn's *The Human Touch: Our Part in the Creation of the Universe*. Unlike the three previous books Frayn's does not focus on a single human behaviour – art, eating, laughter – but subjects human thought itself to philosophical enquiry. Erudite, imaginative, funny, he unbolts chapter by chapter the fabric of the universe. Things that most of us regard as certainties – the laws of science, the dependability of nature – vanish like smoke. It has become apparent, he points out, in the wake of quantum mechanics and the uncertainty principle, that scientific laws are human artefacts with no real existence outside our statement of them. Logic is just a system we have made up, not an inherent condition of the natural world. The universe itself is our invention. All its characteristics exist only as figments of the human brain. Without us it would have no characteristics at all, and so would cease to exist.

But would the universe really cease to exist without human beings? Frayn anticipates and dismisses the obvious objections to this claim with acrobatic agility. Mathematicians, for example, might protest that number must always have existed, irrespective of whether anyone was present to do the counting. On the contrary, Frayn responds, number is something we have imposed on the natural world. To claim that nature is 'doing mathematics' when particles combine or separate would be ridiculous, and to say that number must always have been present in principle, waiting to be discovered, would be like saying that bubble gum or the works of

Shakespeare were always present in principle.

Though it is absolutely lucid, and full of enjoyable anecdotes, Frayn's book takes you to the chilly edge of the intelligible by showing that the intelligible is what our brains can manage, and that beyond it is nothing – or rather, nothing that can be formulated in human thought. You might say that Frayn is quite like an early Christian, in that the early Christians were also interested in what the human brain could not manage, only they called it God. They didn't think He would cease to exist when humans did, but they did think that if God stopped thinking about the universe, even for a moment, it would cease to exist. I once pointed out this similarity to Michael at an event we did together at the Cheltenham Literary Festival. He did not seem entirely convinced.

Reviewers can make enemies. At a *Sunday Times* Christmas party a prominent man of letters refused to shake hands with me when we were introduced because he thought I had given a bad review to a book of his in revenge for a bad review he had given to one of mine. Assuring him I hadn't read his review only made it worse. Ben Macintyre once wrote a piece in *The Times* to say that he and others who thought my reviews hurtful had formed an anti-Carey club, and that his mother, who lived round the corner from us in St John Street, planned to introduce a pair of frilly knickers into the Carey laundry to raise my wife's suspicions. Children are supposed to be distressed and need counselling when their parents are pilloried in the press, but I was disappointed to find that our two thought it all a tremendous hoot.

My worst mistake, if it was a mistake, was reviewing Ted Hughes's *Shakespeare and the Goddess of Complete Being*. I knew Hughes a bit and admired him enormously as a poet, so I was keen to review his Shakespeare book. But when I read it I was aghast. The idea for it originated, he explains, in a dream. Shakespeare appeared to him one night, clad in dazzling Elizabethan finery, and laid on a special performance of *King Lear*. When he woke Hughes found he was in possession of hitherto unguessed-at secrets of the bard's life and works. Chief among these is that all Shakespeare's later plays, including the great tragedies, contain, if you read them properly, a magic formula derived from Babylonian creation myths, which takes the form of a story-line combining – roughly speaking – the plots of 'Venus and Adonis' and 'The Rape of Lucrece'.

I thought the whole thing was appalling nonsense. Worse, it was a kind of betrayal. Hughes was a great poet, exquisitely attuned to the multiple meanings of poetry. What did he think he was doing reducing Shakespeare's plays to this tedious mythical mumbo-jumbo? The only point where the book broke free of its rhapsodic exegetical muddle was in a footnote on page 11 where Hughes describes a huge matriarchal sow, gross, whiskery, many-breasted, a riot of carnality with a terrible lolling mouth 'like a Breughelesque nightmare vagina, baggy with overproduction'. This had nothing to do with the book's argument, but I read it as a magnificent late Hughes prose poem, epitomising his violently divided feelings about women.

Inadvisedly I said all this in my review, and Hughes was furious. He wrote a long, angry reply. I wrote an equally angry response, and the *Sunday Times* printed them on facing pages with glowering photos of each of us. That was in 1992, and I never saw Hughes again. But five years later I reviewed his *Tales from Ovid*, a loose translation from the *Metamorphoses* with lots of magnificent Hughes additions, which I thought one of his greatest things. In 1998, out of the blue, came a letter from him, enclosing a gift – a first edition of Sylvia Plath's *Ariel* – and enclosing, too, a cut-out from a newspaper showing one of those psychological puzzles made of thousands of multicoloured dots, which different viewers will see different shapes in. His letter (which Christopher Reid prints in the *Selected Letters*) was an olive branch, saying that we had disagreed only because we had seen different things in Shakespeare, like two people looking at one of these puzzles. I was shamed by his nobility, and wrote back at once with my own apologies. But he died before it arrived. His widow found my letter later, unopened.

It might be suspected that all this reviewing meant I neglected my faculty duties in Oxford. However, that was not so. Strictly, professors had no obligation to help with the administration of the faculty, and the two other English literature professors, John Bayley and Richard Ellmann, wisely kept clear of all such entanglements. I, less wisely, decided someone should take a lead and that it should be me. I did several stretches as chair of the English faculty board and of its Graduate Studies Committee, and tried to get the gaggle of assorted fellows and lecturers distributed throughout Oxford's thirty-something independent colleges to behave like a coherent faculty. It was deeply resented. For example, when I wrote (at the faculty board's prompting) to various faculty members, suggesting that they might give lectures that related to the syllabus rather than to their own private interests, it caused grave offence. One replied that he regarded lecturing on the syllabus as 'spoon-feeding'. Another accused me of infringing his academic freedom.

The graduate students, on the other hand, especially the Americans, welcomed the idea of belonging to a faculty, as in a real university. I started a regular graduate seminar in Renaissance studies to which graduates from all the colleges could come and exchange ideas and hear visiting speakers, and it is still going strong forty years later. The graduates said they would like to have practice in giving conference papers, as they would have to do when they applied for jobs. So I organised a Faculty Seminar Day one Saturday in Hilary term, planned like a mini-conference. The graduates turned up in droves, eager to give their papers, and the faculty secretaries sacrificed their Saturday to come along and serve coffee and biscuits. Most of the members of the faculty, however, exercised their academic freedom by staying away. I think a total of eight put in an appearance throughout the day.

I also tried to update the undergraduate syllabus. I invited the faculty members who taught literature to a meeting and we resolved to make Anglo-Saxon optional rather than compulsory for first-year students. This evoked furious opposition from a diehard minority in the faculty, and took ten years to accomplish. Reform in Oxford is seldom rapid and never popular. In October 1984 *Private Eye* published a barbed anonymous piece about me, outlining my general unfitness to be a professor and my undistinguished background, and claiming that 'the favourite song at Oxford English faculty parties is the theme tune from *2001 Space Odyssey*. For it is in the year 2001 that John Carey retires from his post as Merton Professor of English Literature.' For all I know this may have been true. But if so it was not the result of negligence on my part, rather the contrary. When I did retire in 2002 Nigel Smith, a colleague who had become a professor at Princeton, proposed to edit a *Festschrift* for me, as I had done for Helen Gardner when she retired. However, Oxford University Press declined to publish it.

Writing

As well as reviewing books, I was writing some myself. The first, after the one on Dickens, was about Thackeray. I'd read *Vanity Fair* as a sixth-former, and it was like nothing I'd read before – garish, glamorous and, for a teenager, enviably raffish and worldly-wise. For those who haven't read it yet, it's about two pairs of lovers in the war-torn Europe of the Napoleonic campaigns. George Osborne is married to Amelia Sedley, and Rawdon Crawley, a fierce young blood from the titled gentry, has been seduced into marriage by Becky Sharp, the most flagrantly immoral woman in Victorian fiction. Both George and Rawdon are in the army, and both fight at Waterloo. Their wives remain in Brussels and listen, all day long, to the fearsome thunder of the cannon. Towards evening, on the battlefield, the French Imperial Guard make their last charge and are repulsed by the victorious English, and Thackeray writes: 'No more firing was heard at Brussels – the pursuit rolled miles away. Darkness came down on the field and city: and Amelia was praying for George, who was lying on his face, dead, with a bullet through his heart.' I'll never forget the shock I got reading that. My sixth-form notions of novel structure were outraged. 'You can't do that,' I thought. 'You can't kill off a major character with half the novel still to go – and just in a subordinate clause!' Afterwards I realised that by making death sudden, casual and unreasonable Thackeray was being realistic.

All this made me keen to get back to him and read him properly. So I bought a complete, multi-volume Thackeray from Blackwell's – for almost nothing – and read it through. It was a terrible disappointment. *Vanity Fair*, I found, was not just Thackeray's first great novel, it was his only one. After *Vanity Fair* his fiction got steadily duller and more pompous until, when you reach stuff like *The Virginians*, it is soporific at a pharmaceutical level. The only comfort was his early journalism, which attracted me by its vitality and colour and its ridicule of anything pretentious or grandiose. Here is the official guide taking visitors round Castle Carabas in *The Book of Snobs*: 'The great 'all is seventy-two feet in lenth, fifty-six in breath, and thirty-eight feet 'igh. The carvings of the chimlies, representing the buth of Venus, and Ercules, and Eyelash, is by Van Chislum, the most famous sculpture of his hage and country . . .'

Thackeray's art criticism, jotted down, I imagined, as he wandered scornfully round the galleries in London and Paris, is equally disrespectful, and his social observation is wickedly funny. A tour de force is *The Second Funeral of Napoleon*, a satire on the grisly pomp surrounding the reinterment of the Emperor's remains in Les Invalides. His travel book *Notes of a Journey from Cornhill to Grand Cairo* characteristically disparages the standard tourist attractions – the pyramids, St Sophia – and notices, instead, the incidentals that give foreign places their foreignness, like the coins in Jaffa, 'made of a greasy, pewtery sort of tin'.

In the Arab quarter of Cairo he finds an old friend who has gone native, and lives on one side of a courtyard full of 'camels, gazelles and other beautiful-eyed things'. They dine together off 'delicate cucumbers stuffed with forced meats' and 'yellow smoking pilaffs' and 'ruby pomegranates, pulled to pieces, deliciously cool'. The joy in food is typical. One of his star turns is *Memorials of Gormandizing*, recalling the triumphs of *haute cuisine* he has munched his way through over the years, mostly in Paris. The account of *perdreau aux truffes* at the Café Foy makes you salivate just reading it. He loved shopping as well as eating, and gives rapturous accounts of the shop windows in the Palais-Royal, which was his Mecca – the glowing centre of commerce's rainbow world, where 'beautiful dressing gowns used to hang, more splendid and gorgeous than any tulips', and wonderful bonnets with 'ravishing plumes of marabous, ostriches and birds of paradise'.

I read everything I could find about Thackeray – including Gordon Ray's magnificent edition of his letters – but the only critic who seemed to have felt what I did about the journalism was George Orwell in an article called 'Oysters and Brown Stout'. Orwell, though, didn't have the space to display Thackeray's brilliance, so I determined to make my book an anthology as well as a book, quoting great chunks of Thackeray that had never been reprinted since the nineteenth century, and giving readers a completely different idea of his writing from anything available on bookshop shelves. (The bookshop situation improved in 1993 when D. J. Taylor published some of the best journalistic pieces in an Everyman Library edition entitled *A Shabby Genteel Story and Other Writings*.)

I poured out my plans to Charles Monteith, who listened patiently and said he would send along a contract for me to sign. I called the book *Thackeray, Prodigal Genius*, to give a sense of him flinging his gifts around carelessly in newspapers and magazines. He did this, I think, partly because he was too proud to want to be thought to take writing seriously, and partly because, contemptuous of the grandiose, he believed that brilliant, ephemeral things could have as much vitality as pompous masterpieces. In Naples, after seeing the gigantic classical statue known as the Farnese Hercules, he wrote to a friend: 'Playing a smart piece on the piano, or cutting a neat figure of eight on the Serpentine, or writing a review, are really as good as that thumping piece of skill.'

There is a drawing of him by Daniel Maclise which exactly catches the Thackeray I wanted to write about. He is lounging arrogantly on a chair like a Regency swell, with his legs wide apart, a notepad on his knee, and his pencil held meaningfully just in front of his crotch. I'd seen this picture only in reproductions and I discovered that the original was owned by the Garrick Club so Charles, who was a member, and I went in search of it. We eventually ran it to earth hanging in the ladies' lavatory. Thackeray, I'm sure, would have been tickled pink by its location. He was fond of bawdy, and had a brilliant gift for the impromptu. "Tis true 'tis titty, titty 'tis 'tis true,' he remarked of an unusually revealing example of female portraiture. I got Charles to put the drawing from the ladies' on the front of my book when it was published in 1977.

The reviews were much better than I expected. C. P. Snow in the *Financial Times* said it was 'a book of flashing panache, utterly liberated from the academic faults'; Margaret Lane in the *Telegraph* agreed it was 'deliberately unacademic' and 'a pleasure to read', and Michael Levey in the *Times*

Educational Supplement said 'nothing could be farther from conventional English literary criticism'. So I felt I was on the right track.

John Donne came next. An odd jump from Thackeray, admittedly, but I'd meant to write a book on Donne ever since I was a graduate student. My D.Phil. thesis had been about Donne the poet, but I wanted the book to be about Donne the preacher and thinker as well, and I wanted to show that they were the same person – that the poems and prose were fabrics of the same imagination. No one had tried to do that before, and no one has since – maybe because the reading you need to do before you start is pretty colossal. The sermons alone fill ten volumes, and on top of that there are devotional and controversial works, including a learned defence of suicide (a solution to life's problems Donne was frequently tempted by).

What had struck me in reading Donne was that he always preferred paradox and contradiction to simplicity. It's this that makes his poetry so demanding when compared with standard Elizabethan love poets. In his writings about religion the same habit persists. Here, for example, is Donne preaching about angels. 'They are creatures that have not so much of a body as flesh is, as froth is, as a vapour is, as a sigh is, and yet with a touch they shall moulder a rock into less atoms than the sand that it stands upon, and a millstone into smaller flour than it grinds.' Whenever he writes about angels it is this paradoxical, contradictory quality that intrigues him. They are 'super-elementary meteors', suspended between God and man; they are six thousand years old, yet have not 'one wrinkle of age in their face, or one sob of weariness in their lungs'; they are 'the riddles of heaven'. By contrast, simple angelic attributes – beauty, wisdom – which attract other writers don't interest him. His religious thinking seeks paradox and contradiction just as his poems do.

To say that is to treat his religious beliefs as imaginative constructs, like the poems, and in my book I argue that that is what religious beliefs are. All of us, I suggest, not just Donne, choose religious beliefs that meet our imaginative needs, and it is because they meet our imaginative needs that we choose them. Some readers – Christopher Ricks among them – found this idea shocking. But it is not necessarily shocking. If we remember Shaw's St Joan telling de Baudricourt that of course God speaks to us through our imagination, it is not shocking at all. At all events, what I tried to do in the book was analyse the imaginative preferences and processes in the poems and show that they were found in the sermons and religious writings too. When Donne chose what theological path to follow through furiously disputed issues such as original sin or the resurrection of the body or the nature of God, he was led by the same imaginative needs as inspired the poems about love and women.

The other controversial claim in the book was that Donne's apostasy was crucial to his development. He was born into one of the foremost Catholic families in the land, at a time when the persecution of English Catholics was becoming ferocious. As a boy he was taken by his tutors to see the public butchering of Catholic priests. He watched devout bystanders praying to the victims' mangled bodies, and remembers being kept awake at night by thoughts of martyrdom. One of his uncles was head of the secret Jesuit mission in England, and his tutors may have hoped to recruit Donne to the cause. Danger came very close. His younger brother Henry, arrested for harbouring a Catholic priest, died in prison, and the priest was hanged, drawn and quartered. Had Donne remained a Catholic it might have meant sharing Henry's fate, and would in any case have debarred him from the kind of career he wanted. So he chose apostasy and worldly advancement, renouncing his Catholic faith and becoming secretary to a leading government official. Ardent Catholics, like those who had brought him up, would certainly have believed that, because of that choice, his soul was damned for all eternity, and in my book I tried to estimate the effects of this on his writing, from the obsession with disloyalty and betrayal in the love poems to the terror of damnation in the *Holy Sonnets*.

Donne is a difficult poet and an intricate thinker, and the challenge in writing about him was to hold the attention of readers who weren't academics. I worked hard at this, and offended some reviewers. One American professor deplored my 'colloquial phrasing and word order', presumably favouring books that put ordinary readers off. I sent Helen Gardner a copy, and thanked her in the preface for her guidance as a supervisor. But I guessed she would be appalled by my emphasis on Donne's apostasy, since she revered him as an Anglican saint. In reply she wrote me a weirdly contorted letter saying that (1) she had at first refused to review the book (for *Encounter*), but had then been persuaded to do so; (2) when she sent in her review to the editor, Anthony Thwaite, she had asked him not to publish it, but to publish a lecture of hers on Donne instead; and (3) Anthony was going to publish the review all the same and (she warned) it was not favourable. This disingenuous farrago was subscribed 'With love and apologies, Helen'. I never got round to asking Anthony what his memories of the episode were, and when I dipped into Helen's *Encounter* review its bossy tone reminded me so forcibly of my mother's shrill, bigoted denunciations of my teenage relationship with Heather that I never finished it.

In any case, reviewers generally didn't agree with Helen. There were glowing assessments by Christopher Hill, Robert Nye, Michael Ratcliffe, Charles Nicholl, Jonathan Raban, Robert Ellrodt and others. The great Anatole Broyard extolled the book in the *New York Times*, the *Washington Post* liked it, and I was excited to get enthusiastic clippings from far corners of America – the *Fort Worth Texas Morning Star-Telegram*, the *Scottsdale Arizona Progress*, the *Sunday Telegram Worcester, Mass.* Best of all were the letters from readers who wrote to say how much pleasure the book had given them. 'Well Donne, Sir!' quipped a Sussex gentleman, and a lady from South Africa wrote, 'Your *John Donne Life, Mind and Art* is one of the best books I have ever read. It is like Mozart in that it makes one happy to be alive.'

That made me happy to be alive too, particularly as I had recently almost died. In January 1981 I'd gone on a British Council lecture tour of India, taking in Delhi, Calcutta, Bhubaneswar, Bombay and Kolhapur. Before I went, the University Medical Officer, Dr Juel Jensen, a charming Danish bibliophile, gave me an anti-malarial drug, Maloprim, with instructions to take it twice weekly and continue after my return. I did, and soon after I got back to Oxford began to feel very ill. My temperature soared, I thought I had flu, and went to bed. Luckily our GP took a blood sample, which showed that something was killing off my white blood cells. I was whisked into the John Radcliffe Hospital and isolated with 'barrier nursing', which meant anyone who came in had to wear mask, gown and medical cap to reduce the risk of infection. The John Radcliffe is a teaching hospital so, soon after I arrived, a group of students, suitably gowned and capped, turned up with an instructor, who told them, 'This is Professor Carey, who has recently returned from India and has a white blood cell count of . . .' I forget the figure, which meant nothing to me, but there was a suppressed gasp from the students, who started to scribble in their notebooks, and I got the impression they were wondering whether to take a coffee break now or wait until I pegged out and have coffee afterwards.

My temperature was so high that I was beyond caring anyway. I was hallucinating a lot. Looking back I realise I thought the room I was in was a whole series of different rooms. At night I was taunted by demons – horribly knowing demons, privy to all the most disgraceful, disgusting and ridiculous things about me. Perhaps they were illusions, but there's no knowing with demons. David Weatherall, the Nuffield Professor of clinical medicine, was in charge of my treatment, along with Sir John Badenoch, who, as a fellow of Merton, was a friend and colleague, and I'm sure they saved my life. Another Merton friend, the pathologist Michael Dunnill, came to see me, and his chat and cheerfulness – thoughtfully put on for the occasion, I suppose – helped to make me feel still part of normal existence. A needle was stuck in my back to take a sample of bone marrow. I saw it in the jar and thought it looked just like the beef gravy my mother used to make from the Sunday roast. Apparently the sample showed a lot of damage and John Badenoch came to warn me, gently, that I might not pull through. Bizarrely, soon after he'd gone, a cleaning lady arrived in my room, smoking, with a mop and bucket, and dusters tucked in her belt. I mumbled feebly that she shouldn't be here and that I'd die if I got an infection. 'You won't die, love,' she said, tapping the ash from her cigarette into her bucket. And she was right. Maloprim, it transpired, destroyed white blood cells in very rare cases, mine being one, but as I had stopped taking it just in time I gradually got better.

All the same, it was a sharp jolt of reality, and so was India. I had never seen poverty on such a scale, nor ever known it to be accepted so casually by those who were not poor. An incident sticks in my mind from a later visit in 1984. I was in Baroda, walking back to the campus for a class with a young Indian lecturer. 'It is hard for us to imagine', he said, 'the slum conditions described in Victorian novels,' and he went on to suggest that the British Council might aid understanding by sending 'illustrative material'. I looked around. All along the university perimeter, on the dirt sidewalk, were neat piles of cooking utensils belonging to pavement-dwelling families. The grown-ups were off doing casual labour. The toddlers could be seen playing almost naked on muck heaps. Slightly older children were patiently sorting piles of plastic bags, rags and bottles for resale. Krook, the rag and bone dealer from *Bleak House*, would have felt quite at home. My Indian friend noticed none of this because he had schooled himself expensively not to. To see what Victorian slums were like he had only to keep his eyes open on a train into Bombay as it passed through the putrid shanty towns. But that would have connected literature too closely with life and he – quite understandably – wanted to keep them apart.

Afterwards I started thinking more about the separation of literature from life, and about how writing that deals directly with life – Thackeray's journalism, for example – is generally thought to be somehow inferior to fiction or drama or poetry. I wondered why this was, and whether it made any sense. Charles Monteith had retired by this time, but the poet Craig Raine had joined the staff of Faber and Faber and he asked me if I'd like to edit an anthology of reportage. It seemed a good way of testing my ideas about literature and life, so I said I would. It meant a lot of reading in unfamiliar historical sources, and took four years, but it was extraordinarily exciting, like – I imagine – panning for gold. I decided at the start that I wouldn't include anything that didn't make me want to read it twice. I also decided not to restrict myself to the work of professional journalists – though they weren't excluded – and to include only eyewitness accounts. All knowledge of the past that isn't just supposition derives from people who can say 'I was there', and the medley of witnesses I eventually collected – travellers, soldiers, murderers, victims, chance bystanders, novelists, explorers – could all say that. My time-span went from ancient Greece to the 1980s, and I didn't just have pieces about major historical events – though there were lots of those, of course. What counted was quality of writing and sharpness of observation. So the book is full of indecorous or surprising glimpses –

the French ambassador peering down the front of Queen Elizabeth I's dress and noting the wrinkles, Joe Louis's nostrils flared like a double-barrelled shotgun as he closes in on Max Schmeling, Mata Hari drawing on her filmy stockings on the morning of her execution, Pliny watching people in Pompeii with cushions on their heads to protect them from volcanic ash, a guest at a dinner party hosted by Attila the Hun observing how people mind their manners, Mary Queen of Scots, suddenly aged in death, with her pet dog cowering among her skirts and her head held on by a single recalcitrant piece of gristle.

The book far outsold anything I had ever written myself – which was galling – and the reviewers competed in searching for superlatives. 'Spell-binding', 'Compulsively readable', 'Wonderful', 'Sensational', 'Endlessly gripping', were some of the plaudits. Jeremy Paxman called it 'Stunning'; Stephen Spender, 'Fascinating, compulsive and horrifying'. In Britain it was called *The Faber Book of Reportage* but in America they called it *Eyewitness to History* and it sold strongly there too. I'd never had so many letters from readers. 'Why wasn't history taught like this in school?' was a question a lot of them asked. 'Could we have another volume please?' was another. A Second World War item I had included was an account of the Japanese bombing of Pearl Harbor, and I got a letter from an American ex-serviceman who had been Bugler of the Guard at the Hawaiian naval base, waiting to sound the call for church, when the Japanese bombers struck. He corrected some facts in the account I had printed.

The sales of *Reportage* evidently suggested to Faber that I might be usefully employed doing another anthology, and a young member of the Faber team, Julian Loose, asked me if I'd like to edit *The Faber Book of Science*. I was not an obvious choice. When I'd done School Certificate science most modern science had not been invented. Obviously the sensible thing would have been to say 'No'. As it happened, though, when I was in Bhubaneswar I'd got interested in the Marxist scientist J. B. S. Haldane, who spent his final years there, and I had looked up some of the science articles he wrote for the *Daily Worker*. Among them I found his essay 'On Being the Right Size', and was captivated. In it he demonstrates that giants, like those he remembered from the illustrated *Pilgrim's Progress* of his childhood, could never have existed. They were, he pointed out, ten times as high as a man, which meant that they were ten times as wide and ten times as thick as well, so that their total weight was a thousand times a man's, or eighty to ninety tons. However, the cross sections of their bones were only a hundred times those of a man's, so every square inch of giant bone had to support ten times the weight borne by a square inch of human bone. As the human thigh bone breaks under about ten times the human weight, the *Pilgrim's Progress* giants would have broken their thighs every time they took a step.

This seemed to me not just beautifully clear, but an example of a new literary form – popular science – which, unlike the old literary forms, depended on explanation and truth. It had originated in the nineteenth century, with Michael Faraday and T. H. Huxley, and was currently enjoying a golden age with writers like Isaac Asimov, Arthur C. Clarke, Freeman Dyson, Carl Sagan, Richard Feynman, Stephen Jay Gould, Steve Jones, Richard Dawkins and Lewis Wolpert

– all of whom I drew on in my anthology. A great boon in researching the book was that Oxford's Radcliffe Science Library is open access – that is, you can wander around the book stack taking volumes from the shelves as you please, and over the course of three years I spent many hours there. I was looking for accounts of science by scientists – astronomers, physicists, biologists, chemists, psychologists – that were arresting and lucid, and I especially wanted eureka moments – the workers in Edison's laboratory putting together the first electric light bulb, or Enrico Fermi activating the world's first atomic pile. I also found treasures in writers who weren't primarily scientists – Ruskin explaining that iron 'breathes', and 'takes oxygen from the atmosphere as eagerly as we do', when it makes rust; or Nabokov waiting among the darkening lilacs to spot the 'vibrational halo' of an olive and pink hummingbird moth; or the Czech poet Miroslav Holub brooding over a dead muskrat, and imagining the adrenalin and stress hormones still sending out their useless alarms in the creature's spilt blood, and the white blood cells still busily trying to perform their accustomed tasks, bewildered by the unusual temperature outside the muskrat's body.

What amazed me when the book was published was how generous scientists were about it. *Nature* gave it a rave review, and it was shortlisted for the 1996 Rhône-Poulenc, the biggest science-book prize. William Hill offered odds of 5–1 on it, as against 3–1 on Richard Dawkins's *River Out of Eden* which was the favourite. The winner was Arno Karlen's *Plague's Progress*. Like *Reportage*, the science anthology sold strongly. In America it was called *Eyewitness to Science* and the TSP book club put in an order for twenty-eight thousand copies. Lots of letters came from readers. The one I've always cherished was from a blind lady in Flintshire. She explained that the book had been read on tape for the use of the blind, and for days she'd got up early in the morning and stayed up late at night to listen to it right through. It was, she wrote, 'absolutely the most fascinating and all-absorbing piece of work I have ever read', and, she concluded, 'I think you may have changed my life. One month ago I had never read a scientific book. I am now halfway through O-level chemistry.'

In case this all sounds disagreeably triumphalist it may comfort readers to know that the book I wrote in between the two anthologies got absolutely terrible reviews. It was called *The Intellectuals and the Masses*, and was essentially a simple study in cultural history. I pointed out that the huge increase in the population of Europe in the nineteenth century caused consternation among many observers. In Britain the situation was complicated by the Education Acts of the 1870s which created, for the first time, a mass reading public and mass-circulation newspapers. Among British literary intellectuals the response to these developments was almost universally hostile. They resented the 'semi-literate' masses, despised their pretensions to culture, and detested newspapers. The more extreme among them, such as W. B. Yeats, D. H. Lawrence and H. G. Wells, considered ways in which the masses, or large sections of them, might be exterminated. Others, more moderately, argued that universal education was the mistake, and should be stopped. Though the intellectuals could not actually return the masses to illiteracy, they could exclude them from high culture by making it too difficult for them to understand, and that is what they did. They created what we now call modernist literature, which cultivates obscurity and depends on learned allusions, comprehensible only to the highly educated. Similar developments, I noted, occurred in other arts such as painting and music. I backed up these points with quotations from T. S. Eliot, Ezra Pound, Wyndham Lewis, Virginia Woolf, George Bernard Shaw, E. M. Forster, Aldous Huxley, and others.

My modest proposals about the social origins of modernism were greeted with howls of fury. Reviewers seemed beside themselves with rage. It was alleged that I hated culture, and wished to condemn the population to 'an endless diet of television soaps, the *Sun* newspaper, and royal scandals'. I was a commissar, an ally of Mrs Thatcher in her war against the arts, a lackey of the Murdoch press, and a puritan with a 'class-based, priggish horror of champagne'. As a professor of literature I had no business criticising literary figures, anyway, I was told. It was 'fouling my own nest' and 'biting the hand that fed me'. Although the reviewers were united in vituperation, their arguments were at times mutually contradictory. One lot thought it monstrous that I should search out illiberal opinions, sometimes from the writers' private correspondence. Others maintained that everyone had always known the writers I mentioned were fascists, so there was nothing original in my findings. *The Times* printed two reviews of the book, side by side. One, by Peter Ackroyd, had evidently not been considered unfavourable enough, so a querulous diatribe by Derwent May was added, just to set the record straight.

Faber and Faber were delighted by all the publicity. An excited Joanna Mackle would phone to say that two or three more reviews had appeared. 'What are they like?' I'd ask. 'Oh, terrible,' she would reply light-heartedly. I thought of Joanna as the most dynamic member of the Faber team, and her laughter was a tonic. So was a letter I received from Ian McEwan, whom I knew slightly, which began: 'Dear John, This spiteful passion in the press suggests you must be doing something right.' Spurred by the excitement, BBC2 decided to feature a discussion of the book on *The Late Show*. Howard Jacobson was chosen as my antagonist, Sarah Dunant was in the chair, and Ian was included as referee. Beforehand Howard and I were kept in separate green rooms, presumably for fear of a fracas. The discussion was a bit chaotic, and the single feature that attracted viewers' notice, apparently, was Sarah's new hairdo. Ian, though, remained calm and judicious throughout, and afterwards he and I went for a drink, over which I explained lengthily and, of course, needlessly, that it wasn't a matter of whether modernist writers were good or bad as writers, I was just trying to account for a cultural change.

The reviewers condemned the book so unanimously that people started to wonder whether it could really be all that bad. Edward Pearce spoke up for it in the *Guardian*, and independent defences were mounted by Julie Burchill, Angus Calder, Laura Cumming and Lucasta Miller – four writers who, so far as I could see, had nothing in common except, of course, their excellent judgement. Nowadays *The Intellectuals and the Masses* is on many university and college reading lists, and no one seems to mind.

I tried out its ideas in several German cities, on lecture tours organised by the Deutsch–Englische Gesellschaft. I was curious to know how my theory would go down in another culture, and, besides, I was keen to see Germany. As a child during the war I had thought of it as an underworld of destruction. The names of its cities – Berlin, Nuremberg, Kiel, Dresden – belonged to a black mythology, as unthinkable to visit as Valhalla. Then, one day in 1995, I found myself wandering round Dresden in the September sun. Paddle steamers thumped cheerfully up and down the Elbe, packed with pleasure-seekers. Two little girls stripped off their frocks and jumped about, shrieking, in a fountain. The stalls in the old market were hung with harvest festival decorations and I bought sausage, bread, mustard and beer for lunch. I had not learned German at school – just after the war it wasn't really an option – but I'd joined a class in the 1970s at the Oxford College of Further Education, taken by an inspiring teacher called Hertha Duncombe, so I could just about make myself understood. In the picture gallery I dawdled happily in front of Lorenzo di Credi's *Holy Family with St John*, Liotard's *The Chocolate Girl* and Vermeer's *Girl Reading a Letter* and *The Procuress*. In the Albertinum were two marvels, Monet's *A Jar of Peaches* and Degas's *Woman with Opera Glasses*. I sat at a pavement table and drank a cup of coffee opposite the bombed ruins of the Frauenkirche, which had been kept unrepaired by the Russians as an anti-war memorial.

I heard many memories of the war. A lady in Berlin, a professor's wife, told me how she and her parents and siblings had been in the city when the Russians arrived. They had escaped from a small east German town in their car.

On the journey they could hear the Russian tanks, and saw Cossacks riding along a riverbank, shaking the ground. In Berlin, the German defenders were jumpy, and people were being executed. In the room where her family found shelter was a woman doctor who was to be executed next morning for 'rash sayings'. She was behind a curtain, and a priest was with her. They told her – in Latin so that no one else would understand – that the Russians were coming and she would be saved. Next morning the Russians behaved well. Her brother, who was a bandsman in the German army, had told them not to hide but to go out and meet the conquerors. They did, and were not harmed.

I'd expected post-war German audiences to be serious and liberal-minded, and alert to the dangers of modernism's anti-democratic animus. The younger members of the Gesellschaft were like that. But among their wealthy elders my views gave some offence. Two or three people walked out of my lecture in Hamburg. At a dinner in Oldenburg I was seated next to a senior academic who berated me for my leftist leanings – not what he expected of an Oxford professor – and described to me in some detail his four-wheel-drive, his skiing holidays and his yacht. There was much talk among the other guests about how cheap it was to hire students as gardeners and waitresses. A young lecturer who was my carer in Bielefeld intimated to me that class distinction was rather carefully observed in the upper reaches of the Gesellschaft. We were dining in a mansion belonging to one of the town's leading families, and she assured me she would never have been allowed inside if she hadn't been looking after me.

In Essen I was taken to see the Krupp family castle, the

Villa Hugel. My guide, a local pillar of the Gesellschaft, was a hale sixty-six-year-old who had been one of Hitler's boy soldiers at the end of the war. The castle was stuffed with artworks. In the hall were large oil paintings, in the English country-house style, showing blond Krupp children on horseback, with woods and fields stretching away behind them. Among the wonders on display was an exhibition of Chinese antiquities, including a terracotta warrior and a 'jade man' – a death suit made entirely of jade pieces held together by gold wire. The Krupp family's vast fortune had been built on the manufacture of armaments, dating back to the nineteenth century. Before the war Alfred Krupp had facilitated Hitler's secret rearmament programme, and after the war he was found guilty at Nuremberg of crimes against humanity, including plundering industries in occupied countries and employing slave labour. One of his factories, for producing artillery fuses, had been sited near the Auschwitz concentration camp and used Jewish prisoners as slaves. No one mentioned any of this as we admired the Chinese antiquities.

On the whole I think the younger members of the Gesellschaft must have prevailed over the old guard, as I was invited back for five German tours in all and German was the first language *The Intellectuals and the Masses* was translated into – Steidl published it as *Hass auf die Massen* in 1996. A city I'd long wanted to see was Heidelberg, because of its John Donne associations, and on my last German trip I was invited to lecture there. Donne had come on an embassy in 1619 and preached to Elizabeth, the daughter of James I, who was married to Frederick the Elector Palatine. Frederick added an 'English wing' to the castle for his bride, with a monkey house, a menagerie, and an Italian Renaissance garden. I was shown an elegant arch which the passionate prince is said to have had built for her overnight, as a surprise. I wondered whether Donne – who had written an epithalamion for their marriage – had been shown it too. Perhaps, like me, he had time to linger in the wooded valley of the Neckar, and ride up to the little walled town of Dilsberg, on its hilltop, and have delicious *Pfifferingen* for lunch.

The Krupp house at Essen with its gorgeous artworks and sinister history stayed in my mind, and I felt vaguely that it symbolised something I wanted to write about. But the idea failed to grow until I was lunching one day with Julian Loose, and he said, 'Why don't you write a book called *What Good Are the Arts?*?' Julian is a man of few words, but the ones he does utter are always worth pondering. So I did a lot of reading in aesthetics, anthropology, psychology and education theory, looking for answers to two questions: 'What is a work of art?' and 'Is there any evidence that exposure to works of art makes you a better person?' I thought at first that the answers to these questions would be easy. I was pretty sure, for example, that *Hamlet* was a work of art and most pop music wasn't, and as I'd spent much of my life reading literary works of art I naturally wanted to believe they'd made me better. But the more I thought and read the less certain I became. People seemed to have been confident for most of the nineteenth century about what did and what didn't count as a work of art. But over the next hundred years those certainties collapsed, and by the start of the twenty-first century anything could be a work of art. An empty gallery had been exhibited as a work of art, a light bulb going on and off had won the Turner Prize, and the Tate had added to its collection a tin can of Piero Manzoni's excrement. Of course, some people don't believe these are works of art, but others do, and there's no way of telling who's right. Nor is it clear what 'right' would mean in that context. What objective test could you apply to identify a 'real' work of art? People have suggested that real works of art are the ones God likes. But, even if you believe in God, how can you tell what art He likes? Does He prefer Beethoven to Mozart or vice versa? Others have suggested that real works of art are those that make people behave better. But that raised the second question I'd asked at the start, and the answer is disappointing. A hundred years of experimental psychology have led researchers to the conclusion that behaviour is a complex outcome of nature and nurture and can't be altered by works of art.

So the idea that there is, or ever could be, a standard test that authenticates genuine works of art seemed to me an illusion. If you value something and get joy and satisfaction from it and think it is a work of art, then it is a work of art for you, even if no one else agrees, and the definition I came up with was: 'A work of art is anything that anyone has ever considered a work of art, though it may be a work of art only for that one person.' This seemed like heresy to some reviewers, but the alternative, so far as I could see, was telling people who thought that – say – a can of excrement was a work of art that they were wrong, and however strongly I felt they were I did not believe there were any objective criteria I could call on in making such an assertion. I noticed, too, that for all their huffing and puffing, none of the hostile reviewers could suggest an objective test for identifying genuine works of art either. What they argued, generally speaking, was that contact with real works of art gave them special, elevated feelings – similar to religious feelings – which they considered very valuable and important, and the kinds of art they disparaged did not. In my book I had offered a paraphrase of this kind of argument, which ran: 'What I feel when I listen to Mozart or look at a Rembrandt is more valuable than what you feel when you look at or listen to whatever trash gives you pleasure.' Such statements make no sense because, apart from anything else, you can't know what another person feels, let alone evaluate it.

To some readers all this will seem blindingly obvious, as it did to me. I'd always assumed that judgements of art and literature were matters of personal taste – what else could they be? – and it was a relief to find that the critics who took the same view included those whose intelligence I most respected. Nick Hornby, Tom Sutcliffe, Blake Morrison and Rupert Christiansen all liked the book, and Melvyn Bragg wrote to say that at several points he found himself shouting 'Yes' out loud. Those who hated it – and there were quite a lot – demanded how it was that I could judge book competitions and teach literature if I didn't value some works more highly than others. But of course I did value some works more highly than others. I'd spent my life valuing some works more highly than others. But I knew that my evaluations were subjective and personal (as, incidentally, all the judgements in this book are), reflecting the kind of person I was and the kind of upbringing I'd had. I didn't think they were absolute or eternal or equivalent to divine wisdom. Naturally

I was prepared to defend what I valued and explain why I valued it, and try to persuade others to value it too, so they could share the pleasure it gave me. But I took it for granted that, whoever you are, the artworks that are most deeply precious to you may not be precious to other people, and that doesn't make you better or them worse.

I believed entirely in *What Good Are the Arts?* and loved talking about it. It seemed to free people to air their enthusiasms, and to defy the art-world pundits. I tried it out on all kinds of audiences and it always seemed popular. I talked to the City Club of Cleveland, Ohio, 'the oldest free speech forum in America', I talked to a committee of civil servants at the Department of Culture, Media and Sport (attracted, I suppose, by its implications for arts funding), I talked to a pre-play audience at the National Theatre and I did my best to implant the seeds of thought into Sir Christopher Frayling, then chair of Arts Council England, in a discussion at the South Bank Centre. At the Charleston Festival, a Bloomsbury stronghold, Howard Jacobson and I debated 'Do the arts make people better?' and a vote taken before and after by the chair, Polly Toynbee, revealed that, even in that rarefied company, fewer thought they did at the end than at the start.

Thinking about infallible judgements, in the arts and other things, and about the kind of people who imagine they're capable of them, got me interested in utopias. While I was working on *The Intellectuals and the Masses* I'd read nearly all the works of H. G. Wells, and it seemed to me that he used utopias to express two aspects of his nature, one benign, the other ruthless, and I wondered whether that was common with utopians. The only real-life utopia I had been to was Israel – on a British Council lecture tour in the spring of 1987 – and the benign and ruthless sides seemed pretty clear there. My hosts were academics, delightful, civilised people. They were strictly orthodox, but also capable of joking about it. One of them had just returned from India and told me how, on his last day there, he had refused to sign his hotel bill because it was the Sabbath. The Indian hotel porter took his refusal to be due to an unfavourable astrological prediction, so accepted it as perfectly reasonable.

They showed me their land with eager pride. Hebrew, they explained, had been a dead language, and had become the language of a modern state – an unprecedented achievement. They told me how in the 1920s the Arabs had driven the Jews out of the port of Jaffa, and the Jews had founded a new settlement on some sand dunes nearby, which was now the city of Tel Aviv. Fifteen years ago, they recalled, the road to Tel Aviv from Bar Ilan – the university where I was based – was a single desert track with no buildings, just sand. Now it was a four-lane highway. That didn't seem an improvement to me, but they were obviously pleased. They liked to see the country growing. More buildings meant more progress. So did more people. There were children everywhere. When I went to Jerusalem I got a taxi to the bus station. But the driver insisted on taking me all the way – for free – when he found I was English. He was fat, voluble, unshaven, generous, and his taxi was a scruffy Ford Escort with a green plastic fan and a pile of orange invitations to his youngest son's wedding. He offered me one, and told me his family history. He had five sons and a daughter. When his daughter was at school the boy in the desk behind insisted on pulling her hair. She told him to stop. The teachers told him to stop. His father told him to stop. He still pulled her hair. 'Now they have three children,' he exploded jubilantly. 'How many children have you? Two? Two! You are sleeping for twenty years! Ha, ha!'

My hosts took me to Galilee for a day. We passed the kibbutz at Kinneret, one of the earliest, dating from 1913, and I was told how it had been founded by Russian émigrés eager to put their communist ideals into practice. It was a utopia within a utopia. Then we drove up to the Golan Heights, beautiful, grassy, covered in wild flowers – poppies, clover, and a yellow flower I didn't recognise. Swifts shrieked overhead, on their way to summer in England. The Heights were officially 'disputed territories', seized by Israel during the Six Day War. But there was clearly no dispute in my hosts' minds. This was their land. I was hardly in a position to disagree, coming from a country that had won half the world by conquest. Besides, their tiny nation was threatened on all sides. Why shouldn't they cling to what they had? For my generation the Holocaust excused anything and everything Israel did to defend itself. Memories of it were still fresh. While I was there John Demjanjuk was standing trial, accused of being 'Ivan the Terrible', a notorious guard at Treblinka extermination camp, where an estimated 925,000 Jews died in the gas chambers. The court proceedings were on TV all day long. We lunched by the Sea of Galilee at Tiberias, and on the way back passed the place where Christ walked on the water and the hill where he preached the Sermon on the Mount – 'Blessed are the peace-makers' – and Nazareth, a sprawling Arab town full of rubbish. My hosts pointed out, correctly, how filthy it was.

Arab–Israeli tension didn't seem high in the brief time I was there. In the Crusader Market, on the way up to the Temple Mount in Jerusalem, Israeli soldiers, looking no older than schoolboys, lounged in shop doorways with sub-machine guns and cans of Coke. My hosts, being orthodox Jews, would not set foot on the Mount, so I went up alone to see the Dome of the Rock, a gleaming hemisphere poised above the city like a spacecraft from some far galactic civili-sation with higher intelligences and a keener sense of beauty than ours. The Arab custodians at the door explained po-litely where I should leave my camera and shoes, and I went barefoot into the shadowy interior, over the rich carpets. It was silent and empty, a place for meditation. So I sat and meditated, thinking how it contrasted with the Christian sites in Jerusalem – the shoving, sweaty crowds doing the stations of the cross on the Via Dolorosa, and the hectoring guides, 'Here Our Lord fell for the second time', and the tourist shops selling tat.

The only Arab I talked to during my stay was a taxi driv-er who took me to the home of a Jewish family, friends of my hosts, who had invited me to share the Sabbath evening meal with them. We got lost on the way, and my driver was terrified, saying it was a very orthodox neighbourhood and closed for the Sabbath and we would be stoned. We weren't, but the evening went badly. I was welcomed, and the father, a well-known neurologist and poet, broke bread and blessed the wine and said prayers. But his son, a brawny, graceless youth, yawned ostentatiously and taunted his mother with a quotation from scripture – the imprecations against Israel's enemies in Psalm 137, 'Blessed is he who shall dash thy children against the stones.' So much for Israel's world-view, he mocked. Everyone was relieved when he mooched off to bed. But it showed me that the Israeli utopia was threatened from within as well as without. My hosts had already told me that the young were not keen to join kibbutzim, preferring an easy life in the city.

I had expected to be moved by seeing the holy places. But everything was so overlaid with buildings and monuments that the places did not seem to exist any more. At the Church of the Holy Sepulchre we were allowed into the tomb three at a time. But it was just an emptiness. I felt nothing except my failure to feel. I said a silent prayer for my two sons, in a desperate bid to register something meaningful, then there was nothing to do except stumble out again, minding not to bump your head.

Perhaps people who read books are doomed to find places that they have read about a disappointment when they actually see them. I had felt a quiver of anticipation when my host mentioned the Vale of Sorec, because I remembered Milton's Samson saying that the place where he met his future wife 'Was in the Vale of Sorec, Dalila'. I always thought it a lovely line, especially because in Milton 'Dalila' is stressed on the first syllable, making it light and dancing. So I asked my host where the Vale of Sorec was, and he pointed to a nearby ravine now used for waste disposal. This kind of shock may explain why utopias – the ones people make up – have no history, but tend to be fresh, green places where humanity can make a new start.

Away from Jerusalem and Tel Aviv it was not so bad – fewer buildings, fewer people. I took a trip through Caesarea to Acre, and drove up Mount Carmel for a view of the coastline and the banana plantations stretching north to Lebanon. I bathed in the Dead Sea at Ein Gedi and ate dates from the oasis with frozen yoghurt. On the way back I got my first glimpse of Jericho, a green patch among the mountains. 'The shady city of palm trees', Henry Vaughan calls it in a poem, quoting Deuteronomy. Bougainvillea clambered purple, white and pink among the palms, and citrus orchards grew even in the middle of the town. It was easy to think of this as the Promised Land, God's utopia, that He showed Moses from the top of Mount Pisgah. On the same trip I climbed up to the fortress of Masada, a bare, giddy rock blazing in the sun, where Jewish rebels held out against the Romans and committed mass suicide rather than surrender. It was gaunt and pitiless but it had a power that the Christian sites, crawled over and desecrated, had lost.

My impression that Arab–Israeli tension was relatively relaxed vanished during a conversation among Israeli academics in one of the universities I visited. The subject of kidnappings by Palestinian terrorists came up, and a professor enquired whether we knew why the hostages taken were never Russians. We didn't, so he explained. The Palestinians had once kidnapped a Russian, he said, and the Russians had sought out the kidnappers' families, taken away two males, castrated them, and delivered 'the parts' back to their relatives. 'Hostage released. No more kidnappings,' he concluded. Everyone agreed it was a good idea, including the lady academics present. I was priggishly shocked at the time.

Later I wondered whether, in their position, I would have reacted any differently.

My *Faber Book of Utopias* was published in time to greet the new millennium, and it contained about a hundred ideal commonwealths, imagined realms and exemplary nowheres. They spanned four thousand years, from an Egyptian papyrus of 2000 BC to modern California, and they displayed many different notions of perfection – communist, fascist, anarchist; all-male, all-female, all-hermaphrodite; rural idylls, sci-fi technocracies. Oscar Wilde once said that a map of the world that did not contain utopia would not be worth having, and when I started out his notion of utopias as symbols of hope rather appealed to me. But my reading, and my brief exposure to the Promised Land, modified that view, and I ended up thinking that the aim of all utopias is to eliminate real people. Real people are changeable, curious, inventive, disobedient, selfish and infinitely diverse – in a word, human. Utopias cannot accommodate such beings. They must be got rid of before utopia can begin, and replaced by a species capable of perfection. That is not a hopeful message, which may be why *The Faber Book of Utopias*, though respectfully reviewed, did not sell very well.

Not long after it was published Julian emailed me to say that William Golding's daughter, Judy Carver, wanted to discuss the possibility of my writing a biography of Golding. It was something I'd wanted to do for a long while. Back in 1984 Faber had decided to publish a *Festschrift* for Golding's seventy-fifth birthday and Charles Monteith asked me to edit it. I was nervous about approaching possible contributors because the payment Faber was offering them – even when I'd got Charles to double the figure he first thought of – was very small. But the response was heartening. Brilliantly imaginative pieces arrived from John Bayley, Craig Raine and Anthony Storr. Seamus Heaney wrote a poem, 'Parable Island', Ian McEwan remembered reading *Lord of the Flies* at boarding school aged thirteen, Peter Green recalled drunken holidays with Golding in Greece, Ted Hughes discoursed learnedly on baboons and Neanderthals and *The Inheritors*.

I travelled down to Golding's Cornish house, Tullimaar, to interview him for the book, and on the first evening, when I went down to dinner, he was bashing away tumultuously on his grand piano – Liszt, I think it was – and Ann, his wife, remarked acidly as I entered, 'You haven't played that for a long time, William.' I held my breath. How would he respond? Smash the piano? But he just shrugged it off, as if such barbs were customary, leaving me even more eager than before to know about his life, marriage and family. The interview was no help. He did his grey-bearded sage act, repeating things he'd said scores of times before. The only thing he objected to, when I sent him the transcript, was that I had inserted '[laughs]' every time he had laughed, and he made me cut them all out, saying that 'laughs' was 'a giveaway' – though what it gave away I'm still not sure. When the *Festschrift* was published in 1986 he seemed genuinely pleased, dubbing it his 'Birthday Book' – 'better than *Festschrift* don't you think', he wrote in his thank-you letter, 'and easier to spell. Anyway the German makes it sound as if we all danced in heavy boots round a foaming barrel or two.'

A bonus I got from editing the *Festschrift* was a letter from Philip Larkin, whom I'd asked to contribute. Golding, he protested in reply, 'isn't a writer I know much about – I don't think I own a single book by him. When *L of the F* came out, I thought it improbable, and never followed up the rest, though oddly enough (in view of what you say) [I'd said I thought *The Inheritors* Golding's best novel] I *did* read *The Inheritors* and found it moving. But on the whole no.' In previous letters we'd discussed the tendency of a certain kind of pretentious English writer to denigrate England, and at the end of his letter Philip recalled how common that was around 1950: 'People said how much better abroad was – no queues (old people and cripples brushed aside), no shortages (flourishing black market) and so on.' I was pleased by this touch of asperity, taking it as a sign that he was fit and well and enjoying retirement. I was wrong. It was the last letter I got from him and he died eight months later.

Though Golding liked his birthday book he was adamant he didn't want me or anyone else to write his biography, and I'd gathered this ban remained in force even after his death in 1993. So I was surprised to hear via Julian of Judy's proposal. She asked me to lunch in Bristol to discuss it, and on the way back to her house we passed some scaffolding where builders were at work. Judy grasped my arm, steering me clear of the danger zone. 'We don't want anything landing on your precious head,' she explained. I felt I wouldn't much like anything landing on it even if it didn't contain an embryonic biography of Golding. Still, I could see what she meant, and the more she talked the more irresistible the project sounded. I would have access to all Golding's working papers, including drafts of the novels and the first version of *Lord of the Flies*, and also a two-and-a-half-million-word private journal that he kept every day from 1971 to his death.

I'd never written a biography before and wasn't sure I was cut out for it. Even calling it 'biography' was, I gathered, passé. Among the cognoscenti it was now known as 'life-writing'. Reading the journal took me six months and was astounding. Among other things it was a dream diary, so it recorded Golding's unconscious as well as his conscious life. He also used it to plan, day by day, the design of the novel he was at work on, correcting and rewriting, and remembering where different strands of the story came from. There was a lot about his childhood and bad relations with his mother and about his son David's terrible breakdown, and this was mixed up with ruminations about God and the universe and taking Ann to get her hair done each week. When I came to particularly fascinating bits I would remind myself, with a jolt, that I was the first person in the world outside his immediate family to be reading this amazing stuff. I remembered Charles Monteith telling me that *Darkness Visible*, the baffling novel which ended Golding's years of silence after David's breakdown, had been put together from fragments he happened to have in a bottom drawer. Now, using the journal, and the green-biro drafts Golding had scribbled (in, as usual, old exercise books from Bishop Wordsworth's School, Salisbury), I found I could unscramble the various states of the novel's composition and clarify at last what it was about.

Judy and her husband Terrell were unstintingly helpful. Gill and I would go and stay with them and I would spend days reading through the archive while Gill photocopied wads of manuscript to take away and study later. When the book was finished they were generous in their praise and, even though I'd included intimate material which, I think, many families would have jibbed at, they didn't ask for a single word to be changed. Naturally, because of Golding's eminence, the book got a lot of press coverage. It was BBC Radio 4's Book of the Week, and Gill and I were asked, on the strength of it, to the Auckland and Sydney literary festivals. While we were away I heard it had been shortlisted for the James Tait Black Memorial Prize for biography.

I immediately thought, 'I bet it won't win,' and I was surprised I cared so much. I had done quite a lot of book-prize judging, and one thing I'd learned was that the result was largely a matter of chance. Since I believed value judgements were subjective, that was no surprise. Almost always, once the winner had been picked, I would think of other books that could just as well have won. When I first chaired the Booker Prize judges in 1982 Thomas Keneally's *Schindler's Ark* won, and I was happy with that, though personally I preferred William Boyd's *An Ice-Cream War*. Next time round, in 2003 (by which time it had been renamed the Man Booker Prize), D. B. C. Pierre's *Vernon God Little* won, though afterwards I felt that Zoe Heller's *Notes on a Scandal* and Mark Haddon's *The Curious Incident of the Dog in the Night-Time* (not shortlisted because two of the judges took against it) would have made very good winners. I'd also judged the annual W. H. Smith Literary Award for several years, along with Philip Ziegler and Hermione Lee and latterly with Lucy Hughes-Hallett and Mark Lawson. It was a more informal set-up – the three judges decided what books to consider, then met and discussed them. The prize was open to non-fiction and poetry as well as fiction and, in later years, to American authors (Mark's idea) and to foreign-language books in translation. So it meant wide reading, and over the years the list of winners – among them Derek Walcott's *Omeros*, Vikram Seth's *A Suitable Boy*, Ted Hughes's *Tales from Ovid*, Philip Roth's *The Human Stain* – looks pretty impressive. But, as always, a list of those that nearly won would look impressive too.

In the middle of writing the Golding book I was asked to chair the first Man Booker International Prize for Fiction, and it seemed too interesting a prospect to miss. It was open to authors worldwide, provided their works were available in translation, and the idea was to judge a writer's whole output rather than just one book. My fellow judges were Azar Nafisi, author of *Reading Lolita in Tehran*, and Alberto Manguel, and we had an early meeting in Alberto's house near Poitiers – a renovated medieval presbytery with an oak-panelled library housing his collection of thirty thousand books. His staggering knowledge of world literature was invaluable in drawing up our initial list of seventy or so writers across the globe who we thought deserved consideration, and this was followed by months of reading. Several names on our list were quite unknown to me. Reading the works of, for example, the Japanese Nobel Prize winner Kenzabur Oe, I found myself entering fields of imagination I had never set foot in before. We had to whittle our list down to eighteen finalists, then to a single winner. How? How do you eliminate, say, Margaret Atwood or Kazuo Ishiguro, or Nobel laureates such as J. M. Coetzee, Naguib Mahfouz and Gabriel García Márquez?

The winner we chose was the Albanian Ismail Kadare – a

survivor of dictatorship, who writes out of the life-blood of a culture largely unknown in the West, and who traces the rift between Islam and Christianity that now threatens to tear our world apart. In his acceptance speech he recalled being inspired by *Macbeth* as a boy, and associating the castle that loomed over the town where he grew up, Gjirokastër, with Macbeth's castle. He was speaking in Edinburgh, and said he was off to Cawdor next day to see Macbeth's real castle. I was delighted with his win, and yet, I thought, what about Günter Grass and Milan Kundera, my personal gods? Weren't they as good? What about Antonio Tabucchi, whose *Pereira Declares*, though relatively brief and under-stated, seemed to me to have a perfection unmatched by any other novel I read in those months? The only way to quieten such doubts is to remind yourself that book prizes, though excellent for selling books and for honouring their recipients, don't ultimately mean anything except the preference of one set of judges at a particular time.

Armed with these consolatory reflections I travelled up to Edinburgh for the James Tait Black awards, resigned to being publicly humiliated, but feeling that, as I'd been short-listed, it was my duty to go. At the preliminary drinks reception I chatted with A. S. Byatt, whose *The Children's Book* was on the shortlist for the fiction prize, and she seemed surprisingly chirpy. We had known each other since the 1980s when we occasionally met as panel members on Philip French's BBC Radio 3 *Critics' Forum* programmes. These were the best arts programmes I ever took part in, on radio or TV, but they were terrifying occasions, particularly the lunches beforehand – cold collations laid out under clingfilm in some chill, anonymous room in Broadcasting House – where everyone strove to appear cleverer than everyone else, and Philip himself was so clearly and effortlessly cleverer than any of us that I would feel crushed before we even got to the studio to be given our final instructions before the drop. Actually my memory was that Antonia had been pretty nervous at these gatherings too, so her sangfroid on the James Tait Black evening mightily impressed me. Only afterwards, over dinner, did it emerge that she knew all along that she had won the fiction prize, having sensibly told the organisers she would not come back from her summer home in the Cevennes unless she had.

Lacking her foreknowledge I sat miserably in the front row while the chairman of the judges carefully analysed each of the shortlisted biographies in turn. His assurances that it was an extremely strong shortlist and that the losers should not be downcast were aimed, I felt certain, exclusively at me. His sympathetic gaze lingered over me while he said it. I think I closed my eyes as a kind of defence mechanism when he drew breath to announce the winner, and when he did it took a moment to sink in that my Golding biography had won. I was far more moved than was appropriate for someone who knew literary prizes to be meaningless. But then, academic matters apart, I had not won anything since the Richmond and East Sheen Grammar School for Boys cross-country run some fifty-eight years before.

12

So, in the End, Why Read?

There are as many answers to that question as there are readers. My answer is that reading opens your mind to alternative ways of thinking and feeling. Read Richard Dawkins
and you think and feel one way about religion. Read George
Herbert and you think and feel another. Book-burners try to
destroy ideas that differ from their own. Reading does the
opposite. It encourages doubt. Think of Donne:

> Doubt wisely, in strange way
> To stand enquiring right is not to stray,
> To sleep or run wrong is.

Reading distrusts certainty. Think of Yeats:

> The best lack all conviction, while the worst
> Are full of passionate intensity.

Reading punctures pomp. Remember Shelley's Ozymandi-
as, a shattered statue:

> And on the pedestal these words appear:
> 'My name is Ozymandias, King of Kings.
> Look on my works, ye Mighty, and despair!'
> Nothing beside remains. Round the decay
> Of that colossal wreck, boundless and bare,
> The lone and level sands stretch far away.

Remember Melville in *Moby-Dick*; 'O young ambition, all
mortal greatness is but disease.' Remember Shakespeare's
Isabella:

> But man, proud man,
> Dressed in a little brief authority,
> Most ignorant of what he's most assured,
> His glassy essence, like an angry ape
> Plays such fantastic tricks before high heaven
> As makes the angels weep, who with our spleens
> Would all themselves laugh mortal.

Reading is contemptuous of luxury. Remember George Eliot writing about Rosamond Vincy in *Middlemarch*: 'in poor Rosamond's mind there was not room enough for luxuries to look small in'.

Reading makes you see that ordinary things are not ordinary. Remember Keats: 'The setting sun will always set me to rights, or if a sparrow come before my window, I take part in its existence and pick about the gravel.' Remember Larkin's wishes for a friend's newborn daughter:

> May you be ordinary,
> Have, like other women,
> An average of talents:
> Not ugly, not good-looking,
> Nothing uncustomary
> To pull you off your balance,
> That, unworkable itself,
> Stops all the rest from working.
> In fact, may you be dull –
> If that is what a skilled,
> Vigilant, flexible,
> Unemphasised, enthralled
> Catching of happiness is called.

Reading is vast, like the sea, but you can dip into it anywhere and be refreshed. Reading takes you into other minds and makes them part of your own. Reading releases you from the limits of yourself. Reading is freedom. Now read on.

Acknowledgements

My chief debt is to my sister Marjorie. Without her memories and her accurate record-keeping I could not have written the first part of this book. I am also grateful to my nephew Adam Thynne for sharing with me his discoveries about family history.

I should like to thank Martin Amis for allowing me to quote from his letter to me (p.230), the Society of Authors as the Literary Representative of the Estate of Philip Larkin for permission to quote from Larkin's letters (pp.269, 285, 342–3) and Faber and Faber Ltd for permission to quote from Larkin's 'Born Yesterday' (p.350).

Several people generously gave up their time to read the book in draft, and offered helpful comments – my sons Leo and Thomas, my niece Jane Thynne, and my friends Peter Kemp and David and Tricia Grylls. I am much in their debt, as I am to my agent Toby Eady for his patience, help and advice and to my outstandingly efficient and discerning copy-editor Eleanor Rees.

Julian Loose and Kate Murray-Browne at Faber and Faber have kept me going with their help and encouragement, and my wife Gill has co-operated unstintingly from start to finish – and after.

Index of Authors and Titles

Index of Authors and Titles

Index of Authors and Titles